JOHN NORDEN'S
THE SURVEYOR'S DIALOGUE (1618)

Literary and Scientific Cultures
of Early Modernity

Series editors:

Mary Thomas Crane, Department of English, Boston College, USA
Henry Turner, Department of English, Rutgers University, USA

This series provides a forum for groundbreaking work on the relations between literary and scientific discourses in Europe, during a period when both fields were in a crucial moment of historical formation. We welcome proposals for books that address the many overlaps between modes of imaginative writing typical of the sixteenth and seventeenth centuries – poetics, rhetoric, prose narrative, dramatic production, utopia – and the vocabularies, conceptual models, and intellectual methods of newly emergent "scientific" fields such as medicine, astronomy, astrology, alchemy, psychology, mapping, mathematics, or natural history. In order to reflect the nature of intellectual inquiry during the period, the series is interdisciplinary in orientation and publishes monographs, edited collections, and selected critical editions of primary texts relevant to an understanding of the mutual implication of literary and scientific epistemologies.

John Norden's
The Surveyor's Dialogue (1618)
A Critical Edition

Edited by

MARK NETZLOFF
University of Wisconsin-Milwaukee, USA

ASHGATE

© Mark Netzloff 2010

Published by
Ashgate Publishing Limited
Wey Court East
Union Road
Farnham
Surrey, GU9 7PT
England

Ashgate Publishing Company
Suite 420
101 Cherry Street
Burlington
VT 05401-4405
USA

www.ashgate.com

British Library Cataloguing in Publication Data
Norden, John, 1548–1625?
John Norden's The surveyor's dialogue (1618): a critical edition. – (Literary and scientific cultures of early modernity)
   1. Norden, John, 1548–1625? Surveyor's dialogue. 2. Surveying – Early works to 1800.
   3. Agriculture – Early works to 1800.
   I. Title II. Series III. Netzloff, Mark.
   526.9–dc22

Library of Congress Cataloging-in-Publication Data
Norden, John, 1548–1625
   [surveyor's dialogue]
   John Norden's the surveyor's dialogue (1618) / edited by Mark Netzloff.—A critical ed.
      p. cm.—(Literary and scientific cultures of early modernity)
   Includes bibliographical references and index.
   Previously published: Printed by T. Snodham, London, 1618.
   1. Surveying—Early works to 1800. 2. Agriculture—Early works to 1800. I. Netzloff, Mark. II. Title.

TA544.N82 2010
526.9—dc22
                                                                            2009050652

ISBN 9780754641278 (hbk)
ISBN 9781409403753 (ebk)

and bound in Great Britain by
ooks Group, UK

Contents

List of Figures

Acknowledgements

At Ashgate, my thanks to Erika Gaffney, an ideal editor, and to Whitney Feininger, Kathy Bond Borie, and Lee Kemsley for their assistance throughout the text's production. Henry Turner first proposed the idea to me of putting together an edition of Norden's text, and I am appreciative of the opportunity he offered to make this remarkable text more widely available.

Thanks to my colleagues in the Early Modern Group at UWM for their comments and suggestions on an earlier draft of the Introduction. This edition as a whole benefited substantially from the thoughtful comments of an anonymous reader. Sukanya Banerjee, as always, was my chief reader, interlocutor, and source of support.

The Newberry Library was of invaluable assistance in reproducing the illustrations from Norden's 1618 text; thanks especially to John Powell for his help.

This text is dedicated to my father, Richard Netzloff, on his well-earned retirement.

Frontispiece   'Competing models of surveying': Title Page from Aaron
Rathborne, *The Surueyor in four bookes* (London, 1616).

Introduction

Surveying and Social Dialogue

The frontispiece of Aaron Rathborne's *The Surueyor* (1616) (see Frontispiece) presents what may be the best-known image of an early modern surveyor. Despite its currency, however, its depiction of the social role and professional training of surveyors differs significantly from that of a contemporary surveying manual, John Norden's *The Surveyor's Dialogue*.[1] In the portrayal of 'Artifex' that appears at the top of Rathborne's title-page, the surveyor is defined primarily in relation to his mastery of the technical aspects of his craft. He is therefore shown at work with the most advanced surveying instrument of the time, the azimuth theodolite. And even though the surveyor is represented in the act of writing, his labor is merely one of transcription, as he provides a record of the labor performed not by him but by his instruments. The survey thus attains a status as fact, as objective and reproducible, because its accuracy is no longer dependent on the individual conducting it.

It is appropriate that this image from Rathborne's title-page is often reprinted in studies of early modern surveying and cartography, for it reproduces key assumptions about the place of technology in these fields. A focus on technological innovation and specialized expertise provided a framework through which an increasingly professionalized group could emphasize the theoretical principles underpinning its practical form of knowledge.[2] In his inclusion of allegorical figures representing arithmetic and geometry at each side of his frontispiece, Rathborne follows other early modern mathematical practitioners, such as Leonard Digges, in presenting classical Euclidian geometry as the theoretical foundation of surveying. Classical precedents conferred intellectual legitimacy to surveying while also countering perceptions of its disturbing innovativeness. This concern emerges early in the first dialogue of *The Surveyor's Dialogue* as well, with the character of the Farmer dismissing surveying as an 'upstart Art' (p. 27).[3]

Possessing a specialized body of knowledge also served as a marker of social distinction for surveyors, a foundation of professional identity that differentiated them from practitioners lacking this level of expertise. Norden refers to this latter group as 'intelligencers' (p. 19), a category that includes surveyors who fail to uphold the standards of the profession—by accepting bribes to alter land

---

[1] Three editions of *The Surveyor's Dialogue* were published in Norden's lifetime (1607, 1610, 1618). Book 6, the final dialogue between the Surveyor and a Purchaser of Land, first appeared in the 1610 edition.

[2] For extended discussion of this point, see J.A. Bennett, *The Divided Circle: A History of Instruments for Astronomy, Navigation and Surveying* (Oxford, 1987) and Bernhard Klein, *Maps and the Writing of Space in Early Modern England and Ireland* (Basingstoke, 2001), p. 51.

[3] All references to *The Surveyor's Dialogue* are drawn from this edition and will be cited parenthetically in the text.

boundaries, for example—as well as those usurping the prerogative of trained specialists, such as tenants who pass on information regarding the value and features of neighboring properties. What unites this suspect class is the mode of information they circulate. 'Intelligence' is subjective knowledge, information deriving from the contestations and competing interests of social relations. The mathematical surveyor, by contrast, offers an 'indifferent' account, one seemingly devoid of subjective interest. It is his mode of knowledge, even more than his technical expertise, which establishes the results of the survey as 'fact'.[4]

But this emergent model of the professional surveyor is offset by a second image located at the bottom portion of Rathborne's frontispiece. Titled 'Inertia strenua', a tag from Horace referring to 'masterly inactivity', this section depicts a surveyor who has misplaced confidence in his technological acumen. Pointing with one hand to his plane table, a fairly basic surveying instrument, with his other arm he makes a sweeping gesture over the hilly landscape in front of him. Ignorant of the technical limits of his instrument, he assumes that he can plot out the land in a simple act of transcription. Norden similarly critiques the privileging of technology in his text, dismissing 'ingenious geometrical conclusions' as nothing more than 'curiosity' (p. 111). Instrumentation, for Norden, is not so much a goal unto itself or a guarantee of accuracy as much as a means for helping the surveyor in a competitive marketplace by speeding up the pace of his labor (p. 133).[5] The instrument featured in Rathborne's first image, the theodolite, was indeed so innovative that it was rarely used by surveyors in the field, a fact that even Rathborne concedes in his appraisal of it.[6] In Norden's text, the Surveyor uses far simpler instruments, most especially the plane table, which was often dismissed as primitive and favored by the 'vulgar'.[7] In addition, Norden's discussion of the technical aspects of surveying is limited to Book 4, an 18-page section that is the

---

[4]   My discussion is indebted to Mary Poovey's *The History of the Modern Fact: Problems of Knowledge in the Sciences of Wealth and Society* (Chicago, 1998).

[5]   A similar emphasis on speed and efficiency can be seen in Norden's commission for a survey of the King's woods in Surrey, Berkshire, and Devonshire: see British Library, Egerton MS 806 f. 42.

[6]   See Rathborne, *The Surueyor in Four bookes* (London, 1616), p. 124.

[7]   The plane table was fairly simple to use: a large sheet of paper would be placed on a flat and level ('plane') board mounted on a tripod and accurately oriented to the compass. The surveyor established two points from which he could see all the features of the landscape he was surveying. With the tripod at one of those points, he sighted to the features along an alidade, marking their direction (not distance) on the paper. When he repeated this form of polar measurement at the other point, the points of intersection marked on the paper provided a scaled outline of the plot of land. Because the surveyor did not have to measure distances with his plane table, he could survey a large area relatively quickly (J.A. Bennett, 'Geometry and Surveying in Early-Seventeenth-Century England', *Annals of Science* 48 [1991] 347).

shortest of *The Surveyor's Dialogue*'s original five books.[8] The comparative length of the remaining sections attests to the emphasis Norden places on other topics: the social role of the Surveyor (Book 1, 26 pp. in *1618*); the history and components of manors (Book 2, 37 pp.); the manorial court system, especially procedures for conducting a Court of Survey (Book 3, 47 pp.); and land management and improvement techniques (Book 5, 46 pp.). Moreover, whereas Rathborne's text includes over 100 geometrical images, Norden's depicts only six figures, and these are fairly rudimentary by the standards of his contemporaries.[9]

All of these choices demonstrate that Norden's text—unlike Rathborne's— was intended more for a general audience than a readership of fellow or aspiring surveyors, and Norden emphasizes not the specialized, technical aspects of the craft but instead the social, legal, and agricultural components of surveying. For Norden, the surveyor possesses a social role that is inextricably linked to the management and preservation of agrarian life. As the Surveyor points out early in his first dialogue with the Farmer, 'plotting', while necessary, is not the 'chief part' of surveying practice:

> for besides the former faculty of measuring and plotting, he must have the understanding of the Latin tongue, and have some sight in the common Laws, especially of Tenures and Customs, and must be able to read and understand any ancient deeds or records, French and Latin, and to judge of the values of land[.] (p. 27)

In the early modern period, surveys were conducted under the jurisdiction of the manorial court system, the Court baron, and were typically known as Courts of Survey in reference to their authorizing body and institutional context. The survey was not primarily a technical endeavor conducted by an individual surveyor that produced a visual document in the form of an estate map. On the contrary, as Norden's passage indicates, it was instead a textual process that entailed the collection and interpretation of deeds and other legal documents. The result of a survey was not a 'map' *per se* but a textual inventory of land boundaries and features.[10] It is appropriate that when *The Surveyor's Dialogue* was republished in the eighteenth and nineteenth centuries, Books 4 and 5 were deleted, an

---

[8] At 14 pages, Book 6 is the only section shorter than Book 4. As a point of contrast, Rathborne devotes most of his text to explaining the geometric foundations of surveying and the use of instruments, with a consideration of the social and legal aspects of surveying relegated to the last of his text's four sections (*The Surueyor*, pp. 175–228).

[9] For discussion of the use of such graphic figures, alternately described as 'plots' or 'plats', see Henry S. Turner, *The English Renaissance Stage: Geometry, Poetics, and the Practical Spatial Arts 1580–1630* (Oxford, 2006).

[10] For example, Norden's survey of the manor of Halimote in Berkhamsted, Hertfordshire provides a list of tenants, their properties, and annual rents without including any estate maps: see 'Perambulatio, &c. de Halimote' (1616), British Library, Landsdowne MS 905 f. 98.

excision of those sections dealing with the technical aspects of surveying and the surveyor's instruments.[11]

Early modern surveying did not always produce objects that were primarily visual in form. In some recent critical discussions of early modern surveying, surveys are presented as a subset of cartography, and there is an underlying assumption that all surveys were intended to produce a visual record in the form of an estate map.[12] But surveying began to be equated with mapping only in the late sixteenth century, relatively late in the development of both fields, a period which Peter Eden describes as the 'golden age of estate cartography'.[13] The fact that Norden's Surveyor is not a cartographer therefore distinguishes his text's depiction of its subject from the institutional and intellectual changes marking both fields. Even though Norden had produced a series of county maps as part of his *Speculum Britanniae* series, and was well-versed in the cartographical aspects of surveying, this facet is mentioned only once in *The Surveyor's Dialogue*.[14] In the first book, Norden's Surveyor imagines a scenario in which the results of his survey will enable a landlord, 'sitting in his chair', to be able to 'see what he hath … upon the sudden 'view' (p. 25). This passage, one of the most frequently cited references to Norden's text, does indeed demonstrate the significant conceptual effects of estate surveying, illustrating what Bernhard Klein describes as 'an

---

[11]   The 1738 edition printed Books 1–3 only, while the 1853 text included Book 6 alongside the first three dialogues. In addition, the 1853 edition deleted sections referring to outdated practices such as feudal service (Book 2) and early modern instrumentation (Book 3); this latter omission reflects the extent to which surveying instruments had become standardized and professionalized by the nineteenth century. For a list of variations among the editions, see the Textual Notes.

[12]   On estate maps, see P.D.A. Harvey, 'English Estate Maps: Their Early History and Their Use as Historical Evidence', in David Buisseret (ed.), *Rural Images: Estate Maps in the Old and New Worlds* (Chicago, 1996), pp. 27–61, as well as his *Maps in Tudor England* (London, 1993), pp. 79–93.

[13]   Eden, 'Three Elizabethan Estate Surveyors: Peter Kempe, Thomas Clerke and Thomas Langdon', in Sarah Tyacke (ed.), *English Map-Making, 1500–1650* (London, 1983), p. 76. Among other discussions of early modern surveying, see Jess Edwards, *Writing, Geometry and Space in Seventeenth-Century England and America* (London and New York, 2006); David Buisseret (ed.), *Monarchs, Ministers, and Maps: The Emergence of Cartography as a Tool of Government in Early Modern Europe* (Chicago, 1992); J.A. Bennett and Olivia Brown, *The Compleat Surveyor. Published to Accompany a Special Exhibition at the Whipple Museum of the History of Science* (Cambridge, 1982).

[14]   Frank Kitchen has provided a comprehensive account of Norden's biography and career as a cartographer and professional surveyor in several works: 'Cosmo-Choro-Polygrapher: An Analytic Account of the Life and Work of John Norden, 1547–1625' (unpublished D. Phil. Dissertation, University of Sussex, 1992); 'John Norden (1547–1625), Estate Surveyor, Topographer, County Mapmaker and Devotional Writer', *Imago Mundi* 49 (1997): 43–61; and 'John Norden,' *The Dictionary of National Biography*, vol. 41 (Oxford, 2004), pp. 5–7.

increasingly desocialized conception of agrarian space'.[15] The social function of surveying is thus transformed from 'overseeing the relationships between landlords and tenants to overseeing the land as a thing in itself', as Crystal Bartolovich has commented.[16] Nonetheless, Norden's allusion to a landlord poring over his estate map is, after all, a hypothetical scene, and it presents an ideal of a desocialized model of possession that is at odds with the contested terms of property and tenure in early modern agrarian England.

Rathborne's image of the surveyor alone with his instruments and Norden's reference to a landlord sitting at home with his estate map share an underlying assumption about the work of surveying. Whether at the stage of production or consumption, this labor is embodied in the figure of the solitary, individual subject. By contrast, a distinguishing feature of Rathborne's careless surveyor is the social context in which he operates, with an emphasis placed on the tenant farmers who assist him as he conducts his perambulation of the manor. If he depends too much on a faulty instrument, the plane table, he is even more dangerously reliant on the information that tenants provide him. One of the dominant concerns of Norden's opening dialogue is, in fact, the Surveyor's need to counter the opposition of the tenant Farmer and induce him to cooperate with the survey. As a practicing surveyor, Norden was acquainted with the widespread resistance that a survey could generate: in one instance, he noted that 'We coulde not procede in the survey of this manor for that of nere 100 tenantes not 30 appeared'.[17]

When a survey was conducted in the early modern period, this process was organized under the jurisdiction of the Court baron, a context that challenges the image of an avaricious landlord foisting a survey on unwilling tenant farmers. The manorial court system was not administered by the Lord himself but instead conducted under the auspices of his steward (estate manager) and bailiff (legal officer), and all of its proceedings were reviewed and authorized by a jury of freeholder tenants.[18] In other words, the assumption that a landlord would hire a surveyor, who would then produce an estate map for the landlord's eyes only, misrepresents the complex process that constituted a Court of Survey. It is appropriate, then, that the longest section in Norden's text is Book 3, which provides step-by-step instructions for calling and administering a Court of Survey (pp. 79 and ff.). Although surveys often authorized actions that had deleterious social effects—from raised rents and fines, and the enclosure of commons or wastes, to

---

[15]   Klein, *Maps and the Writing of Space*, p. 59.

[16]   Crystal Bartolovich, 'Boundary Disputes: Surveying, Agrarian Capital and English Renaissance Texts', unpublished Ph.D. dissertation, Emory University, 1993, p. 18.

[17]   Qtd in Eric Kerridge, *Agrarian Problems in the Sixteenth Century and After* (London, 1969), p. 30.

[18]   On the early modern manorial court system, see especially Christopher Harrison, 'Manor Courts and the Governance of Tudor England,' in C.W. Brooks and Michael Lobban (eds), *Communities and Courts in Britain, 1150–1900* (London: Hambledon Press, 1997), pp. 43–59.

a redrawing of tenants' land boundaries—this process did not occur outside the law.[19] What distinguished agrarian change in this period, however, was that the legal foundation of surveys was increasingly undermined, particularly as a result of limits imposed on the contributing authority of both a professional class of manorial officials and an elite of landholding tenant farmers (or freeholders).

Because early modern surveys entailed a process of social negotiation, Norden's selection of the literary convention of the dialogue provides an appropriate framework in which to depict his Surveyor's experience in the field. The formal qualities of the text also differentiate *The Surveyor's Dialogue* from other contemporary surveying manuals. Whereas the earliest publications in English treating the geometric aspects of surveying were similarly written in dialogue form, this convention had flourished in the mid-sixteenth century and was rarely used by the early Jacobean period.[20] The changing form of these texts derived in part from a shifting rubric for the organization of knowledge, a 'decay in dialogue' that accompanied the growing influence of Ramist logic. As Walter Ong has argued, Ramism organized knowledge according to a spatial logic associated with visual perception.[21] Its characteristic taxonomies, which broke down subjects into a chain of adjuncts and subcategories, attempted to create transferable, reproducible models for knowledge production, a process that fixed objects of inquiry by transforming them into charts on the printed page. One can see this influence bearing on Norden's text in his fourth book, where he offers a series of graphic forms to explain how a plot of ground can be measured (p. 127). However, even at this moment, the dialogue form itself reveals the ways that the surveyor's 'plot' results from a process of construction involving human agents. As Virginia Cox has argued in her study of the early modern dialogue, this literary form 'has the effect of calling attention to the act of communication itself'.[22] In this sense, rather than emphasizing its referential content, the facticity of the information presented,

---

[19]   In legal terms, enclosure could begin only with the prior approval of five independent referees and two surveyors as well as a guarantee that displaced tenants would be relocated or compensated (Joan Thirsk [ed.], *The Agrarian History of England and Wales*, vol. 4: 1500–1640 [Cambridge, 1967], p. 254).

[20]   Other texts on surveying or geometry written in dialogue form include Robert Recorde, *The Pathway to Knowledg* [*sic*] (London, 1551, with eds in 1574 and 1602); William Cuningham, *The Cosmographical Glasse* (London, 1559); Edward Worsop, *A Discouerie of sundrie errours and faults daily committed by land-meaters* (London, 1582); Rooke Churche, *An olde thrift newly revived* (London, 1612).

[21]   Walter J. Ong, *Ramus, Method, and the Decay of Dialogue* (Cambridge, MA, 1958), p. 287. Also relevant to this point is Steven Shapin's *A Social History of Truth: Civility and Science in Seventeenth-Century England* (Chicago, 1994).

[22]   Virginia Cox, *The Renaissance Dialogue: Literary Dialogue in its Social and Political Contexts, Castiglione to Galileo* (Cambridge, 1992), p. 5.

the text foregrounds its own terms of representation as a way of illustrating the process in which knowledge is constructed and transmitted.[23]

The dialogue form is characteristically *un*formed, a protean quality that is reflected in its application to a diverse range of texts and genres. As Jon R. Snyder has noted, it is a form especially well-suited for those 'marginal' kinds of texts that do not conform to traditional definitions of genre.[24] *The Surveyor's Dialogue* is similarly difficult to categorize: while the text's comparatively brief discussion of the geometric and mathematical aspects of surveying distinguishes it from other surveying manuals, its fairly utilitarian use of the dialogue convention also creates challenges for analyzing it in terms of its literary qualities. But by hewing so closely to the context of spoken dialogue, and thereby creating a text that has a 'low level of literization',[25] Norden also facilitates its pedagogical function. The dialogues themselves stage scenes of learning that provide models for readers' own acquisition of knowledge.

From his opening debate with the Farmer onwards, the Surveyor quite literally has a lot of explaining to do, a pedagogical context that is sustained throughout the remaining dialogues. Whereas the Surveyor initially has to justify his presence in the first book, different skills are called for in Book 2, his dialogue with the Lord, an absentee aristocratic landowner who needs to be informed about even the most basic aspects of the manorial system, from its origins and history to the kinds of feudal services that can still be demanded from tenants. The Farmer reappears for the following three books, but in a new identity as the Bailiff, the Lord's legal officer. The longest section, Book 3, emphasizes not only the physical work of conducting a survey, following the Surveyor and Bailiff as they travel the bounds of the manor and question a Jury of tenants, but also its underlying legal basis, with the Surveyor enumerating the procedures that comprise a Court of Survey. The relatively brief Book 4 outlines instructions for measuring land and converting it into mathematically determined 'plots', and includes a series of geometric images and tables to demonstrate these calculations (pp. 127 and ff.). Book 5 provides an extended discussion of techniques of soil management and agricultural improvement, covering such issues as deforestation and fen drainage, while Book 6, the shortest of the dialogues, offers an exchange between the

---

[23] For Cox, the exchanges among speakers in a dialogic text are also replicated by a 'literary transaction' between the text and readers (ibid., pp. 4–5). Another dialogic feature of Norden's text is provided by his marginal notes, which sometimes offer a perspective distinct from that of the main text: for discussion, see Bartolovich, 'Boundary Disputes', p. 58.

[24] Jon R. Snyder, *Writing the Scene of Speaking: Theories of Dialogue in the Late Italian Renaissance* (Stanford, 1989), pp. 7–8. Among other discussions of the early modern dialogue, see Lynne Magnusson, *Shakespeare and Social Dialogue: Dramatic Language and Elizabethan Letters* (Cambridge, 1999); Dorothea B. Heitsch and Jean-Francois Vallee, intro., *Printed Voices: The Renaissance Culture of Dialogue* (Toronto, 2004), pp. ix–xxiii; Kenneth J. Wilson, *Incomplete Fictions: The Formation of English Renaissance Dialogue* (Washington, DC, 1985).

[25] Snyder, p. 9.

Surveyor and a Purchaser of Land in which the latter is advised to lease property rather than owning it as a freehold tenant.

The thematic versatility of *The Surveyor's Dialogue* is reflected in the frequency with which it has been cited in critical studies from a range of fields: not only early modern surveying, but also mathematics, geometry, and the history of science, mapping and the history of cartography, agrarian and agricultural history, and economic history, especially Marxist studies of the history of capitalism. These studies seldom consider the text's literary qualities, however, and in most cases *The Surveyor's Dialogue* is treated as a historical document and plumbed for its referential content. As a result, discussions tend to be short and highly selective, rarely referring to more than a passage or two from the text. Despite the frequency with which the text is cited, no published critical study has analyzed *The Surveyor's Dialogue* in its entirety.[26] But attention to the whole of the text leads to some unexpected results, including a sense of the importance of several topics that have not received due critical attention, from the representation of the agrarian poor, and the emergence of a national market, to changes occurring to the natural landscape such as deforestation, issues that will be discussed later in the Introduction. Through its dialogic form, the text offers multiple perspectives on these developments, even at those moments when it attempts to quell critique and offer a defense of the status quo. The unsettled status of these topics is additionally evinced by a number of textual cruxes. Norden made several key revisions to his final edition of 1618, particularly in Book 5's discussion of enclosure and deforestation, changes that reflect the complexity of his own position. Particularly in these sections, the text's form and conventions of representation are integral components of its engagement with social and historical contexts.

---

[26]   The only extended discussions of *The Surveyor's Dialogue* have been chapters in dissertations: see Bartolovich, 'Boundary Disputes', pp. 16–61 and Kitchen, 'Cosmo-Choro-Polygrapher', pp. 240–58.

Manorial Culture

Freehold

The Surveyor's Dialogue is so immersed in its various contexts—the legal, agricultural, and scientific discourses of its time—that it offers particular challenges for a modern reader unfamiliar with the specialized languages of these fields. The first context that is necessary to explain is the complicated workings of tenure, the terms regulating property ownership and relations of service in the early modern period. A discussion of agrarian social relations is complicated by the fact that a manor possessed several different forms of tenure: freehold, copyhold, and leasehold. If a tenant was a freeholder, this designation referred to the terms of tenure rather than the tenant's class status. Consequently, a tenant could at the same time be a freeholder of one property and a copyholder of another. Freehold tenure closely approximated ownership of the land, and it granted tenants the full right to sell or transfer holdings as well as confer property to stipulated heirs. Freehold provided a security of tenure due to the fact that it fell under the jurisdiction of the common law, thereby providing tenants with a legal foundation to title outside the manorial system.[1] Over the course of the early modern period, freeholders increasingly removed themselves from ties to their erstwhile manors, an independence that was generalized with the abolition of feudal tenures in 1660.[2]

One finds freeholders often referred to as 'yeomen' or 'capitalist farmers' in critical discussions of agrarian relations. As these terms indicate, freeholders formed an elite among the tenancy, an intermediate class situated below the gentry but above customary tenants. The landowning class of a typical village was split between two relatively small elites: the local gentry, the traditional landowners and social superiors, along with a prosperous, socially mobile contingent of freeholder tenants. Through their ownership of their land, both of these groups were differentiated from two much larger classes: the tenant farmers who possessed their land through copyhold (customary) tenure, a population three or four times the size of the number of freeholders, and the unpropertied poor—servants, cottagers, and wage-laborers—who comprised as much as two-thirds of the rural population.[3] Freeholders also formed the professional class of agrarian England: the Lord's stewards and bailiffs, the officials administering his estate, were drawn from the manor's freeholders, as were members of the Juries who oversaw the proceedings of the manorial court and authorized the results of surveys.

---

[1]   Richard Lachmann, *From Manor to Market: Structural Change in England, 1536–1640* (Madison, WI, 1987), p. 38.

[2]   Christopher Hill, *The Century of Revolution, 1603–1714* (1961; New York, 1982), p. 127; Bartolovich, 'Boundary Disputes', n. 33, pp. 208–9.

[3]   Raymond Williams, *The Country and the City* (New York, 1973), p. 102.

A discussion of freehold tenure is especially relevant to an analysis of Book 1 of *The Surveyor's Dialogue*. Although the Surveyor's interlocutor is referred to as 'Farmer' throughout this initial dialogue, he is more accurately described as a freeholder. Recognizing the precise character of this figure's social position significantly alters the conventional reading of this section. Past discussions of the text have assumed that the Farmer is a customary tenant because of his initial resistance to the kinds of innovations achieved through surveys, from a limited access to commons, and an increase of fines and rents, to a more precise demarcation of property boundaries. But in defending custom the Farmer is concerned less with tenants' customary rights than with the ability of commercial farmers to possess a form of tenure that secures title to their land as absolute property: 'and for freeholders' deeds, their Land is their own, and whether they may be compelled to shew them or not, I cannot tell' (p. 37). His ultimate defense of the Surveyor's presence therefore does not reverse or contradict his earlier position; it merely stems from his realization that the survey will benefit his economic interests as a freeholder.

One can assume an implied readership of freeholder tenants for *The Surveyor's Dialogue* due to the fact that the text addresses representatives of this class in five of its six books. The dialogues featuring the Farmer, the Farmer in his guise as Bailiff, and the Purchaser of Land thereby provide pedagogical templates for readers, and they offer rudimentary instructions on the components of surveying, from its legal process (Book 3) to land measurement (Book 4) and improvement techniques to the soil (Book 5).[4] But even as the text confers knowledge that will enable freeholders to advance their position in an increasingly market-oriented environment, it also expresses an ambivalence regarding the effects of their social mobility. If rents have increased along with property values, the Surveyor attributes these changes to ambitious freeholders who have driven up prices through competitive land auctions (p. 23). Freeholders are closely associated with agrarian capitalism throughout the text, and the Surveyor's frequent admonitions to the Farmer and his counterparts are intended to ensure that this class sustains its position in a managed way. In Book 6, for example, he advises the Purchaser of Land to acquire land on shorter-term leases rather than the more stable but less profitable terms of freehold tenure. This recommendation derives from a concern that freeholders will take on the attributes of the landed gentry as they acquire wealth and position, and, in becoming 'gentlemen', will consequently opt out of the risky market in favor of sustaining their wealth for posterity. Risk and uncertainty thus become encoded in the terms of agrarian social relations, a

---

[4]   The intended readership of *The Surveyor's Dialogue* distinguishes it from other early modern texts on agriculture, which generally addressed an audience of gentlemen farmers (Andrew McRae, 'Husbandry Manuals and the Language of Agrarian Improvement', in *Culture and Cultivation in Early Modern England: Writing and the Land*, Michael Leslie and Timothy Raylor [eds] [Leicester, 1992], pp. 44–5, and *God Speed the Plough: The Representation of Agrarian England* [Cambridge, 1996], p. 145).

social logic in which freeholders are integral to the formation of capital. While they are differentiated from small landowners and customary tenants due to their acquisition of wealth and consequent social mobility, they are also denied the security that derives from stable land title or the acquisition of rank, estate, and other forms of social capital.[5]

Copyhold and Custom

Over the course of the early modern period, freeholder tenants were increasingly differentiated from the larger mass of customary tenants and agricultural laborers. Copyhold tenure itself had initially emerged as an effort to stabilize agrarian social relations in the aftermath of the Black Death in the fourteenth century. The ensuing scarcity of labor rendered laborers far more valuable as well as mobile, forcing landlords to offer their tenants better terms and a security of tenure in the form of copyhold.[6] Tenants were consequently ensured a fixed rent, the right to renew their leases with a limited fine, and the ability to pay their rent in cash rather than through feudal duties of service.[7] Copyhold tenure thus coordinated aspects of feudal service with market dynamics, a juxtaposition that carries over into Norden's discussion in Book 2. Norden insists on preserving the distinctive rituals of feudal service, even if solely in ceremonial form. Because tenants—freeholders as well as copyholders—'still owe services unto their Lords' (p. 39), the Surveyor lists the various fines and gifts that tenants must provide their landlords. Feudal service provided continuity with the past, a way of enshrining tradition and ensuring that tenants stay in place. Yet Norden also recognizes that this economy of symbolic deference is always already shaped by the conditions of the market. Even in his analysis of the genealogy of villeinage, or bond-servitude, he acknowledges that these terms of service exist in name only, and are ultimately incompatible with market relations, 'for if the Lord buy or sell with his bond Tenant, it is an immediate enfranchisement of the Tenant and his posterity' (p. 75).

The defining feature of copyhold was the security it provided: a guarantee of fixed rent and protection from arbitrary fines or eviction that was backed by the written deed (copy) entered into the roll of the manorial court. But alongside its legal foundation, copyhold also acquired the force of unwritten 'custom'. There was an underlying assumption that the terms of copyhold derived not from specific social conditions or legal arrangements but from customary practices preserved from 'time immemorial'.[8] Because of this correlation, copyhold tenure

---

[5]   Norden therefore refuses to see freehold as analogous to absolute property, insisting that it offers only 'conditional' title to land (p. 39).

[6]   See Richard Lachmann, *Capitalists in Spite of Themselves: Elite Conflict and Economic Transitions in Early Modern Europe* (Oxford, 2000), p. 175.

[7]   Lachmann, *From Manor to Market*, pp. 38–9.

[8]   The classic analysis of this issue is J.G.A. Pocock's *The Ancient Constitution and the Feudal Law* (1957; New York, 1967), esp. pp. 30–55.

is often referred to as 'customary' tenure. One of the most significant changes affecting early modern agrarian society was an overarching erosion of the rights of customary tenants. At the beginning of the early modern period, customary tenants formed nearly two-thirds of all landholders in England and were 'by far the most important class in the agricultural life of the country'.[9] By the end of the seventeenth century, only one-third of tenants retained their land through customary tenure, and this number would dwindle even further over the course of the eighteenth century.[10] But as copyhold tenure declined in practice, the idea of custom assumed a new importance. The defense of custom offered a language for articulating popular protest against the unequal terms of economic improvement. Although often steeped in nostalgia and traditionalism, it also provided a framework through which new rights could be asserted.[11] As C.E. Searle notes, custom 'was not something fixed and immutable. … On the contrary, its definition was highly variable in relation to class position, and accordingly it became a vehicle for conflict not cohesion'.[12] Moreover, the conflicts centering on definitions of custom were often battles that pitted groups of the tenancy against one another. The 'internal divisions' among intermediate groups such as freeholders and copyholders played a role as significant as landlord-tenant relations in transforming definitions of tenure and property.[13]

Custom also possessed a specific, localized meaning in the early modern period. When Norden mentions 'custom', he is referring to the customary practices of individual manors. Custom, in this context, is thought of solely as 'the custom of the manor' rather than as a more generalized or abstract principle. But just as the theory of custom possessed a semantic flexibility, the practices of copyhold tenure were similarly variable and amorphous throughout the early modern period.[14] At times, this would benefit tenants, who could lay claim to land title or specific rights based on prior, 'customary' use, and even reinforce their rights through vague recourse to historical precedent. But the ambiguity of custom also gave landlords greater latitude in implementing changes against copyhold tenants, and, in fact, half of customary tenants lacked security of tenure, making them

---

[9]   R.H. Tawney, *The Agrarian Problem in the Sixteenth Century* (1912; New York, 1967), p. 41.

[10]   E.P. Thompson, 'Custom, Law and Common Right', *Customs in Common: Studies in Traditional Popular Culture* (New York, 1993), p. 114. For a recent assessment of critical views regarding the decline of customary tenure in the early modern period, see Henry French and Richard Hoyle, *The Character of English Rural Society: Earls Colne, 1550–1750* (Manchester, 2007).

[11]   Thompson, p. 1. For a related discussion, see Andy Wood, 'The Place of Custom in Plebeian Political Culture: England, 1550–1800', *Social History* 22 (1997): 46–60.

[12]   Qtd in Thompson, p. 110.

[13]   Williams, *The Country and the City*, p. 40.

[14]   Sir Edward Coke similarly noted that 'should I go about the catalogue of several customs, I should with Sysiphus … undertake an endless piece of work' (qtd in Thompson, 'Custom', p. 137).

vulnerable to the effects of change, which ranged from raised rents and fines to eviction from their holdings.[15] Norden's own recommendations similarly erode the foundational conditions of copyhold tenure. Instead of ensuring fixed fees, for instance, he argues that landlords must respond to market conditions and retain their power to raise rents and entry fines (p. 23).

Throughout his text, Norden is highly skeptical of any claims deriving from custom. As a consequence, he never refers to it as an abstraction but only in reference to the particular practices of a specific social unit. Custom is limited to a strictly legal definition in his mind, one that renders it synonymous with copyhold tenure.[16] Instead of positing custom as unwritten or unchanging[17] its basis, instead, is entry in the court-roll of the manor. These records constitute a historical authority that underwrites social stability: 'ancient Records, and books of *Survey* of great antiquity' (p. 143) are 'so much the more certain, by how much the more ancient' (p. 80). But Norden is at pains to explain why landlords are nonetheless able to abuse their authority, and he can only feebly lay blame on a lack of records, in which case 'neither memory or record can reform them' (p. 26). By contrast, the Farmer in Book 1 offers a critique of this emphasis on material records: deeds may not only be altered or counterfeited (p. 37), they also require interpretation, and, ultimately, can create as many disputes as they settle (p. 24). The focus on material documentation becomes, in the Farmer's comic reformulation, an image of the surveyor carrying his 'whole trunk full of records' (p. 31) over the course of his survey. Since the Farmer possesses a dual role as the manor's Bailiff, the figure responsible for the manor's records (p. 80), this satire also reflects on the limits of his own knowledge. Indeed, the Surveyor later reprimands the Farmer/Bailiff for the latter's carelessness, noting that his errors will be enshrined for posterity (pp. 85, 145).

Leasehold: Agrarian Capitalism and Neofeudalism

Norden generally consigns customary tenure to the past, casting it as a residual practice that was slowly being phased out in most manors. As the Surveyor notes in his second dialogue with the Lord, customary rights were established at the initial formation of the manorial system, and neither Lords nor tenants had the authority to create new customs (p. 55). Any changes to tenure could occur only outside the customary realm with the introduction of market-based adjustments to entry fines, rents, and the terms of tenure itself. Leasehold tenure, the third and most innovative form of tenure, thus began to compete with and increasingly

---

[15]   John E. Martin, *Feudalism to Capitalism: Peasant and Landlord in English Agrarian Development* (London, 1983), pp. 118, 128.

[16]   See Norden's discussion of custom on pp. 49 and ff.

[17]   Except in the case of the Lord's property, which the Surveyor presents as 'all such Lands, as have been time out of the memory of man, used and occupied in the Lord's own hands' (p. 49).

replace both freehold and copyhold forms of tenure. As Robert Brenner has argued, the transfer of land from the customary sector to leasehold was instrumental in forestalling the development of 'peasant proprietorship'.[18] There were positive effects stemming from these changes, including the elimination of the coercive, non-economic forms of surplus extraction that had typified feudal terms of service. However, the dwindling opportunities for most tenants to gain direct ownership of their land also helped create an environment in which producers 'had no choice, in order to maintain themselves, but to buy and sell on the market'.[19]

As Crystal Bartolovich has noted, one of the underlying conflicts running throughout Norden's text is a tension between 'market' and 'manor' discourses.[20] While the Surveyor consistently endorses economic innovations such as leasehold that accelerate the development of market-driven models of land ownership and commerce, he also attempts to preserve the social stability that he associates with manorial society. A distinctive quality of the text is this division it insists on maintaining between economic and social spheres. Yet this disjunction is itself a symptom of emergent market relations, reflecting the assumption that the 'market' can be held at a safe distance from social relations, and that change can be contained so as not to disrupt the imputed tranquility of the domestic space. The manor, in this context, is defined not only as 'home', the geographic space of residence, but also more broadly as the space of social habitus, the conceptual frame of reference that defines ways of thought and structures of feeling.[21] The dominant feudal language of *The Surveyor's Dialogue* reveals more than just the residual influence of feudal relations, or an inability to conceptualize newer, more capitalist dynamics. Rather, the recourse to feudal traditions as a way of conferring social and conceptual stability is itself what transforms this older social system. Feudalism is not only revived—it is reinvented. As a result, the neofeudal environment presented by Norden is one that already contains the capitalist attributes whose development he is trying to forestall. As Ellen Wood has noted, capitalist relations arose when class groups, in conflict with one another, tried to 'reproduce themselves *as they were*'.[22] Change, in other words, was effected precisely by the attempt to stay in place and

---

[18]   Robert Brenner, 'Agrarian Class Structure and Economic Development in Pre-Industrial Europe', in T.H. Aston and C.H.E. Philpin (eds), *The Brenner Debate: Agrarian Class Structure and Economic Development in Pre-Industrial Europe* (Cambridge, 1985), p. 47.

[19]   Brenner, 'The Agrarian Roots of European Capitalism', *Brenner Debate*, p. 214. The point of reference for discussions of agrarian capitalism is, of course, Marx's analysis of 'primitive accumulation' in volume 1 of *Capital* (see *Capital: A Critique of Political Economy, volume one*, trans. Ben Fowkes [Harmondsworth, 1976], pp. 873–913). Richard Halpern provides an invaluable analysis of Marx's critical paradigm in *The Poetics of Primitive Accumulation: English Renaissance Culture and the Genealogy of Capital* (Ithaca, NY, 1991), esp. 1–15 and 61–100.

[20]   Bartolovich, 'Boundary Disputes', p. 30.

[21]   I am drawing on Pierre Bourdieu, *Outline of a Theory of Practice* (Cambridge, 1977) and Raymond Williams, *Marxism and Literature* (Oxford, 1977), pp. 128–35.

[22]   Ellen Meiksins Wood, *The Origin of Capitalism* (New York, 1999), p. 45.

sustain traditional hierarchies and social practices. The 'unintended consequence' of these changes, Wood adds, was that classes were forced to adapt to 'market imperatives' in order to maintain social position and economic stability.[23]

Professionalism and Value

Over the course of the text, it is the Farmer/Bailiff, the Surveyor's interlocutor in four of the six dialogues, who illustrates most fully the effects of emergent market conditions. When he first appears in the opening book, the Farmer insistently defends his own and other tenants' customary ties to the land. But his gradual support of surveying results from an appreciation of the Surveyor as a uniquely professional figure, a mediator ultimately working independently of the landowners who employ him.[24] This professional role serves as a model for the reconstitution of the Farmer's own identity. When the Surveyor encounters him again in Book 3, the Farmer is referred to as the Lord's Bailiff, the manorial official in charge of arranging for freeholder tenants to serve as jurors in manorial court proceedings, a professional identity he retains over the course of the remaining dialogues. Erasing his customary ties to the land, as well as his economic interest in the Court of Survey being conducted, the Farmer is thereby similarly transformed into an official—the Bailiff—whose identity is predicated by his expertise rather than his interests.[25] When he announces his desire to become a professional surveyor as well (p. 32), the Farmer correlates the social claims of surveying—its ability to settle disputes objectively—with its professional foundation as a set of transferable skills and an acquirable body of knowledge.

As the Surveyor conducts his survey over the course of Books 3 and 4, he and the Bailiff engage in a series of knowledge transactions.[26] Along with other freeholder tenants, the Bailiff supplies the Surveyor with the information he requires for his survey as they accompany him on his perambulation of the manor in the third book. In Book 4, the Surveyor converts the raw data drawn from his informants into geometrically determined 'plots', abstracting the land from the

---

[23]   Ibid., p. 45; on this point, also see Brenner, 'Agrarian Class Structure'.

[24]   Professionalism is a topic that has only recently begun to receive critical attention, and my own analysis is indebted to Eric Ash's illuminating discussion of 'expert mediators' in *Power, Knowledge, and Expertise in Elizabethan England* (Baltimore, 2004). For an extended discussion, also see Edward Gieskes's *Representing the Professions: Administration, the Law, and Theater in Early Modern England* (Newark, DE, 2006).

[25]   In another instance correlating professionalism and objectivity, the Lord is angered by what he perceives as the unwarranted impartiality of the Surveyor, who will provide an indifferent account both to tenants and the landlord employing him (p. 65).

[26]   This term derives from Lisa Jardine and William Sherman, 'Pragmatic Readers: Knowledge Transactions and Scholarly Services in Late Elizabethan England', in Anthony Fletcher and Peter Roberts (eds), *Religion, Culture and Society in Early Modern Britain* (Cambridge, 1994), p. 102.

verbal context of dialogue and negotiation. Dialogue remains integral even in this section, however, with Book 4 depicting a reciprocal exchange, a pedagogical context in which the Surveyor instructs the Bailiff in the rudiments of triangulation and land measurement. The legitimacy of the Surveyor's craft is ensured through its replication; the fact that the Bailiff could conduct his own survey and arrive at the same results confirms the status of surveying as an objective body of knowledge, instrumental in character and transferable in its applications. Surveying, in this context, functions merely as a closed system, one that deals exclusively with questions of measurement, calculation, and the gathering of information.

But the rules of this language game shift when the Bailiff presses for the referential content of the survey, that is, the monetary value assessed to individual plots of land. It is at this point that the Bailiff's identity is reconstituted once more: no longer a professional officer of the manor, he becomes, instead, a 'stranger' in the dominions of his Lord. Shifting to the third-person, the Surveyor declaims that 'he is no true Surveyor for the Lord, that will make the same known to strangers' (p. 144). Even though, he notes, 'there are some things which may be public', others are to be insistently kept 'private, and to be concealed', even from the professional managers of the estate (p. 145). Withholding the property values from the Bailiff, the Surveyor advises him to consult another surveying manual and improve his technical knowledge rather than inquire into matters beyond his concern (p. 145). To preserve rights of property, the content of the survey must remain concealed.

Norden's recommendation is in keeping with the institutional secrecy that surrounded the production and dissemination of early modern surveys, documents that in most cases did not circulate among a wider audience. As J.B. Harley has noted, early modern mapping was a technology whose value was contingent on the secrecy of its information.[27] The survey functioned not only as an instrument of capital, used to assess and assign value, but also as a form of capital itself, albeit one whose value depended on the concealment rather than the circulation of its contents. In practice, early modern surveyors had their own capital interest in preserving the secrecy of their surveys: unbeknownst to the tenants providing them with information, surveyors could claim for themselves any previously 'concealed lands' that they had uncovered in the course of their work.[28]

Even as this information is withheld from him, the Bailiff's curiosity about land values testifies to the final transformation he has undergone over the course of the text. By seeing the land in terms of value, and in relation to fluctuating terms determined by market conditions, the Bailiff assimilates himself to an emergent logic of agrarian capital. But even as he embraces the market so fully,

---

[27]   Harley, 'Silences and Secrecy: The Hidden Agenda of Cartography in Early Modern Europe', *Imago Mundi* 40 (1988): 61. For a related discussion, see my chapter 'Forgetting the Ulster Plantation', in *England's Internal Colonies: Class, Capital, and the Literature of Early Modern English Colonialism* (New York, 2003), esp. pp. 187–8.

[28]   Kerridge, *Agrarian Problems*, p. 27.

he is denied access to any knowledge of its workings. Book 4 concludes with the Surveyor dropping a bombshell on the Bailiff and informing him that the survey has in fact ascertained his poor job performance, that he has not 'been so careful and provident for the Lord's profit' (p. 145). It is this revelation that provides the context for Book 5, the longest dialogue in the text, in which the Surveyor instructs the Bailiff on the latest techniques for improving agricultural production: soil management, including irrigation and drainage, the planting of hedges, trees, and forests, and the production of agricultural commodities for a national market.

The Country and the City

Books 5 and 6 of *The Surveyor's Dialogue* have remained the most overlooked portions of a text that is itself read far too selectively. But these final two dialogues provide invaluable accounts of the social effects of emergent market relations in agrarian England. In Book 5, the Surveyor's description of techniques of agricultural improvement creates a framework of a national market, one that denaturalizes local customs by comparing them to other regions, thereby offering a mode of analysis that enables a transition to agricultural production for the market. Book 6 consists of the Surveyor's encounter with a Purchaser of Land, a freeholder tenant who had earlier appeared as a member of the Jury for the Court of Survey. Moreover, these final books—like the text as a whole—are significant in terms of what they do not discuss, particularly in terms of two key omissions: Norden's steadfast refusal to acknowledge the Midland Rising, a popular rebellion occurring at the same time he was initially composing his text in 1607, and his scant reference to the practices of enclosure that were at the center of ongoing disputes in the Midlands and elsewhere.

A National Market

Drawing on his background as a writer of devotional texts,[1] Norden concludes Book 6 on an apocalyptic note, envisaging the demise of the values associated with agrarian culture.[2] The dominance of market relations is likened to the spread of disease: All that is solid melts into air, and the erosion of boundaries separating agrarian England from its urban counterpart ensures that neither region is able

---

[1] Norden wrote 24 devotional texts, the most popular of which was *A pensiue mans practise* (London, 1586). This text, which went through 17 editions by 1640, was augmented with second and third parts in later editions (*The pensiue mans practise. The second part. Or the pensiue mans complaint and comfort* [1593] and *A progress of pietie, being the third part of the Pensiue mans practice* [1598]). For discussion, see Alfred W. Pollard, 'The Unity of John Norden: Surveyor and Religious Writer', *The Library* 7, 3 (1926): 233–52 and Frank Kitchen, 'Cosmo-Choro-Polygrapher', pp. 152–73. Kitchen also provides a bibliography of Norden's religious writings (pp. 349–63).

[2] Norden himself traversed urban as well as rural contexts, with much of his personal and professional life centered on London. A longtime resident of Middlesex, his map and description of that region was the most successful volume in his *Speculum Britanniae* series (*Speculum Britanniae. The first parte of an historicall description of Middlesex* [London, 1593]). He also composed several maps of London, including maps of the City and Westminster in his *Middlesex* volume, along with two later maps: *The view of London bridge from east to west* (London, 1597; republished in 1624) and *Civitas Londoni* (London, 1600).

to fend off this decay (p. 201). Contradicting this concluding sermon, however, Norden's text as a whole attests to the economic interdependence of rural, seemingly neofeudal England and its emergent urban counterpart, the rapidly sprawling metropolis of London. It illustrates the ways that the formation of capital creates the conditions for an 'unprecedented kind of *internal* market',[3] a circuit of production and circulation that elides boundaries separating rural from urban markets. In this context, the housewives of Hertfordshire and Middlesex produce their goods for the London market, 'as they do all other vendible things else' (p. 165), and even an object like a fish-pond, traditionally associated with the pleasures of rustic retreat, becomes a commodity 'vented very beneficially' to an urban clientele (p. 173). Literalizing the eroding grounds of regional distinction, Norden notes that the land itself has become transformed and associated with mobility and commodification, with rural soil and limestone transported to London while the city's waste is taken to its western suburbs for conversion to compost (p. 181).

A figure of uncertain provenance, the Surveyor himself embodies the distinctive placelessness that accompanies capital formation. It is never stipulated, after all, where the Surveyor has come from, where his home is located, or where he will be employed next. Lacking ties to any region or locality, the Surveyor instead brings with him a national frame of reference.[4] This changing sense of place is a perspective that is increasingly shared by the Farmer/Bailiff, whose shifting social position—as he moves from tenant farmer to manorial official to aspiring surveyor—is marked by a growing knowledge acquired through extensive domestic travel.[5] Assuming the universalized position of the professional subject,[6] the Bailiff begins to refer to the customs of his 'country' (p. 188) *as* customs—as local, subjective, and open to reform and improvement. Those tenants who oppose such innovations become associated, in his mind, with 'country willfulness' (p. 151): the refusal to comply with the new terms of the market is reinscribed as a stubborn adherence to an outmoded sense of regional specificity.

Norden's Surveyor imagines the nation as a serialized, interlocking network of localities, and his analysis is insistently comparative, drawing analogies from the practices and commodities of other regions: the price of wheat at Royston, Hertfordshire (p. 23); the unit of measurement used in Shippon, Berkshire

---

3   Wood, *Origin of Capitalism*, p. 40.

4   The most influential discussion of Norden in the context of English nationhood is Richard Helgerson's 'The Land Speaks' essay, included in his *Forms of Nationhood: The Elizabethan Writing of England* (Chicago, 1992), pp. 107–47. But whereas Helgerson links mapping and surveying with a sense of the particularity of place, my own discussion emphasizes the abstracting power of market relations.

5   The Farmer mentions having traveled to London, where he saw surveyors advertising their services (p. 24), and later reveals knowledge of Somerset (p. 182) as well as the problem of flooding in the East Anglian Fenlands (p. 150); these details counter his later self-deprecating remark that 'I have been no great traveller' (p. 165).

6   On this point, see Sukanya Banerjee, *Becoming Imperial Citizens: Indians in the Late-Victorian Empire* (Durham, NC, 2010).

(p. 58); the practices of inheritance found in Kilmersdon, Somerset (p. 94); the production of cider in Devon (p. 164). The emergence of a national market in turn leads to the creation of regional specialization, with the commodities of a region increasingly standing in for the lost distinctiveness of local identity. In representing a national market, Norden additionally transforms the model of exchange, moving away from a local, customary basis to a generalized abstraction of a national market. He therefore advocates the standardization of units of measurement, for example (p. 142); in order to facilitate the movement of goods between regions, any quaint customs and practices that impede the circulation of commodities are seen as expendable.[7]

The creation of a national market is therefore also predicated by its exclusions. Norden's text never mentions Scotland, for instance, and contains few references either to Wales (pp. 164, 180) or areas of the North Country (pp. 99, 102). If the market creates a network linking together the nation's constituent 'countries', those regions excluded from economic development are also excised from the mental map of the nation.[8] However, demonstrating how inclusion in the national market is not solely a demographic factor attributable to agricultural output, an odd feature of the text is that it never even mentions the Midlands. Norden's image of England has an absent geographic center, and his discussion omits an entire swath of the nation: Oxfordshire, Warwickshire, Northamptonshire, Leicestershire, Nottingham, Rutland, Huntingtonshire, Bedfordshire.[9] There was no economic justification for this exclusion, since the Midlands constituted one of the most commercially viable and productive areas of the country.[10] Nor did this exemption result from Norden's professional specialization, for while he was employed most

---

[7]   Appropriately, Norden was the first cartographer to indicate roads on his maps when he included this feature as part of his county map of Cornwall (*Speculi Britanniae Pars: A Topographical and Historical Description of Cornwall* [London, 1728]). In addition, one of Norden's most popular texts, *England An Intended Guyde, for English Travailers* (London, 1625), consisted of a series of charts marking distances between towns in each county, while a general chart providing distances between towns in England and Wales was sold as a separate broadside (*A table shewing the distances betweene all the Cities and Shire Townes of England* [London, 1625]). For discussion of Norden's 'road maps,' see Garrett A. Sullivan, *The Drama of Landscape: Land, Property, and Social Relations on the Early Modern Stage* (Stanford, 1998), pp. 129–34.

[8]   Literal markets—that is, market towns—were likewise unevenly distributed throughout England and Wales, with the greatest concentration in the southwest (Dorset, Somerset, Gloucestershire) and southeast (Suffolk, Kent) (Thirsk [ed.], *The Agrarian History of England and Wales*, vol. 4, p. 496).

[9]   Norden provides a thorough survey of agricultural practices in England, referring to 30 of 39 counties in the course of his text. Significantly, eight of the nine counties not mentioned in his text are located in the Midlands.

[10]   Thirsk (ed.), *The Agrarian History of England and Wales*, vol. 4, p. 496.

often in the West Country and Home Counties, he worked on several occasions in the Midlands as well.[11]

The Midland Rising

There was a more direct reason for Norden's omission of the Midlands from his view of England's national market. As he composed his text in 1607, one of the largest agrarian protests of the early modern period—the Midland Rising—was taking place throughout the region. What had begun that April as a series of protests against the enclosure of arable land by large landowners in Northamptonshire soon grew into a mobilization of more than 1,000 rioters. Over the next two months this rebel group conducted a series of attacks against enclosures, and expanded their activities throughout Warwickshire and Leicestershire before being violently suppressed by the local militia on 8 June.[12] Acknowledging the significance of the Midland Rising counters the assumption that early modern England lacked any major instances of popular revolt in the century from the 1540s to the 1640s. On the contrary, approximately 125 enclosure-riots took place in the Jacobean period alone.[13] The Midland Rising was the largest, most organized, and most sustained of these efforts. It was also a protest distinctive for its ideological foundation. By casting themselves as 'Diggers' in their seizure of commons, the rioters articulated a model of popular protest, a precedent that would later be consciously invoked by Gerrard Winstanley and other radicals in the 1640s and 1650s.[14]

Previous discussions of Norden's text have noted that the Rising occurred roughly around the time that *The Surveyor's Dialogue* was first published.[15] But this context is more than a coincidence, and Norden in fact wrote his text in the months

---

[11]   Norden would have been especially acquainted with Northamptonshire. His description of the county, begun in 1591 under the direction of Lord Burghley and intended for inclusion among his proposed series of county maps, was published posthumously as *Speculi Britanniae Pars Altera: Or, a Delineation of Northamptonshire* (London, 1720). Norden also surveyed estates in Huntingtonshire and Leicestershire, although in 1619, a year after the publication of the third and final edition of *The Surveyor's Dialogue* (Kitchen, 'Cosmo-Choro-Polygrapher', pp. 23–31, 388, 400).

[12]   On the Midland Rising, see Steve Hindle, 'Imagining Insurrection in Seventeenth-Century England: Representations of the Midland Rising of 1607', *History Workshop* 66 (2008): 21–61; Roger B. Manning, *Village Revolts: Social Protest and Popular Disturbances in England, 1509–1640* (Oxford, 1988), pp. 82–107; and Martin, *Feudalism to Capitalism*, pp. 161–79.

[13]   Manning, *Village Revolts*, p. 82.

[14]   James Holstun, *Ehud's Dagger: Class Struggle in the English Revolution* (London, 2002), pp. 372, 382.

[15]   See Bartolovich, 'Boundary Disputes', p. 33 and Klein, *Maps and the Writing of Space*, p. 59.

following these events.[16] He therefore omits any reference to the Rising in order to suppress the memory of a context whose implications threaten to undermine his entire project.[17] But the Rising nonetheless manifests itself within the text, often in vague allusions such as the references to unspecified forms of 'disorder' and 'complaints' that pervade the first dialogue with the Farmer (p. 35). The text's gaps often take on a willfully perverse form: when Norden's Surveyor includes a sample document of a precept calling a jury of tenants to the manorial court, he dates his letter 3 June, with the court to open 10 June 1607, the same week as the bloody skirmish that ended the Midland Rising (p. 83). In other words, Norden deliberately sets his dialogues at exactly the same time as the Midland Rising, insistent to have business carry on as usual in Beauland Manor, undisturbed by the most tumultuous events in agrarian England during the Jacobean period.[18]

The context of the Midland Rising bears on the text in other ways as well. Given Norden's flourishing second career as the writer of popular devotional tracts, many of which appealed to a nonconformist audience, it is surprising to find that he generally avoids theological topics in *The Surveyor's Dialogue*. But because the ideological program of the Rising was one of militant Protestantism, such references possessed a dangerous topicality. In the second book, for example, the Lord dismisses the Surveyor's infusion of religious language as something that 'digress[es] from our present matter' (p. 67) and grows increasingly uncomfortable with the implications of the Surveyor's use of scripture.[19] At the conclusion of that book, the Lord reminds his interlocutor that he has 'heard all thy discourse with patience', and also grumbles that 'there is no comfort in a discontented people' (p. 77). Ultimately, however, the Lord has little cause for concern; even though the Surveyor draws on scripture to curtail the actions of landowners—to be moderate in enforcing forfeitures, for example (p. 61)—he most often directs his biblical citations against tenants, as when he warns that God will punish them if they lie or withhold information from the survey (pp. 33, 85).

---

[16] Although the 1607 edition's dedicatory epistle to Robert Cecil is signed 1 January 1607 (sig. A4), one must keep in mind that the New Year began on 25 March in the early modern period, and that the text would therefore have been completed by 1 January 1608, more than six months after the violent suppression of the Midland Rising.

[17] My discussion draws on Pierre Macherey, *A Theory of Literary Production* (1966; London, 1978), esp. pp. 85–9.

[18] The second-largest anti-enclosure riot of the period, in Ladbroke, Warwickshire, also took place during the first week of June 1607 (Manning, *Village Revolts*, p. 82). This event is additionally noteworthy due to the involvement of a local landowner, William Shakespeare. For discussion of the impact of these events on Shakespeare's drama, see Richard Wilson, 'Against the Grain: Representing the Market in *Coriolanus*', *The Seventeenth Century* 6 (1991): 111–48.

[19] In Book 1, the Surveyor similarly objects to the Farmer's application of scripture to 'matters of politic and civil society' (p. 28).

Enclosure

Although the literature of agrarian complaint is often seen as an Elizabethan phenomenon, the practices of enclosure that were critiqued in these texts persisted—and even accelerated—throughout the Jacobean period.[20] One of the more glaring omissions in *The Surveyor's Dialogue* is that the text—in its first published version from 1607, at least—contains only one reference to enclosure. Even in this instance, Norden imagines enclosure merely as a localized and instrumental strategy for land improvement, one that he lists alongside the building of hedges and watercourses. Moreover, instead of associating enclosure with the threat of depopulation, of tenants uprooted from the land, Norden isolates this practice to the conversion of 'wastes and unprofitable commons' to agricultural use and production (p. 90).[21] Early modern complaint literature had diagnosed enclosure as a systematic practice that was being implemented on an unprecedented scale throughout England. Norden, by contrast, distances his own dialogue from this literary tradition of protest and social debate, and confines the topic, instead, to a private, commercial sphere of individual landlords making improvements to their property. In addition, Norden resituates the geographic location of the text, transposing it from the Midlands—the site of ongoing, active resistance to the conversion of land to pasture—to the arable farming regions of the West Country and Home Counties. He thereby creates a pacified space, one associated with improvement and cultivation rather than depopulation and enclosure, a solitary landscape populated by free commercial farmers and unencumbered by social conflict.

Commons and Cottagers

But the wastes that Norden associates with innocuous reclamation efforts were themselves sites of contestation and protest, especially in the Jacobean period, when nearly half of land disputes centered on the appropriation of wastes and commons for private use.[22] Moreover, these areas were not unpopulated but instead home to the most destitute and marginal classes of manorial society, especially the cottagers who resided in the undeveloped, outlying areas of estates.[23] Significantly,

---

[20]   McRae provides a comprehensive survey of sixteenth-century complaint literature and its relation to agrarian reform in *God Speed the Plough*, pp. 23–57.

[21]   As Ellen Wood notes, 'enclosure' broadly refers to the extinction of common and customary use rights, and is not limited to the physical fencing-in of a plot of land (*Origin of Capitalism*, p. 83). For a similar point, see Martin, *Feudalism to Capitalism*, p. 132.

[22]   Manning, *Village Revolts*, p. 84. Norden himself wrote an unpublished treatise on this topic: see 'Reasons to prove that the inclosing of Wasts [*sic*] and Common Forest grounds and chases are Lawful, Profitable [and] Necessarie to the King and people' (1612), British Library, Additional MS 38445, ff. 5–9.

[23]   For discussion of early modern cottagers, see Netzloff, *England's Internal Colonies*, pp. 204–10. J.M. Neeson discusses the later history of these groups in *Commoners: Common Right, Enclosure and Social Change in England, 1700–1820* (Cambridge, 1993).

cottagers and smallholding tenants, those groups most vulnerable to enclosure and the privatization of commons, comprised the mass of participants in the Midland Rising. Whereas most surveying manuals, as Andrew McRae has noted, are characterized by 'their distinct *lack* of people',[24] *The Surveyor's Dialogue* is exceptional in extending its purview even to the social role of cottagers. In Book 3, during his circuit of the manor's boundaries, the Surveyor overrides the Bailiff's suggestion that cottagers be omitted from the survey, rebutting the latter's view of this group as a temporary presence and unprofitable feature of the landscape (p. 124). But Norden includes the cottagers in his survey in order to press that they 'be reformed by the Lord of the Manor' (p. 99). Altering their social position, he transforms them from customary tenants to squatters illegally occupying the fringes of the Lord's property. He also reconstitutes their social identity, recasting them as 'savages' removed from civil society (p. 99). The commons, as well as the displaced populations inhabiting these spaces, are rendered as antithetical to stable manorial society, a strategy necessary to elide the kinds of displacement and uneven development that are byproducts of the formation of capital.

State and 'Common weale'

Opposition to enclosure was also shared by the English state, which attempted to forestall these changes through statutes limiting enclosure and depopulation.[25] As a result, the interests of the state and customary tenants were often aligned against those of large landowners. This was the case with the Midland Rising, as rioters petitioned the central government to intervene on their behalf and curb the actions of local landowners. Ultimately, though, the English state sided with local officials and sanctioned the violent suppression of the revolt.[26] The protests of the Midland Rising were directed primarily against large landowners who were members of the traditional rural gentry. Norden's text, by contrast, depicts smaller landholders resorting to enclosure as a way of maximizing production and increasing their social standing, and he is unusual in that he places blame solely on ambitious tenants, freeholders who have become 'powerful and mighty' by appropriating commons 'without the Lord's license' (p. 89). As they disrupt traditional hierarchies and become middlemen in the manorial economy, these social climbing tenants take

---

[24] McRae, 'Husbandry Manuals', p. 42.

[25] On the failure of state efforts to regulate enclosure, see Tawney, *Agrarian Problem*, pp. 313–400.

[26] The English state finally chose to act following the Rising, and brought charges against several of the enclosing landowners who had been targeted by the rioters. (See Edwin F. Gay, 'The Midland Revolt and the Inquisitions of Depopulation, 1607', *Transactions of the Royal Historical Society* 18 [1904]: 195–244.) Although the Rising had attempted to act in the name of the state, and create a popular mechanism for enforcing violations of the statutory prohibition of depopulation, the state enforced its own laws only once these unsanctioned agents of their authority had been delegitimized and punished.

on the traits of their former masters and are likened to the enclosing magnate, the aristocratic landowner conventionally cast as the villain of agrarian society: as the Earl of Leicester had memorably phrased it, 'I am like the ogre in the old tale, and have eaten up all my neighbors'.[27] By correlating enclosure with social mobility, Norden critiques this practice without diagnosing its underlying causes.

During his career as a professional surveyor, Norden's most prestigious and lucrative assignments were for the English state rather than private landowners.[28] Given this personal history, it is surprising that he makes relatively few references to the state's intervention in agrarian and manorial relations. In representing Beauland Manor as 'a little Commonwealth' (p. 34), a microcosm of the body politic, manorial society becomes a state unto itself, and the text rarely refers to a social world or public authority outside the social unit of the manor. But when Norden revised his text for its third edition in 1618, he added a second reference to enclosure, a passage that marks a significant shift from his earlier position. Rather than isolating these changes to waste areas, he depicts enclosure as producing wide-scale 'devastation' (p. 172). Moreover, contradicting his insistently privatized view of economic relations, he also voices support for recent statutes that attempted to curb enclosure (p. 172).

This reference to enclosure is one of several changes that Norden made to Book 5 for the final 1618 edition of *The Surveyor's Dialogue*.[29] Another significant revision is a passage that immediately precedes his allusion to the 'devastation' of enclosure, one in which Norden uses the same term to describe the effects of deforestation (p. 171). The rapid and unprecedented disappearance of England's forests was one of the most visible changes to the rural landscape in the early modern period.[30] Earlier in the text, the Bailiff estimates that two-thirds of the forests in his region had been cut down within the preceding 20 years alone

---

[27]   Qtd in Maurice Dobb, *Studies in the Development of Capitalism* (New York, 1947), p. 227.

[28]   For discussion of Norden's professional work for the state, particularly as Chief Surveyor of the Duchy of Cornwall beginning in 1605, see Kitchen, 'John Norden … Estate Surveyor, Topographer, County Mapmaker, and Devotional Writer': 51–6 and Heather Lawrence, 'John Norden and his Colleagues: Surveyors of Crown Lands,' *The Cartographic Journal* 22 (1985): 54–6.

[29]   Some changes are far less bold: in his Preface, for instance, Norden tempers his critique of ambitious freeholders and declares his intention to 'caution' them (*1618*) rather than demand a 'prevention' of abuses (*1607, 1610*) (p. 8). Other, more neutral revisions include an added paragraph outlining the duties of the manorial court in Book 3 (p. 105) and a reference to Varro and Roman practices of soil management in Book 5 (p. 173). For a list of variations among the editions, see the Textual Notes.

[30]   For discussion of early modern deforestation, see the work of Oliver Rackham, especially *History of the Countryside* (London, 1986) and *Trees and Woodland in the British Landscape* (London, 1976). Peter Linebaugh offers a wide-ranging survey of political responses to ecological change in *The Magna Carta Manifesto: Liberties and Commons for All* (Berkeley, 2008).

(p. 165). In contrast to the visible effects of enclosure, and the vocal protests it elicited, deforestation is characterized by an absence. The disappearance of trees from the landscape brings about a comparable vacuum at the level of discourse, an inability to represent the magnitude and implications of such radical changes to the physical environment. This impasse provokes an important shift in the tenor of Norden's text. Initially, forests had been conceptualized solely in terms of their commodity form as timber, with the Surveyor instructing the Bailiff how to enumerate trees and underwoods in order to calculate the profit they could generate (p. 122). But a dawning awareness of the effects of deforestation leads to a search for alternative models of value.

It is at this point that Norden seeks recourse in a classical tradition of husbandry, a literary framework that serves to counter his general endorsement of a market-driven ethos of agricultural improvement. In part, the citation of Roman models enables Norden to reintroduce the state as the overriding authority responsible for managing agrarian change, and he follows classical precedent in recommending the appointment of public officials to serve as consuls, or forest wardens, to 'have charge of the Woods' (p. 171). But, he adds, citing Virgil's fourth *Eclogue*, 'Si [canimus] silvas, silvae [sint] consule dignae' ['If our song is of the woodland, let the woods be worthy of a consul'].[31] Virgilian pastoral, a tradition hinging on the simultaneity of pleasurable rustic retreat and 'the threat of loss and eviction', provides a rubric through which to articulate a eulogistic critique of the intrinsic losses that accompany an ethos of agrarian improvement.[32]

Countering the insistently privatized context that defines manorial relations throughout the text, it is the loss of England's forests, and the absence of the kind of public space they represent, that necessitates a reimagining of the commons. And the form this representation takes is that of the 'common weale': the common good, or public interest, but also the common wealth, the profits that rightly belong to the public domain.[33] These references fall into three main categories in the text: A number invoke the commonwealth as a way of describing 'profit', and consequently figure the nation primarily in terms of a national market. In other instances, the term relates to a model of professionalism based on public service rather than private employment and patronage; such 'Surveyors of the Commonwealth' (p. 17) represent an outside legal authority able to arbitrate disputes within the privatized sphere of the manor (pp. 8, 30). Lastly, other

---

[31]   Virgil, *Eclogue 4*, l. 3 (*Virgil, I: Eclogues, Georgics, Aeneid I–VI*, H. Rushton Fairclough (trans.), Loeb Classical Library [Cambridge, MA, 1999], p. 49).

[32]   Williams, *Country and the City*, p. 17; also see Heather Dubrow, *Shakespeare and Domestic Loss: Forms of Deprivation, Mourning, and Recuperation* (Cambridge, 1999), pp. 80–141. For a related discussion, see Joan Thirsk, 'Making a Fresh Start: Sixteenth-Century Agriculture and the Classical Inspiration', in *Culture and Cultivation in Early Modern England*, pp. 15–34. Elsewhere in the text Norden paraphrases Ovid's *Heroides* as a way of memorializing the effects of deforestation: '*Iam seges est ubi quercus erat*' ['now are fields of corn where woods once stood'] (p. 104 and n. 112).

[33]   See the Index for a full list of textual citations of 'commonwealth'.

allusions to the commonwealth invoke this idea when referring to local, private violations of the public good, from illegal cottages (p. 98) and poaching (p. 103) to enclosure (p. 172) and deforestation (p. 171).

The reintroduction of a social discourse of the commonwealth is one of the most significant features of Book 5 of *The Surveyor's Dialogue*. It is perhaps appropriate that this political language finds its place in the section of the text concerned most fully with the use of the land. In the overlapping political and agrarian registers of this section, Norden's text illustrates an example of what Julian Yates has productively termed as 'agentive drift'.[34] Moving away from the image with which we began, the model of surveying found in the Rathborne frontispiece, the subject of the text no longer remains the solitary surveyor asserting his centrality through an instrumental authority over technology. Instead, the surveyor and his interlocutors themselves assume an instrumental position, and are situated as the stewards of a social body and physical landscape left in their care.[35] The political thus becomes coterminous with what we would now describe as the 'environmental'.[36] In this context, property is no longer figured as the right *over* things, but as the rights *of* things,[37] a transition that enables a different set of questions to be posed relating to the reciprocal obligations binding subject and object in the creation of a social body.

---

[34]   Julian Yates, 'Towards a Theory of Agentive Drift; Or, A Particular Fondness for Oranges in 1597', *Parallax* 22 (2002): 47–58.

[35]   On ideas of stewardship, see Sullivan, *The Drama of Landscape*.

[36]   On this issue, see Michel Serres, *The Natural Contract* (Ann Arbor, MI, 1995), esp. pp. 42–6, and Bruno Latour, *Politics of Nature: How to Bring the Sciences into Democracy* (Cambridge, MA, 2004).

[37]   See Thompson, 'Custom', p. 135. (Thompson derives this point from volume 2 of Blackstone's *Commentaries on the Laws of England*.)

The Text of this Edition

Copy-Text

The copy-text used for this edition is the 1618 version of *The Surveyor's Dialogue*, the third and final edition published in Norden's lifetime.[1] Emendations and corrections to the copy-text have been placed within square brackets in the text. Textual variations—in which the 1618 edition differs from its predecessors—are also marked within square brackets. All emendations and variations among the early modern editions are listed in the Textual Notes. Two of the most significant revisions that Norden made to the 1618 edition—added references to enclosure and deforestation—are discussed above (pp. xxxviii–xxxix).

Orthography

This edition provides the first modern-spelling version of the entire text of *The Surveyor's Dialogue*. The intention, first and foremost, has been to produce a copy of the text that will extend its reception to a wider audience. The 1618 edition is unnecessarily difficult to read due to its orthographic inconsistencies, particularly relating to place names and technical terms. Readers interested in consulting the text in its original, early modern form can easily find digitalized, downloadable copies of all three early modern editions in the EEBO (Early English Books Online) database; a printed facsimile version of the 1618 edition is also available as part of the English Experience series.

Typography

This edition follows the 1618 text in using italic font for such features as speech prefixes, place names, and technical terms. In order to make the text more readable, italic font has been removed from the speeches of the Surveyor's interlocutors and Book 3's list of the components of a Court of Survey. Any errors in the 1618 edition resulting from missing or misplaced type have been corrected as well. All changes are noted in the Textual Notes section.

---

[1]   The specific copy of the 1618 text used for this edition is the facsimile version available in the English Experience series (Amsterdam and Norwood, NJ, 1979). That text derives from the Cambridge University copy (Syn.7.61.77), but draws the pages of Book 6 (sigs. R4r–S4v) from the Bodleian Library copy (4⁰.B.32 Art).

Norden's Marginal Notes

Marginal notes from the 1618 edition have been reproduced as footnotes and are placed within quotation marks in order to distinguish them from explanatory notes.

Figures and Tables

This edition reproduces most of the original graphic images from Book 4 of the 1618 edition of *The Surveyor's Dialogue*. This set of images includes six geometrical figures, which Norden uses to explain triangulation and the mathematical calculation of land size; two representative pages among a set of 20 tables that tabulate the size of an acre; and two tables for converting breadth and length of acreage.

Text of
The Surveyor's Dialogue

THE
SURVEYOR'S
DIALOGUE,

Very profitable for all men to peruse, but
especially for *Gentlemen, Farmers, and Hus-*
bandmen, that shall either have occasion, or be willing to buy, hire, or sell Lands: As in the ready and perfect
Surveying of them, with the manner and Method of
keeping a Court of Survey with many necessary rules,
and familiar tables to that purpose.

As also,
The use of the Manuring of some Grounds, fit as well
for LORDS, *as for* TENANTS.

Now the third time Imprinted.

And by the same Author enlarged, and a sixth Book newly
added, of a familiar conference, between a PURCHASER,
and a SURVEYOR of Lands; of the true use of both, being
very needful for all such as are to purchase Lands,
whether it be in Fee simple, or by Lease.

Divided into six Books by J.N.

PROV. 17:2
A discreet servant shall have rule over an unthrifty Son, and he shall
divide the heritage among the brethren.

Voluntas pro facultate.[1]
LONDON:
Printed by THOMAS SNODHAM, 1618.[2]

---

[1] *Voluntas pro facultate*   Norden's personal motto, which he included on the title-pages of several of his texts: 'will for knowledge'.

[2] *Thomas Snodham*   A printer specializing in sermons and other devotional texts, including Norden's own *A Poore Mans Rest* (1620), Snodham also published several plays, such as Jonson's *The Alchemist* (1612) and Tourneur's *The Atheist's Tragedy* (1611), was well as the 1616 edition of Shakespeare's *The Rape of Lucrece*. The 1610 edition of *The Surveyor's Dialogue* had been printed by William Stansby, who also printed three of Norden's devotional texts: *A Loadstarre to spiritual life* (1614), *A Pensiue Soules Delight* (1615), and *An Eye to Heauen in Earth* (1619). Hugh Astley was the printer of the text's initial edition in 1607.

To the right Honorable Robert, Lord Cecil, Baron of Essendon, Viscount *Cranbourn, Earl of Salisbury, Principal Secretary to the most high and magnificent Prince, JAMES, King of Great Britain, France, and Ireland, Master of his Majesty's Wards and Liveries, of his Majesty's most Honorable Privy Council, and Knight of the most Noble Order of the Garter.*[1]

As the earth (right honorable) was given to man, and man (after divine) was enjoined the care of earthly things, every man in several place, quality and state, the greatest receiving thence greatest dignities, even to be called *Princes of the Earth*, so is it not the least regard, that men of whatsoever title or place, should have of the lawful and just means of the preservation and increase of their earthly Revenues. And that especially, by justly achieving, and rightly using Dominion and Lordship, which principally grow (omitting public office and authority) by Honors, Manors, Lands, and tenants, for according to the largeness of Revenues, are the means to enable the Honorable, to shelter the virtuous distressed, and to cherish such, as by desert may challenge regard. And according to their will and power therein, is the vulgar reputation of their Magnificence. But (my good Lord)

---

[1]   Norden dedicates his text to Robert Cecil as a way of extending the patronage he had received from the Cecil family. The support of Lord Burghley, Robert Cecil's father, had enabled Norden to begin his county maps, the *Speculum Britanniae* series. The *Middlesex* volume (1593), which was dedicated to Burghley, advertised this connection by featuring portraits of Norden and his patron flanking the frontispiece. Burghley's interest in Norden's work was also reflected in his heavily annotated personal copy of this text (British Library, Harleian MS 570). After Burghley's death, Norden's association with the Earl of Essex cost him Robert Cecil's support in 1599, but he gradually regained favor shortly before writing *The Surveyor's Dialogue*. Cecil helped Norden attain the post of Surveyor of the Duchy of Cornwall in 1605, and Norden in turn produced a map of the Ulster plantation for Cecil in 1610 (C.H. Coote, 'John Norden', *Dictionary of National Biography*, vol. 14 (New York, 1909), pp. 550–53; Frank Kitchen, 'John Norden', *Dictionary of National Biography*, vol. 41 (Oxford, 2004), pp. 5–7).

as mine endeavor in this rude Dialogue, tendeth but, as it were, to the plow, so I omit to wade into the impassable censure of honor and dignity, wishing it ever deserved reverence. And as touching Land-revenues, wherewith many are (but especially the Honorable are, or ought to be principally) endowed, I presume only in this simple Treatise to discourse so far (according to my slender capacity, and weak experience) as concerneth the ordinary necessary means of the maintenance and increase of Land-revenues. And because the true and exact Surveying of Land, is the principal, I have herein endeavored, more of Desire than of Power (for the use and benefit of all sorts of men, having to deal with land, both Lords and tenants), to shew the necessity and simple method thereof; most humbly entreating your good Lordship (the fruits of whose, and of your honorable Father's favors, I have many ways tasted) to vouchsafe me your Honorable pardon for presuming, and your like patience in accepting at my hands this second time,[2] this little Mite; which, were it as great, as any well-wishing heart can intend good, it were (together with my poor self) in truest service unfeignedly your Lordship's. It may therefore please the same to accept it, so shall others the more willingly embrace it, or the less disgrace it, humbly recommending it to your gracious favor.

At my poor house at Hendon,[3] *[27 Martii, 1610.]*

Your Lordship's ever to be commanded,
                                        Jo. Norden.

---

        2   The 1607, 1610, and 1618 editions all begin with the same dedicatory epistle to Robert Cecil; the 1618 edition reprints the date of Norden's signature from the 1610 text.
        3   *Hendon* In Norden's era, a village in Middlesex; now a northwest suburb of London. Norden's 'poor house' is described in later documents as a mansion with 16 hearths. Many of Norden's texts feature this declaration of poverty, despite the fact that his annual salary as a Surveyor may have averaged around 200 pounds, a small fortune by early modern standards (Kitchen, *DNB*).

To the benevolent Readers, especially to Landlords, Tenants, and Surveyors of LANDS.

As God in his high and incomprehensible wisdom, hath given unto man two beings, a Spiritual, and Corporal, so hath he enjoined him two prescript cares: the one of divine and heavenly, the other of human and earthly things. And although the first be as far more excellent than the second, as the brightest Sun exceedeth the blackest darkness, yet hath he not omitted, to give unto all men an express commandment, to be mindful of the second. Although it must be confessed, that no man taking an extraordinary care, can add, as of himself, one jot of increase of any good thing, neither can he of his own proper industry, assure himself of any part of true prosperity in this life; yet must he not therefore dissolutely neglect his uttermost lawful endeavor, to advance his own welfare; which he neither can do, without fear and trembling, if he call to mind the cause why the earth bringeth forth unto us of [its] own accord, nothing but the very tokens of our original disobedience, wherein is imprinted this *Motto* or *Poesy* of our shame: *With the sweat of thy face thou shalt eat thy bread, all the days of thy life.*[1] And this without exception of persons, whereby it appeareth, that none is exempted from labor and travail, in one kind or other, to maintain his estate here. Our Fathers of fame began it. *Adam* digged the earth, and manured it. *Tubal* wrought in Metals. *Noah* planted a Vineyard. *Abraham*, *Lot*, *Moses*, *David*, *Eliseus*, *Amos*, and many other godly and great men were Shepherds. *Gideon* was a Thresher of Corn. *Jacob* and his sons the Patriarchs were Herdsmen, *Joseph* a Purveyor of Corn in Egypt. *Paul* made tenants. *Matthew* was a Customer, or Toll-gatherer. *Peter*, *Andrew* and others were Fishermen, and *Saul* a keeper of Asses. If these men began the way of labor in so many kinds, who may say he is free in one kind or other? And he that in respect of his greatness of birth or wealth, will pretend a privilege of idleness, or vain and unprofitable exercises, doth discover his forgetfulness, or neglect of the duty in earth, which every man, even the greatest oweth unto the Commonwealth, his own family and posterity: And he is censured even by the mouth of God, *Worse than an Infidel*, that neglecteth these duties.[2] And none is excused, or exempted out of this *Law of provision for his family*, be he never so high or mean. Not that such men as are honorable by birth, office, or advancement should till the earth, or be Shepherds or Herdsmen. But that they should, according to their greatness, execute

---

[1] *With ... life*   Genesis 3:19: 'In the sweat of thy face shalt thou eat bread, til thou returne to the earth' (Geneva Bible, 1560 edition).

[2] *Worse ... Infidel*   1 Timothy 5:8: 'If there be any that prouideth not for his owne, & namely for them of his household, he denieth the faith, and is worse then an infidel'.

great place in the Commonwealth, whereof (after the care of Divine things, in respect of God that gave them their greatness) they should have care to perform some service, in respect of the King, under whom they enjoy their greatness: to shew love and diligent regard, to aid their inferiors, in respect of whom they have the imputation of their greatness; to be provident in providing things necessary for their Families, that have an interest to partake of their greatness; and, lastly, in respect of their posterities, that are to become the more great by their greatness. And how can they do thus, unless they look into, and use the means of the increase and preservation of their greatness? And for as much as the same consisteth, for the most part, in the revenues of land, what greater care ought they to have, than to maintain, and lawfully to augment the same, which decaying, their Honor and honorable reputation diminisheth. To preserve or augment Revenues, there must be means: the means are wrought by Knowledge, Knowledge had by Experience, Experience by view, and due observation of the particulars, by which Revenues do or may arise. Wherein are to be considered the Quantities, and Qualities of Land, with the present Rents, and estimate values by a reasonable improvement: which duly found, to have a due regard to proportion yearly distributions and expendings with the annual Incomes, in such sort, as always the present year may rather add unto the next than the next to be charged with the year past. For when the present year shall expend more than the Revenues of the same may bear, the year following cannot but be surcharged, and so will it surcharge the future, so long, that either he shall be forced to strike the topsail of his improvident wasting, in time, or, at length, through the furious blasts of excessive prodigality, be blown under the water of disability, by overswelling the sails of his vainglory. I speak not this in the way of attachment, but of [caution]:[3] And so I trust, all men will take it, and accept of my poor endeavor in this kind, considering that necessary it is, that all men should know what it is to have Revenues; namely, first to know them, and then to use them to their own advancement, and to the good of others. And because it is not the work of the Honorable, and of such as have high and serious Commonwealth employments, to be personal actors of their own affairs in this kind, they are to use the service of such as are fit in knowledge, and in just dealing, to [travail] in this kind of business, by whose faithful and sincere informations, they may know what is just and right to be done and demanded. And in all favor and clemency to deal with such, as are in this manner within the compass of their [revenues], and by whom, and by whose labors they maintain their greatness; for (no doubt) there is none but well considereth, that how great or powerful soever he be in Land Revenues, it is brought in unto him by the labors of inferior tenants, yea, *The King consisteth by the field that is tilled.*[4] And there is none of these inferiors, of ordinary

---

[3]   In a revision added to his 1618 text, Norden substitutes 'caution' for the more direct reading found in the 1607 and 1610 editions, 'prevention'. For discussion of key variations among the three texts, see the Introduction, p. xxxviii.

[4]   'Eccles. 5:8' (Ecclesiastes 5:9). Norden's phrasing closely approximates that of The Geneva Bible; his preference for this particular translation reflects the nonconformist

discretion, but well knoweth, that what he enjoyeth, is by the favor of his Lord in a sort; and therefore ought there to be such a mutual concurrence of love and obedience in the one, and of aid and protection in the other, as no hard measure offered by the superior, should make a just breach of the loyalty of the inferior; which kind of union is no ways better preserved and continued between the Lord and tenants, than by the Lord's true knowledge of the particulars that every tenant holdeth, and a favorable course in Fines and Rents, and by the tenants' love and thankfulness in all ready service and duty towards the Lord. And to that end, it is (no doubt) expedient, that Lords of tenants have due regard of their own estates: namely, of the particulars of all their tenants' lands, and that by a due, true, and exact view and survey of the same, to the end the Lord be not abused, nor the tenants wronged and grieved by false informations, which commonly grow by private Intelligencers,[5] and never by just Surveyors. And because the office of a Surveyor (duly weighed) is an office both necessary, expedient, and of trust, it behooveth him to be first honestly and uprightly minded, and, next, skillful and judicious in the faculty. Then can he not, but by industry and diligence, produce an exact discovery and performance of the work he undertaketh, to the true information of the Lord, whose benefit and uttermost lawful profit he is to seek, in a good conscience, dissuading him yet from distasteful Avarice, the greatest blemish that can befall a man, seeking true reputation and renown by his Revenues. For too much severity afflicteth the hearts of poor tenants, who (by common experience) are found to be more firmly knit in the bond of true duty, loyal affection, and ready service unto their Lords, by their Lord's frugality, sweetened sometimes with the cheerful drops of true liberality, than by the extremes of austerity, vain prodigality, or compulsive exactions. And yet not so, as Lords of tenants should be so overswayed with abused lenity, or careless looking into their own, as may breed contempt in tenants; but rather that they should keep such an even and equal hand over their tenants as may continue mutual love, and in them a loving fear; and not to seek the increase of Revenues so much for vainglory's as for virtue's maintenance: which will appear by doing good to deservers, by their virtuous life, a work of true virtue; when, contrarily, vainglory seeketh idle and vain reputation, by unjustly achieving, and either prodigally consuming, or too miserably increasing Revenues; which I must leave to every man's own fancy, wishing all to fashion their ways in this kind, to God's glory, the King's service, the good of the Commonwealth, and to other such ends, for which God hath given them greatest earthly blessings;

---

position also expressed in his devotional writings. For discussion of his religious texts, see the Introduction (p. xxxi) and n. 143, p. 67. All Biblical passages cited in the notes will be drawn from the 1560 edition of the Geneva Bible; when the verse numbering of the Geneva edition differs from other translations, the more commonly used numbering will be listed parenthetically following Norden's original citation.

[5] *Intelligencers* Untrained Surveyors who rely solely on information gained from tenants rather than using measurement and instrumentation. The term also encompasses tenants who profit from passing on information relating to land boundaries. For discussion, see the Introduction (p. xiii); Norden also refers to 'intelligencers' in Book 1 (p. 19).

recommending unto you this simple rude lump, of which, if some more skillful, will bestow the relicking, and bring it to his true shape, my self with many others, should thankfully embrace it. In the meantime friendly accept it, and in kindness afford sparing reproof.

ECCLES. 7:13.[6]
Wisdom is good with an inheritance.

Yours, J.N.

---

6   Eccles. 7:13 (Ecclesiastes 7:11).

The Author to His Book

Look ere thou light into the hands of some:
Some lay but traps to catch thee in disgrace;
Disgrace thou none, be silent where thou come,
(Yet thou shalt come where *Momus*[1] is in place):
    Place thee with those, whose hearts aright do see,
    And seeing, judge, in favor, faults that be.

Faults be in thee; who says he doth not err,
Errs, in conceit, that he alone is free:
And such, not free, will sure thy faults transfer,
And for one fault, transfer them 10 in thee:
    Not thee in this, but me they discommend,
    That I abroad do thee so basely send.

Base I thee send: excuse me what thou can;
If thou cannot, plead thus to seeming friends:
Alas, my friends, abortive I began:
Who me began, thus meanly forth me sends,
    That I might tell him, how I pass the taunts
    Of taunting tongues that seek their praise by vaunts.

I vaunt it not, but am content to be,
Where meanest be, that blush to shew their face:
Who sees my face, a picture base may see;
Yet may he see, far fairer find disgrace.
    Disgrace not him, that sends me for good will:
    But will him well. Requite not good with ill.

Invidia sibi, et [alis] venenum.[2]

---

[1]   *Momus*   the figure in Greek mythology associated with satire and unfair derision. Bacon similarly invoked Momus when referring to the risks incurred in building a country estate: 'Neither is it ill air only that maketh an ill seat, but ill ways, ill markets: and, if you will consult with Momus, ill neighbours' (*The Works of Francis Bacon*, [eds] Spedding et al., vol. 6 [London, 1878], p. 481).

[2]   *Invidia ... venenum* ['Envy's hisses are another poison'].

The Contents of the Six Books
of *The Surveyor's Dialogue*

The first Book.

Containeth a communication between a Farmer and a Surveyor of Land: wherein is proved, that Surveys of Manors and Lands, are necessary both for the Lord and tenant, and in what manner tenants ought to behave themselves toward their Lords, in respect of their tenures.

The second Book.

Is entreated between the Lord of a Manor, and a Surveyor, concerning the estate of a Manor, of the parts and profits thereunto belonging, and how the Lord of a Manor ought to deal with his tenants.

The third Book.

Containeth the manner and method of keeping a Court of Survey, and the Articles to be inquired of, and the charge: how to enter and enroll Copies, Leases and Deeds, and how to take the plot of a Manor.

The fourth Book.

Sheweth the manner of the casting up of the quantities of Acres of all sorts of grounds by the Scale and Compass, with Tables of computation, for ease in accompting.[1]

The fifth Book.

Sheweth the different natures of grounds, and whereunto they may be best employed, how they may be bettered, reformed and amended, fit for all Farmers and Husbandmen.

[The sixth Book.

Containeth a brief conference between a Purchaser of Land, and a Surveyor: wherein are some points necessary to be considered of such as are able and willing to Purchase Land in Fee simple, or by Lease.]

---

[1]   *accompting*   accounting.

THE SURVEYOR'S DIALOGUE, BETWEEN a FARMER and a SURVEYOR: Wherein is proved, that Surveys are necessary and profitable both for Lord and Tenant: and wherein is shewed how Tenants ought to behave themselves towards their Lords.

THE FIRST BOOK.

Farmer   Sir, I am glad I have so happily met with you, for if I be not mistaken, you are a Surveyor of Land.

Surveyor   Admit it so, Sir, what then?

Farmer   I have heard much evil of the Profession, and to tell you my conceit plainly, I think the same both evil and unprofitable.[1]

Surveyor   You seem to be but a young man in years, and are you so deeply seen in the abuse of this faculty, that you can so peremptorily condemn it?

Farmer   Call you it a Faculty? What mean you by that word?[2]

Surveyor   Ability to perform a thing undertaken.

Farmer   Then this faculty of yours, I say, is a vain faculty, and a needless work undertaken.

Surveyor   Speak you this by conjecture, by report of others, or by due experience of your own?

---

[1]   'Surveying rashly condemned'.

[2]   'Faculty'.

Farmer   I speak, indeed, as induced to the opinion I hold, by all the three reasons.

Surveyor   Then needs must you be either partial or malicious in the first two, and deceived in the third: for he that speaketh by conjecture hath not experience,[3] and he that speaketh by report, is as a trunk to convey an uncertain sound coming from one to the ears of others; and if you speak by experience, then have you a pretense to have skill in the art; and by your own experience, it seemeth, you condemn yourself to have abused the same, and so condemn a general necessary profession, in respect of your own particular error in the same.

Farmer   No, Sir, I am willingly unskillful in that contemptible vanity. But my experience groweth, by tasting of the evil that hath followed the execution of the thing, by some like unto yourself.

Surveyor   This is a general condemnation, rashly pronounced against all for the abuse of some, and they only spew out greatest scandals, that are by examination in this business found most deceitful against their Lords;[4] and therefore no marvel though the profession be [condemned] and condemned, of such as are to be condemned, for the offender cannot speak well of the apprehender, nor scarcely of the most just Judge.

Farmer   You speak as if you knew some abuse in me: I tell you, you do me wrong to attach me so.

Surveyor   Belike you think it free for you to censure other men at your pleasure, and to judge them after you own vain conceit, and yet no reply must take hold of your vain quarrel, that riseth of mere malice against the innocent.

Farmer   Innocent? How can that be, when you pry into men's Titles and estates, under the same (forsooth) of Surveyors, whereby you bring men and matter in question often times, that would (as long time they have) lie without any question.[5] And often times you are the cause that men lose their Land; and sometimes they are abridged of such liberties as they have long used in Manors, and customs are altered, broken, and sometimes perverted or taken away by your means. And, above all, you look into the values of men's Lands, whereby the Lords of Manors do rack their Tenants to a higher rent and rate than ever before; and therefore not only I, but many poor Tenants else have good cause to speak against the profession.

Surveyor   Be you not offended at the comparison which I will make to your allegations. Why should not such persons as are inhibited by the laws of the

---

3   'Conjecture often deceived'.
4   'The most faulty findeth first fault'.
5   'The pretended causes why Surveyors are condemned'.

Realm, to commit certain acts within the Commonwealth, cry out against them, that by the same laws are appointed Magistrates and Officers to see these laws executed upon them, as Rogues, Beggars, and other like vagabonds? For if such officers and overseers were not, these offensive persons might have their wills: so should it follow, that men of peace, and good members of the Commonwealth, should be endangered to be sacked of that they have, by such lewd persons. Necessary therefore is it that there should be such as should see unto, inform, punish, and reform these. And by your assertions you may as well intend, under like reason, against keeping of Courts in a Manor, wherein many abuses are found out, reformed, and punished, which without such Courts, would lie smothered, festering so long, that there would be few sound members left within the same.

Farmer   It seems you compare Tenants of Manors that are (many of them) honest, civil, and substantial men to Rogues and vagabonds. You forgot yourself.

Surveyor   My plain words are, that as well these evil members of the Commonwealth, may speak against the Surveyors of the Commonwealth, which (to speak only of the under officers) are the Justices of the peace, Constables, and such like, as may Tenants of a Manor speak against the surveying of their Lands within the same.

Farmer   That were strange: for by the one, the whole state of the Kingdom is kept in peace, and by the other, many millions disquieted, that might live quietly in their Farms, tenements, Houses and Lands, that are now daily troubled with your so narrow looking there into, measuring the quantity, observing the quality, recounting the value, and acquainting the Lords with the estates of all men's livings, whose ancestors did live better with little, than we can do now with much more, because by your means rents are raised, and Lands known to the uttermost Acre, Fines enhanced far higher then ever before measuring of Land and surveying came in;[6] and therefore I think you cannot but confess, that other men, as well as I, have good cause to speak of you and your profession, as I do.

Surveyor   I perceive that the force of your strongest argument is, as before I said, your fear and unwillingness that the Lord of the Manor, under whom, and in whose Land you dwell, should know his own;[7] and that you think it better for you, that he should continue still ignorant of what he hath, and that your estates should be always hidden, and what injury you do should be concealed, than that he should be acquainted with what you hold, and your abuses, encroachments, usurpations, intentions, and wrongs discovered.

Farmer   Sir, we acknowledge that the Lord ought to have his rent, and that is all, and our services at his Courts; but the Land we have, is our own.

---

[6]   'Frivolous objections against the Survey of Lands'.

[7]   'The faulty are afraid to be seen'.

Surveyor   Howsoever you may account them yours, yet the Lord hath such an interest and property in them, as he may also call them his; nay, I may say, you are not in such sort your own, but next under the King, you may be said to be the Lord's.[8]

Farmer   Fie upon you, will you bring us to be slaves? Neither law, nor reason, least of all religion, can allow what you affirm, and therefore, as I before conceived, so I may now protest, that you, and such as you are, are even the cords whereby poor men are drawn into servitude and slavery, and therefore I say again, it is pity any of you have any employment in the Commonwealth.[9]

Surveyor   What, Sir, because I say you are in some sort the Lord's? I tell you, that I mistake it nothing at all; for as the King is Supreme head and Prince, and defender of all his Subjects, so under the King is every Lord of a Manor chief and head over his Tenants, namely, over such as hold of him: and he hath a kind of command and superior power over them, as they are his Tenants, and for that cause he is called, and they do acknowledge him to be their Lord.[10] And what doth the word Lord import, but a ruler or governor?[11] If he be your Lord, then are you his, to be governed in causes determinable within the Manor, and, as I will hereafter prove, the Lord of the Manor may command his Tenants to accompany him into the field against the enemies of the King, by [reason] of some tenures, and they are to follow and be commanded and directed by him; and if they refuse the service, the Lord may distrain for it, or may enter upon their Lands, and resume it as his own in some case: so that I may well say, that in a sort, even your Lands and yourselves are the Lord's. The use and occupation is yours, but if the Land were so yours as were none above you, you might then call it yours; but so is none but the Kingdom, which the King holdeth of none but of God. And no man is so absolute within the Kingdom, but he holdeth his Land of some Manor, or person, or of the King. And of whom such Land is holden, the same is called the Lord of that Land after a sort, because it is held of him by some kind of rent or service, and by possibility this Land may come unto, and by law be cast upon the Lord of whom it is holden, as if you be so willing as you seem, to talk of these Mysteries, you shall anon perceive. And therefore you cannot but say, that the Land and yourselves are in some sort the Lord's. And therefore is it not lawful for the Lord of the Manor to enquire and examine of the things in those kinds belonging unto him? And if there be clean and plain dealing among Tenants, they need not fear who look into their lands and estates.[12] But if there be deceits and wrongs against the Lord, policy willeth you to banish any man, and to bar all the means that may discover them, though equity and honesty be contented to discover all things, to the manifestation of truth. Are

---

8   'Tenants may be said to be the Lord's men'.
9   'A rash censure'.
10   'The Lord of a Manor, under the King, is head of his Tenants'.
11   'A Lord, why so called'.
12   'The innocent need not fear to be looked into'.

not these the matters of chief importance that disquiet you? The measuring of your Lands, the observation of the quality, and estimating the value of your Lands.

Farmer   It is true: for these are the causes our rents are increased, and our fines raised, and this would the Lord never do, if such as you did not enkindle the Lord's desire, by your too severe scrutations, examinations, impositions, and imputations; for were the Lords of Manors ignorant of these things, as in former times, poor Tenants might have things at the rate they had in former times.

Surveyor   My friend, if I compare you to a dead image,[13] be not offended, for I perceive you have eyes to see, and yet you see not; you have a heart to understand, and yet your understanding is amiss.

Farmer   I am beholding to you, Sir, to make me worse than a beast, for a beast hath the things you say I want: How prove you what you have said?

Surveyor   Because you impute your great impositions unto the act of an honest Surveyor, when I will assure you and prove, that the cause is in and of yourselves.

Farmer   Then indeed you might account us brutish, if we would work our own woe.

Surveyor   I perceive, though you may be a good worldly Farmer, you are but a mean observer of the course and carriage of things passing daily under your nose. He that hath seeing eyes, and an understanding mind, may easily see and perceive, that there is no Manor, nay, no Farm be it great, or little, far off, or near hand, but hath been and daily is discovered by private intelligencers,[14] lurking in or near the same, prying into estates, aiming at the quantity, wide, short, or over, seldom hitting right, observing also the quality, and glancing at the value of every man's Land, and thereof secretly and under hand do inform the Lords of the Farm, and they being credulous overmuch, and not a little covetous, build their demands both of Rents and Fines, upon these most deceivable informations, whereby the Lord is abused, and the Tenant wronged; whereas were the things seen, viewed, and surveyed by a judicious and faithful Surveyor,[15] who upon due consideration, and discreet observation of all particulars, gives in a true and indifferent certificate unto the Lord, using rather his uttermost endeavor to moderate and mitigate the Lord's excessive demands than aggravating the validity beyond reason or a good conscience, you would be of another mind; and I protest, I hold that Surveyor a

---

[13]   *dead image*   Norden refers to The Wisdom of Solomon 15:5, a passage from the Apocrypha frequently cited by iconoclastic Protestant writers: 'Whose sight stirreth vp the desire of the ignorant: so that he coueteth the forme that hathe no life, of a dead image'.

[14]   'Private intelligencers and not honest surveyors, give false informations to their Lords'. On 'intelligencers', see the Introduction (p. xiii) and n. 5, p. 9.

[15]   'The course of an honest Surveyor'.

very bad man, that will either for affection or bribe, carry a partial hand between the Lord and his Tenants; yet sith he holdeth as it were the beam of the balance, he should rather give the better weight to the weakest, respecting nothing but a charitable course to be held by the Lord, for whom he travaileth with the Tenant, against whom if he speak not, he shall be often suspected of the Lord to be partial. But if there be equal consideration on all sides, the Lord will believe the Surveyor deals justly, and the Tenant rest satisfied, willingly to leave, or readily to accept, as his own judgment agreeth or disagreeth with the things propounded. For this have I observed, that often times Tenants consider not when they are kindly used, neither see they at all times when they are abused.

Farmer   Truly, I believe you in part; for indeed there are even amongst us, in the Manor wherein I dwell, officious fellows, that to procure the Lord's good opinion, will pry into men's estates, and indeed as you say, into the quantity, quality, and value of men's Lands, and give false information often times; and I know it is a foul abuse, and, of the two, I rather allow a true survey than a false report: for such fond fellows as are thus busy in other men's causes,[16] are of all men [least] to be believed; for they speak always for affection or gain; for they will extenuate the value of them they love, or have gain by, and aggravate the same, as their hope is of the Lord's reward: all this I know without your report. But what is that to the thing you charge your Tenants withal, that they are the cause of their own hard measure? Clear yourself of this slander.

Surveyor   That can I easily do by experience, and I think I shall have the whole world to witness it for your further satisfaction, who cannot yourself be ignorant of the same thing, for you have in part confessed it: for the former Informers, of whom you last spake, are even Tenants themselves; yet I accuse them not all, nay, I excuse none in particular. For I have seen and observed among them a kind of madness, as I may call it, but in the best sense it is a kind of ambitious, or rather avaricious emulation, wherein they strive one to outstrip another in giving most,[17] as where myself have had business of this nature, namely, of letting, setting,[18] or selling of Land for years or lives, being, or near being determined, in Farms or other like, whereby the Lord hath been at liberty to dispose thereof at his will, for best advantage, by choice of a new Tenant, Proclamation to that effect hath been made in open Court, where I have seen, and it is daily in use, that one will outbid another, in so much as I have wondered at their emulation, and could not have asked what they have raised it unto themselves. And should any that is in authority in this case (who in duty is not to hinder the Lord) or the Lord himself, inhibit such hot spirits to climb as high for the Lord's advantage, as the ladder of their own will, and supposed ability will willingly carry them? This is not as one Swallow in a summer, but they are many, and everywhere winter and summer, and yet are other men accused and

---

[16]   'Officious Informers dangerous for Lord and Tenant'.

[17]   'Tenants striving in lowing and bidding, enhanceth Fines and Rents'.

[18]   *setting*   leasing.

condemned for them and their faults, if their will (though willful) be a fault; but I should think it greater madness for a Lord, willfully to refuse what is so voluntarily offered, and so willingly given. Now, who is the cause of raising Rents and Fines?

Farmer   I know, such rash and overforward men there are in the world not a few, almost in every Manor, who are especially pricked forward to this emulation through envy and avarice, having means to achieve their desires. But this bidding and overbidding is in things, wherein the Lord is at his liberty to take a Tenant whom he list. But in customary tenements of inheritance the case is otherwise, where the Rent is and the fine (for the most part) certain, what needs the Lord to have this surveyed, or any freehold Lands?[19]

Surveyor   It is fit the lord should know what his Tenant holdeth, be it free or customary, though at this day there be a needless niceness in some freeholders of Manors, who seem to conceal their estates, and to kick against the view of their Lands; but if they knew what they did, they would reform that error.

Farmer   Call it you an error, for a freeholder to refuse to shew his estate to the Lord, or not to suffer his land to be surveyed?

Surveyor   I may well so call it; nay, I may call it a great fault, or any injury done against the Lord, and hurtful to himself. There is none (it may be you know it) that holdeth Land of a Lord, but he holdeth the same by some kind of Rent or service, and when he comes to take up his Land after the death of his ancestor, or upon purchase, but he doth or ought to do homage and fealty, or one of them, unto the Lord of whom he holds it:[20] the doing whereof, how ceremonious it is, if you be a Tenant to any such Land, you know, and wherein he maketh a solemn vow and oath, to be true Tenant unto the Lord for the Land he holdeth. And sometimes the Tenant of such a tenure, is forced to be aided by his Lord for the same Land, if he be impleaded for it: now, if such a Tenant refuse to shew his estate, or to permit his land to be seen, how performeth he his oath, to be true Tenant, and to do such services as are due unto the Lord? Among which, this, of permitting the Lord to know his own, is not the last, nay, he ought by his oath of fidelity, to further it by all means, both by his proper knowledge and evidence, not only his own, but other men's lands, and thereby he shall not only not prejudice himself, but he shall fortify his title so much the more, by having his evidence enrolled and his land recorded in the Lord's book of Survey,[21] that when his heir shall take up the land, or he alien[22]

---

[19]   On the distinctions of freehold, copyhold, and leasehold forms of tenure, see the Introduction (pp. xxi and ff.).

[20]   'Homage and fealty by freeholders'. Norden discusses the preservation of feudal service in Book 2 (pp. 49 and ff.).

[21]   *book of Survey*   the written record of deeds and leases kept in the manorial court.

[22]   *alien*   transfer ownership.

the same, it appeareth that he is true Tenant unto such lands, for such rent, and for such services;[23] but there be so many scruples thrust into men's heads, by such as have a pretended skill in matters of policy in this kind, and Lords of Manors have been so remiss in taking knowledge of the things in this manner appertaining unto them, that questions of Titles and tenures are daily had and moved,[24] to the great trouble often times both of Lord and Tenant, as is seen by experience daily, as well of land holden of the King as of inferior Lords, which may be reconciled, if Tenants were not too curious and Lords too negligent. Besides this, there are other reasons to move the Lord to know what Land is holden of him, and by what title, rent, and service: for Freeholders may forfeit their land, and their land may escheat[25] unto the Lord; if then he should be ignorant what land it is, where it lies, and how much it is, he may be easily abused for want of records; and so are many Lords of Manors, who for want of due knowledge of their Tenants, and of their land and tenures, other men are entitled to their right.

Farmer   You have said more than I heard or dreamed of, and it holdeth in some sort by reason; how it is by Law I cannot dispute: but in all that you have said, you have not satisfied me in the thing before I spake, touching the fines of customary Tenants of inheritance, which (as I said before) have been of late raised far higher than in former times, by your Surveyors.

Surveyor   You strike always one string, and I find the sound of your meaning: you would always be as easily charged in your Fines as might be, and in that I blame you not; it is every man's case to bear as light a burden as he can. But if you remember what I spake before, touching of the cause of this raising of Fines, where I proved it came most by your own means, you may be the sooner satisfied in this, for it is in nature like the former. Although this kind of Tenant hath seldom any competitor, to emulate his offer, because the Tenant leaveth commonly one either in right of inheritance, or by surrender to succeed him, and he by custom of the Manor is to be accepted Tenant, always provided, he must agree with the Lord, if the custom of the Manor hold not the Fine certain, as in few it doth; now this composition is commonly made by demand of the Lord, and offer of the Tenant.[26] The Lord asketh according to his conceit of the value of the thing, and either his knowledge must arise by his own experience, or by information: the information is either by secret intelligence of some officious neighbor, or by due judgment of an indifferent Surveyor, namely, such a one as carrieth equal respect to Lord and Tenant. And, although, as you acknowledge, former times did afford Tenants more favor in rating and arbitrating

---

[23]   'A needless niceness in freeholders to shew their deeds and Lands to the Lord, or his Surveyor'.

[24]   'Some Lords too remiss in surveying their Land'.

[25]   *escheat*   reversion of ownership to the Lord of the Manor; also see Norden's discussion in Book 2 (pp. 45–8, 62–3).

[26]   'Information hurtful in Fines of Land of inheritance customary'.

Fines, as you suppose, if you consider it well it is now as then it was.

Farmer　You much mistake it; for I will shew by ancient Court-rolls, that the Fine of that which is now 20 pound, was then not 13 shillings and four pence: And yet will you say they are now as they were then?

Surveyor　Yea, and I think I err little in it. For if you consider the state of things then and now, you shall find the proportion little differing:[27] for so much are the prices of things vendible by Farmers now increased, as may be said to exceed the prices then, as much as twenty pound exceedeth thirteen shillings four pence.

Farmer　You speak far from truth, and I marvel you will err so much, pretending to be a man of that reach, that men employ you to overreach others.

Surveyor　To shew you then an instance, look into the Chronicle in the time of Henry the sixth,[28] and you shall find, that a quarter of Wheat, was sold at Royston in Hertfordshire for twelve pence:[29] and I trust, if you be a Farmer, you are a corn seller, and I think, if a man offer you thirty times as much for a quarter, you will say it is better worth.

Farmer　Was it possible that Corn was then and there so cheap, and to rise since, to this rate? It is very strange.[30]

Surveyor　Not at all: for since there grew such an emulation among Farmers, that one would outbid another (which in the beginning was little seen), it grew at length that he that bought dear, must sell dear, and so grew the prices of things by degrees to this rate as now they be;[31] and a Farmer gets as much by his Farm now, as then he did.

Farmer　You err therein, I assure you: for else could Farmers keep as good houses and hospitality now, as they did then, and alas, you see how unable they are.

---

[27]　'Former Fines and Rents, and the present, not unequal'.

[28]　'John Stow'.

[29]　'Wheat at 12 pence the quarter'.

[30]　The unprecedented rate of inflation over the course of the sixteenth century has often been described as a 'price revolution'. There is some dispute about how sharply prices of agricultural goods rose during this period: some estimates calculate a steady hike of 600 percent from 1500–1640; others offer a more conservative figure—167 percent between 1540–1600—while still acknowledging that the problem was at its most acute near the end of the sixteenth century (John E. Martin, *Feudalism to Capitalism: Peasant and Landlord in English Agrarian Development* [London, 1983], p. 131; Joan Thirsk [ed.], *Agrarian History of England and Wales*, vol. 4 [Cambridge, 1967], p. 605).

[31]　'Rents of Land and prices of things grow together'.

Surveyor   It is true, and the reason is manifest;[32] for where in those days Farmers and their wives were content with mean diet, and base attire, and held their children to some austere government, without pride, haunting Alehouses, Taverns, dice, cards and vain delights of charge, the case is altered: the Husbandman will be equal to the Yeoman, the Yeoman to the Gentleman, the Gentleman to the Squire, the Squire to his superior, and so the rest,[33] everyone so far exceeding the course held in former times, that I will speak without reprehension, there is at this day thirty times as much vainly spent in a family of like multitude and quality, as was in former ages whereof I speak. And therefore impute not the rate of grounds to a wrong cause: for to tell you truly, both Lord and Tenant are guilty in it, and yet they may be both content; for they are the Sea and the Brooks: for as the Rivers come from the Sea, so they run into the Sea again.

Farmer   To tell you truly, you have said more than I have heard, and indeed it stands with some reason; and you have in part satisfied me, that the cause of our complaint[34] is not so grievous, as I and infinite other have supposed it.[35] Yet to tell you, as I and others have found, there be some of your profession have either none at all, or little, or very hard consciences, and for the most part such as have least skill, and such indeed I think unnecessary for Lord, or Tenant; for they cannot but abuse the one or other by their reports, and the records which they make, may breed quarrel many years after. And therefore as the Surveyor is a member (as you hold) not only tolerable, but necessary, I wish there were fewer, and they honest, just, and skillful; for, to tell you truly, we have thought among us Countrymen, that there are more than can be employed, as it seemeth by their public declarations of their want of work; for as I have passed through London, I have seen many of their Bills fixed upon Posts in the streets,[36] to solicit men to afford them some service;[37] which argueth, that either the trade decayeth, or they are not skillful, that beg employment so publicly: for *vino vendibili suspensa hedera non est opus*,[38] a good workman needs not stand in the streets or market place.

---

[32]   'The causes why things have grown to this extremity'.

[33]   *yeoman*   a prosperous tenant farmer (freeholder) who owns and works his own land, and whose annual wealth exceeds 40 shillings (R.H. Tawney, *The Agrarian Problem in the Sixteenth Century* [1912; New York, 1967], pp. 27–8). In spite of their wealth and degree of prestige, the status of yeomen was significantly lower than that of gentlemen. Also see Robert C. Allen, *Enclosure and the Yeoman* (Oxford, 1992).

[34]   *complaint*   In using this term, the Farmer situates himself in relation to a sixteenth-century tradition of agrarian satire and social critique. For discussion, see Andrew McRae, *God Speed the Plough: The Representation of Agrarian England, 1500–1660* (Cambridge, 1996), pp. 23–57.

[35]   'Unskillful Surveyors unnecessary'.

[36]   'Surveyors' Bills upon polls in London'.

[37]   In a rare example of this kind of advertisement, the surveyor Ralph Agas published a broadside offering his services: *To all persons whom these presents may concerne* (London, 1596) (STC 195.5).

[38]   *vino ... opus* ['good wine does not require the sign of an ivy bush'].

Surveyor   I confess, in this you have said truly: for none that is indeed fit for employment, will, or needs to crave it, in such manner, for they will be sought unto and solicited. But every one that hath but a part of the Art, nay, if he can perform some one, two or three parts, is not thereby to be accounted a Surveyor:[39] As some Mechanical men and Country fellows that can measure a piece of Land, and, though illiterate, can account the quantity by the parts of money, as a penny to a perch,[40] a groat to a day's work, ten groats to a rood, and consequently, a mark to an acre, which manner of casting sufficeth, and satisfieth them in their small accounts; but the manner of their measuring is often erroneous, as I will shew you hereafter, if leisure serve. Some have the skill of plotting out of ground, and can neatly delineate the same, and by Arithmetic can cast up the contents, which is a necessary point of a Surveyor's office, but not all.

Farmer   Saving your tale, Sir, we poor Countrymen do not think it good to have our Lands plotted out, and methinks indeed it is to very small purpose: for is not the field itself a goodly Map for the Lord to look upon, better than a painted paper? And what is he the better to see it laid out in colors?[41] He can add nothing to his Land, nor diminisheth ours; and therefore that labor above all may be saved, in mine opinion.

Surveyor   They that speak at any time against anything done, or propounded to be done, do either shew their reasons against it, or else they conceal their conceits, and without any good argument, inveigh only against the thing. And I know your meaning in misliking plotting of your Land, and yet you utter not what you think:[42] for a plot rightly drawn by true information, describeth so the lively image of a Manor, and every branch and member of the same, as the Lord sitting in his chair, may see what he hath, where, and how it lieth, and in whose use and occupation every particular is, upon the sudden view; which Tenants mislike, not that the thing itself offendeth them, but that by it they are often prevented or discovered of deceitful purposes. For a Tenant that is both a freeholder and a copyholder for life, or by indenture for life or years, holding these lands intermixed,[43] may easily

---

[39]   'The perfection of a Surveyor's office consisteth not in one part'.

[40]   *perch*   a unit of measurement equal to 5-1/2 yards (16-1/2 feet), or 1/160th of an acre. A *rood* is one quarter of an acre, and is equal in size to 40 square perches. An acre is 4,840 square yards.

[41]   Estate maps were often used for ornamental and decorative purposes: see P.D.A. Harvey, 'English Estate Maps: Their Early History and Their Use as Historical Evidence', in David Buisseret (ed.), *Rural Images: Estate Maps in the Old and New Worlds* (Chicago, 1996), pp. 27–61, as well as his *Maps in Tudor England* (London, 1993), p. 27.

[42]   'A plot of Land necessary'.

[43]   ['Great abuses that grow by Farmers and Tenants that are freeholders'.] As the Surveyor rightly notes, Tenants could own separate plots of land under different forms of tenure. A freehold tenant, in other words, could hold another plot by custom while also

(unless the Lord for life or years, be very especially butted[44] and bounded in their copies or leases, as seldom they are, through the sloth of some stewards, or for default of a true survey to guide them) appropriate unto himself copy or leased land for free, and especially having time enough to alter names and properties, to remove meres,[45] and to cast down ditches, to stock up hedges, and to smother up truth and falsehood under such a cloak of conveniency, as before it be suspected or found out by view, it will be clean forgotten, and none shall be able to say, 'this is the Land'; whereas if it be plotted out, and every parcel of free copy leased, and the rest be truly distinguished, no such treachery can be done against the Lord, but it shall be most readily reconciled.[46] And I dare presume to say, that the want of due plots and descriptions of Land in this form, hath been the occasion of infinite concealments, and losses of many men's Land, and many intrusions and encroachments have been made, and so long continued, that now neither memory or record can reform them, besides infinite other abuses, which are daily done, to the prejudice of Lords, for want of such a monument to be always at hand for their instruction.

Farmer   You aim unhappily, I think, to some men's purposes: but for my part, I promise you I had no such thought in me, and yet what you say, may indeed be easily wrought in most Manors, if they be as the Manor is wherein I am a Tenant; for I am persuaded, there hath not been any view taken of it, or perambulation made, or survey had within the memory of any man alive. And to tell you truly, I think the Lord hath much wrong both by his own Tenants, and by confining[47] Lords: for so the Lord have his rent, and his other duties of us, he is contented; but I may tell you, if he did better look into it, it would be better for himself and his hereafter;[48] yet we wish he would let it rest as it doth, for we may do in manner what we list, and if a Surveyor come, we shall not do as we have done, nor hold that that some have held long without any trouble: but that I leave. Then you say, that plotting is the chief part of a Surveyor's skill.

Surveyor   I say not so, but I say it is necessary for him that is a Surveyor, to be able to do it, and that he be painful and industrious,[49] and having this quality with the rest more necessary, he may be then called a Surveyor.

Farmer   What are they, I pray you?

---

leasing other holdings. The distinctions freehold, copyhold, and leasehold thus referred to the terms of tenure rather than the status of the tenant.

[44]   *butted*   to mark out and define boundaries of land.

[45]   *meres*   lakes.

[46]   'Want of plots of Land prejudicial to Lords'.

[47]   *confining*   neighboring.

[48]   'Tenants commonly wish not for Surveyors'.

[49]   'Who is a Surveyor'.

Surveyor   To little purpose I think I shall tell you; yet because you may know that every one that hath the name, is not indeed a Surveyor:[50] for besides the former faculty of measuring and plotting, he must have the understanding of the Latin tongue, and have some sight in the common Laws, especially of tenures and Customs, and must be able to read and understand any ancient deeds or records, French and Latin, and to judge of the values of land, and many other things, which if time will permit, I will hereafter declare more at large unto you.

Farmer   Why is there such a precise knowledge required in a Surveyor?

Surveyor   Because they are employed in such businesses as concern greatest persons in their estates; for although men be endowed by the providence of God, and of his bounty, with honors, Manors, Castles, Houses, Lands, Tenements, Woods, and other like revenues, which indeed are the sinews and ligaments which conjoin and tie honor and hability[51] together,[52] yet if these be not managed, guided, and carefully continued and increased by a discreet and honest Surveyor, for and in the name and behalf of his Lord, and the Lord again proportion his expense and charge, according unto or within the compass of his known incomes, the Lord may be disabled to maintain that which he hath gotten, the title of honor; and where honor is without means, it wanteth the substance, and hath only the shadow of itself to delight in.

Farmer   It behooves not only men of Nobility, but inferior men also to look unto themselves, for the preservation of their estates, but they indeed that have but little may quickly view it: *Sufficit exiguo strigilatio curta caballo*.[53] But he that hath many Honors, Manors, Lordships, Tenements and Farms, cannot himself take view of them all with ease; for indeed they lie for the most part dispersed in many parts, and they must be aided by the skillful and industrious travail of some judicious Surveyor,[54] who finding by his view and examination, the true values and yearly possibilities of his Lord's Lands, may be a good mean to retain his Lord within compass of his revenues, and to work him to be good to his Tenants; and by that means the Surveyor shall deserve praise, and his Lord win more honor. But I marvel how such great persons did before Surveying came up: for this is an upstart Art, found out of late, both Measuring and Plotting.

Surveyor   You speak I think, according to your conceit, but I will prove it far otherwise,[55] that measuring, plotting, and surveying hath been used in all ages of old. As for description, it was used in Egypt by *Ptolemy* the King, who described

---

50   'What a Surveyor must be able to do'.
51   *hability*   ability.
52   'Revenues the sinews of Honor'.
53   *Sufficit ... caballo* ['A bald head is quickly shaven'].
54   'A discreet Surveyor may be a good mean to manage the Lord's revenues'.
55   'Plotting of Land, and measuring, is very ancient'.

the whole world. And where the River *Nilus* in Egypt overflowed the banks (as at this day it doth about harvest) the violence of the inundations were such as they confounded the marks and bounds of all the grounds that were surrounded, in such sort as none knew his own land; [whereupon] they devised to measure every man's land, and to plot it, so that afterwards always at the water's recess, every man could find out his own land by the plot.

Farmer Truly that was a most excellent invention, and I think it indeed a most necessary course to be held in some grounds that I know in England, which are subject to like confusion:[56] many Marsh lands near the sea coast in Kent, Sussex, Essex, Suffolk, Lincolnshire, Cambridgeshire, and other Shires confining the Sea, or subject to great waters,[57] and if they were thus plotted out as you say, I must needs confess it were a good work, howsoever these kinds of grounds should be hereafter surrounded, increased or diminished by the force of the Sea's continual rage, whereunto they are daily subject; for by that means, if the ditches, which are the ordinary meres, metes and bounds[58] between several men's lands, be confounded, this device might after the winning of these surrounded grounds again, truly reconcile them, and allot every man his own, which otherwise will be impossible to bring to true appropriations. And this in my conceit, is not the least part of your profession, to lay out grounds in their true forms, that every several parcel may be distinguished from other; for I know where great strife hath risen by confounding one Manor with another, where the Sea hath won and lost ground, and devoured the true bounds, of which I am not alone witness; and it is daily seen, that questions do arise by like casualties, where Towns, Houses, Fields, Woods, and much Land hath been and are daily devoured, and in some places augmented, Rivers by force turned out of their right courses, upon other confining lands; whereof time hath taken such hold, as the truth is now brought in question, to the stirring up of quarrels between parties, which if these places had been formerly laid out in plot, the doubt would be easily answered. In these things I cannot but agree with you, that your profession may steed men that have use of your travail in this kind, although no such art hath been used, nor is it reported to have had any use in the word of God.

Surveyor Is there a necessity to produce the use of this, from examples out of the word of God, when these indifferent things are left to the discretion of man, for matters of politic and civil society? If every profession should be driven to fetch authority from the use in sacred things,[59] many things plentiful amongst us that live in a Commonwealth would be found profane; but because you seem to

---

[56] '[Grounds] subject to surrounding, fit to be plotted'.

[57] Norden discusses the drainage of the Fens and other early modern land reclamation projects in Book 5: see n. 11, p. 150.

[58] *Mere* lake; *mete* boundary line.

[59] 'Every matter in modern use among men, cannot be proved to have had use in holy Scriptures'.

urge it, I will not stick to let you know, that it is not without example in the Old Testament. If first you will have the proof of measuring, look into the 2 Chapter of *Zachary*, and there shall you find, that the Prophet reporteth, that *he saw a man with a measuring line in his hand, and he asked him whither he went? And he said unto him, To measure Jerusalem, that I may see what is the breadth thereof, and what is the length thereof.*[60]

Farmer   I do remember now that I have read such a thing indeed, but, as I take it, this measurer was an Angel of God.

Surveyor   Then is the warrant of measuring so much the more strongly confirmed unto men. But you may perceive that measuring was then in use in other things: for had not there been the use of the measuring line before, how could the Prophet have known it to be for that purpose?

Farmer   Yes, being a Prophet.

Surveyor   He could not have called a thing by [its] proper phrase (to the understanding of other) that had not been in use before, neither could his relation thereof have been understood of them to whom he declared it, unless they also had before known the like.

Farmer   Can you prove the like of Surveying?

Surveyor   *Joshua* commanded the children of Israel, that every Tribe should choose out three men, that he might send them through the land of Canaan, to view, survey and to describe it: for so is the word, *Ye shall describe the land into seven parts, and bring them hither to me.*[61] And what description could they make, without viewing and surveying the places?

Farmer   It is true that you say, such a view was taken at that time, that every Tribe might have his portion of inheritance. And surely in these Surveyors was much trust reposed by Joshua, the chief head of the children of Israel; for, according to their report, did Joshua divide to every Tribe his portion.[62] This surely was a work of great discretion and judgment in the Surveyors, and great providence in Joshua: for, indeed, he could not travail in all those parts himself, and therefore he did wisely to appoint such as were fit to perform the service; and it makes me remember your former defense of the profession,[63] in travailing for great persons, who cannot afford time nor pains to view their own Lands themselves. And it is not every man's gift

---

[60]   This biblical episode is described in Zechariah 2:1–2.

[61]   *Ye shall ... to me*   Norden refers to Joshua 18:6.

[62]   'Joshua 18. Surveying proved by Scripture'.

[63]   'Every man cannot equally divide Lands into many parts'.

to be able to divide Lands into equal, or certain unequal parts, that men that are parties therein, may hold them equally dealt withal, unless it be such a one as hath skill in dividing and apportioning, which thing comes often in use among men in this Commonwealth. And further authorities, or better warrant than these you have produced, for my part I will require none, unless you can and will voluntarily shew some later examples within our own kingdom, done in our forefathers' times, for I like not novations[64] and new devices that our forefathers have not seen or done.

Surveyor   If you had time and experience to look into and to understand what hath been done concerning this matter long ago, you should find in the records of the *Tower*,[65] even before the Conquest, matter to satisfy you, that this profession was then in use, and there shall you find the fruits. And since the Conquest, the book called *Domesday*, lying in the *Exchequer*, will confirm you I think sufficiently, that it is not as you say a new invention. [Besides], the same art hath been in sum and substance established by act of Parliament, and called *Extenta Manerii*:[66] upon which Statute, that learned Judge Master *Fitzherbert*,[67] hath written a little commodious and compendious Treatise; so that if you stand upon any further authorities, I will leave you to the present use thereof, which men of best discretion and greatest revenues do hold and continue, and none spurn against it, but the malicious or ignorant.

Farmer   I confess, I was lately ignorant of the things which now in part I know, but I was never malicious: as for the records and Statute whereunto you refer me, I believe you without further search, and for mine own part I am sorry that ever I have so with others backbitten the profession, and slandered the honest professors thereof; for I now do well see and plainly understand, that the same is lawful and expedient, and not any way hurtful unto the Tenants, if the Surveyor be skillful and honest, and his information (given by faithful and willing assistants, which are the Tenants themselves) be true, and his help of the Lord's records ready; for these are the two pillars,[68] upon which a Surveyor must of force build his work, information and record, as I take it, although record be always preferred before verbal intelligence: yet if records be never so authentic and true, of things unknown to him that hath the examination of them, what can be effected or done

---

[64]   *novations*   innovations.

[65]   Contemporary published guides for consulting records held at the Tower and other sites included Thomas Powell, *Direction for Search of Records Remaining in the Chancerie, Tower, Exchequer* (London, 1623) and Powell and Arthur Agard, *The Repertorie of Records* (London, 1631).

[66]   '3 Edward I. Extenta Manerii'. The statute *Extenta Manerii* (1276) first codified 'Directions for making Survey of a Manor' (H.C. Darby, 'The Agrarian Contribution to Surveying in England', *The Geographical Journal* 82 [1933]: 530).

[67]   *Fitzherbert*   Norden is referring to John Fitzherbert's *The Boke of Surueyinge* (London, 1523), an immensely popular work that went through 12 editions by 1567.

[68]   'The Lord's Records and the Tenants' informations are the pillars of a Survey'.

but as by a blind man that knoweth his face is to his way, but how and where to step he is uncertain? And although he desire none to bear him, because his legs are sound, yet he will not refuse to be led by the hand the way he would go. So a Surveyor, in my poor opinion, that hath a bundle, nay, a whole trunk full of records of several tenements, and parcels of land, whose names he can read, whose butts[69] and bounds he can relate, but yet he sees not the way of himself to go to them, or can say without discretion, 'This is this or that piece of land', and therefore I know that Tenants must give aid to a Surveyor, or else he will fail, though not in his art yet in the truth of his work.

Surveyor   You have said well, and it appeareth your apprehension is good in this business, and indeed the aid of the Tenants is a good help in this case, especially when records are also present; for if record and their information concur, then is the Surveyor in the right way.[70] But many times if the Surveyor cannot help the Tenants by his records when they are at fault, he shall hardly find which way his game goes; for a skillful Surveyor carrying his record in his hand, in his perambulation of a Manor, shall after the first entry be able to guide himself, and go from place to place, from field to field, even by his own evidence, if they be truly made, and the butts and bounds right, especially if the names continue unaltered, and that the Tenants can avow it as he citeth it, and nothing then is to be altered, but the names of owners, who change often. And for this business,[71] the fittest men to accompany the Surveyor abroad are the most ancient and longest inhabitants within the Manor, for the Surveyor's instruction, and the youngest, to the end they may also learn to know the like, to give like aid by their experience to posterities.

Farmer   Methinks it were a good course (if I be not too saucy) that a Surveyor should after his perambulations made, and the particulars entered, publicly read the same before the Tenants in open Court, to the end that they may approve or reprove what is true or mistaken, for the best may err in setting down of many things.

Surveyor   I like your advice well, and surely he that doth not so, and compare it also with former records, doth not as behooveth. But I know, and have found by trial, that Tenants think it a hard imposition,[72] once in their lifetime to attend such a business; they had rather do any work, than to do their Lord service, and themselves this good: for many of them are so wise in their own conceits, as they think them fools that give any assistance unto this work; and some so willful, that if they knew that they and theirs should be forever benefited by it, they will stand aloof, and any small occasion of their own will easily withdraw them from it; and some again are so worldly, that they think no day well spent, but that is spent upon their present

---

[69]   *butts*   borders.
[70]   'The Surveyor by the Lord's records may in some things guide the Tenants'.
[71]   'The ancientest Tenants fittest to guide the Surveyor'.
[72]   'Tenants unwilling to accompany the Surveyor'.

profit; and lastly, some are so given to their vain delights, as neither love of their Lord, or fear of forfeiture of their tenements, or doing good to their neighbors, or securing their posterity, can get any duty in this behalf to be done by them.

Farmer   As far as I conceive, the Lord of a Manor may force his Tenants at such a time, to give their [attendance]; else, you may well think, not a few would find excuses enough to absent themselves.

Surveyor   You say well, and therefore hath the Law provided a punishment for those that will not do their duties in this,[73] or in anything that the Lord hath to do within his Manor, for ordering of his Tenants. And because Tenants should not be forgetful of their duties, they were in former times, and may be still summoned to the Lord's Court every three weeks at this day.[74] And the Lord's remissness in calling them, hath bred in many places a kind of contempt, whereby groweth their slackness in times of their Lord's service. But the Lord of a Manor hath power to punish them, if the pain be within the compass that the Court will bear, which is large enough to weary him that is most arrogant.

Farmer   You have satisfied me in many things whereof I doubted; you have cleared the profession itself of many slanders, and, for my part, I will henceforth speak more sparingly, and advise such as I hear too forward to be better advised. And were I persuaded fully, that I my self might be a Surveyor, and yet retain a good conscience, I would wish I were also capable of the same faculty.

Surveyor   And if I were persuaded, that you would give an indifferent ear, and afford an impartial censure of what I would deliver unto you, I could be contented to bestow some time to shew you what were fit to be done, to the attaining unto such a measure of knowledge in the same, as might enable you to stead yourself and your friends in that kind of office.

Farmer   I would think it well: if I could attain but to some part of this faculty, I would leave the rest to better capacities; but my desire is far from it,[75] if I may not be assured that the practice is lawful, for I would deal with nothing, wherein I might stand fearful that God alloweth it not.

Surveyor   I like you well: I wish him that you seem to fear, to favor all your honest desires, and mine, and that his blessing may follow every our good endeavors; for whosoever undertaketh any profession,[76] be it never so lawful or expedient and necessary for Church or Commonwealth, and hath not the grace and favor of God

---

73   'The Law punisheth Tenants that will refuse to aid him in his Survey'.

74   For discussion of the manorial Court baron, see pp. 46–8, 82–4, below.

75   'A good mind'.

76   'No profession without the fear of God can prosper'.

to guide him, he may for a time seem to prosper in it, and to flourish and ruffle it out with shows of great blessedness, but it is but like Jonah's Gourd, that grew up in one night very great and fair, but withered the next morning.[77]

Farmer   That I thank God I have learned, and to tell you truly, for my part I had rather live in a mean estate in my calling, free from bribery, extortion, and wrong, serving God, than to get infinite wealth thereby, yea, although not the world, but mine own conscience can reprove me for it:[78] for I see such riches continue not many generations, neither hath it a promise of any blessing, although I know, that they that can so rise and flourish, and brave it out, are the men best accounted of; for they are held wise and [politic], and to have skill in their profession, whereas others that bear not the mind to deal corruptly cannot keep way with them in shew, and thereby are condemned to be simple fellows,[79] and their honest carriage and mean rate in the world maketh their ability to perform what they undertake suspicious; yet had I rather of the two, choose the last, howsoever my reputation or employment be regarded in the world.

Surveyor   You are in the right way of a good conscience, which is a continual feast; such as feast, and of such sweetness, as the world cannot see or understand the same: but happy is he whose conscience accuseth him not;[80] for howsoever men may seem to set a good face on evil actions, as if he could not accuse himself by his due examination of his own heart, yet it will come to pass that his conscience will one day bewray it, to his intolerable terror, and he shall be forced to accuse, judge, and condemn himself, without any further witness. And this I tell thee is the end of all such as fear not God, and live not uprightly and justly in their callings; for it is not the calling itself that corrupteth the man, but the man may be corrupted in his calling and abuse his best profession; therefore, I say, see that thou find thine inclination apt unto this profession, and in thy desire though tremble not to attempt the same,[81] for some professions are more natural than others to every man, and all mysteries and sciences whatsoever, are attained by some with greater facility and ease than by others; and some by small industry, study, and endeavor shall attain quickly to that perfection in some faculty, wherein another shall never excel, live he never so long, and be he never so studious and painful.

Farmer   I find mine inclination in conceit, pliable unto this course of life; how it will succeed, must be seen by practice, but that is the least doubt: all my fear is, whether I may do it and yet serve God?

---

[77]   *Jonah's Gourd*   Norden refers to Jonah 4:6.

[78]   'The bravest is accounted most skillful'.

[79]   'The simply honest, most suspected'.

[80]   'Though the wicked seem not to see their own errors, God seeth them, and will discover them'.

[81]   'Some are naturally inclined to some profession'.

Surveyor   Know this that if thou be already of a godly conversation, having the true fear of God sealed up as it were in thine heart, and dost not desire this profession, as *Simon* the Magician did,[82] for lucre's sake, only as he desired divine knowledge, thou mayst assure thee, this profession will not hurt thee, although the workman is worthy of his hire: for none will force thy labor for nought, *operarius dignus mercede*[83] and *dulcis labor cum lucro*.[84] If men did not get by their honest pains, it were mere slavery to undertake any kind of faculty.[85] But to come to the lawfulness of it, know, that it is the manner of the execution, and not the matter of the profession that woundeth the conscience. Every man is not born nor bound to one faculty or trade, neither consisteth the commonwealth of one member, but of man, and every one a several office, too long to express them all in kind. Is not the eye Surveyor for the whole body outward,[86] and the heart the searcher within? And hath not every commonwealth overseers of like nature, which importeth as much as Surveyors?[87] And is not every Manor a little commonwealth, whereof the Tenants are the members, the Land the body, and the Lord the head? And doth it not follow that this head should have an overseer or Surveyor of the state and government of the whole body? And follows it of necessity, that the office is unlawful? An unjust officer maketh not the office unjust, no more than a crabbed face impaireth the fair glass wherein it looketh, or a dusky cloud corrupts fair water whereon it lowreth. In case of Survey of Land, against which you have so much inveighed, if you consider it in reason, and make it your own case, you will say perchance, 'the case is altered'.[88] You have now peradventure a small Farm: Will you be careless and dissolute of the state thereof? Will you not weigh and consider with yourself what land is fit for Pasture, what for Arable, what for Meadow, and the like? And will you not command your servant to view it daily, that no trespasses be done therein, and to see unto the hedges, ditches, fences, water-courses, gates, and such like? Will you not regard the estate of your Cattle, their number, health, and safety? And have you not a continual watch over all your servants and children, and to the preservation of things within and without? If you do thus in one small Farm, what would you do in many? Could you see unto them all yourself? If you had as many Manors, would you lie at home and receive the rents and fines that your Tenants would bring you, without consideration of the estates or values, quantities or qualities of the things for which you receive money? And why have you this

---

[82]   *Simon the Magician*   Simon the Magus had converted to Christianity in the first century CE on the assumption that it would increase his magical abilities: see Acts 8:9–25.

[83]   *operarius dignus mercede* [drawn from 1 Timothy 5:18: 'the labourer is worthie of his wages'].

[84]   *dulcis ... lucro* ['good labor is its own reward'].

[85]   'The manner of the execution, not the matter executed, hurteth'.

[86]   'Surveyors of the body'.

[87]   'A Manor is a little Commonwealth'.

[88]   'Private and mean men Survey their small things, even their little Farms'.

care, or would you look into these things?[89] Is it not, because it is your living and livelihood, by which you and yours are maintained? And how much the more it is neglected, so much the more it decayeth; and if it decay in quantity, you cannot continue equal in quality. And can you therefore think it a hard course in that Lord (that having his Lands which are his livelihood, dispersed in divers parts of the Realm to which, through greater employments of importance,[90] he cannot personally resort; if he could, it is neither for his experience, nor fit for his calling to travail therein) to authorize and send such as may take view of his revenues, and of the estates of his Tenants, who are by custom and law in many things bound unto him; and that by such his substitute, he may be truly advertised of what he hath,[91] and how his means do arise, that he may proportion his charge and expenses accordingly? And [whether] he be abused by his Tenants , or his Tenants by his officers, or one Tenant by another, or the Lord wronged by confining Lords, by intruding too far into his lands, how rents be answered, and customs continued, how freeholders do perform their suits unto his Courts, how his tenements are maintained and repaired, how his Woods are preserved, his fishings, fowling, and prerogatives maintained? All which, by how much the more they are neglected and let run without view or survey,[92] so much the more doth the Lord weaken his estate, and prejudice his heir, wherein, it cannot be denied, he offendeth God, deceiveth the King, and defraudeth the Commonwealth: God, in that he is careless of his blessings bestowed upon him; the King, in that he willfully disableth himself to do him the service he oweth him in body and goods; and the Commonwealth, in that he disableth himself to give it that assistance, that his quality and place ought to afford, and, consequently, sheweth himself unworthy to oversee matters of State and Commonwealth, that is careless to see unto his own.[93] Furthermore, where a due and true survey is made and continued, there is peace maintained between the Lord and his Tenants, where, if all things rest between them confused, questions and quarrels arise to the disturbance of both. In private families, if there be none oversee and to manage things domestical, what disorders, what outrage, what uncivil and ungodly [courses], and what spoil and ruin of all things do follow? The like of necessity, where Tenants are left unto their own wills; and yet, as the unruly company in a family could be contented to be masters of themselves, and have no controlment, so Tenants can well brook their Lord's absence, and that they might be their own carvers, and that the Lord should have what they would yield of their own accord. I speak not of the honestly minded; but where a multitude is without a guide or governor, there is disorder, and disorder breedeth complaints, and complaints are unsavory to a kind Landlord, who must be forced for redress, to punish the offenders; and the most offensive will speak most of their wrong,

---

[89]   'If Revenues decay, a man's estate decays'.

[90]   'Great Statesmen cannot survey their own Lands'.

[91]   'The charge imposed upon a Surveyor'.

[92]   'Wherein Honorable persons do offend in neglecting their Revenues'.

[93]   'True Surveys continue peace between Lord and Tenant'.

and will soonest exclaim against any course that may keep order.[94] So that, to conclude, I affirm, that it is most requisite and expedient for due [order's] sake, that every Lord of a Manor should cause his Lands to be duly seen, and truly Surveyed and certified,[95] and once in seven or ten years to have it reviewed; for the inconveniences that grow by the neglect thereof, are of so many kinds, and they so dangerous (like the most perilous disease long concealed), that they work contempt in the Tenants, and loss to the Lord. Now, to keep this upright between the Lord and his Tenants, I think you cannot deny, but a true and honest Survey is necessary and lawful, and may be performed with a good and safe conscience, and in the fear of God, if (as I have said) the conscience be not before stained with the corrupt desire of unlawful gain;[96] and (as I said before) I think few or none will mislike the course, but such as are far gone in some disease of deceiving their Lord, which cannot endure to have this kind of salve to come near the sore.

Farmer　Truly, Sir, I know not how to answer you, but do consent to that you affirm; for mine own part I cannot but confess, I can find nothing in mine experience to contradict your speech. But pity it is that Surveyors should be ignorant or unhonest: for the one especially abuseth the Lord, and the other wrongeth both Lord and Tenants.

Surveyor　But whether is there cause in your conceit, to approve or reprove the profession, as it is simple in itself? Deliver your mind plainly: leave not a scruple in the minds of your Neighbors, that have exclaimed with you against them that never offended them, reproving as much as they durst, Lords, for looking into their own lands;[97] and, unless Lords were dead images or Pictures of men, having only the name of Lords, and could not at all command their Tenants, that could neither hear, see, nor consider what were fit to be done with their own proper Revenues, I cannot but wonder, that any should spurn against them herein.

Farmer　I think you speak something too forcibly against Tenants in general; for surely all are not opposite to this course, though some be.

Surveyor　I condemn none; but I reprove some, that of mine own knowledge have given testimony of their inward dislike, by their [outward] murmurs;[98] for what is done with an evil will, cannot be said to be done at all. Such as come cheerfully to the service, are dutiful, and I hold it impiety to abuse them; but the unwilling deserve little favor.

---

[94]　'The faulty will first find fault'.

[95]　'A Survey must be renewed once in seven or 10 years'.

[96]　'None mislike true Surveys, but deceivers'.

[97]　'Lords that will not look to their own Lands, are of dead Images'.

[98]　'Evil will is never dutiful'.

Farmer   What should Tenants principally do in such a business?

Surveyor   Nothing but that Law, Custom, and Duty requireth at their hands:[99] to give their best aid to the Surveyor; to travel with him about the Circuit, Butts, Bounds, and limits of the Manor; to inform him of the same, and of every particular man's Land, and Rent; to shew him their copies, leases and deeds, to the end he may enter and enroll them all together in a fair book, for the Lord's use, and for a perpetual record for themselves.

Farmer   For information, and shewing the particular grounds and bounds of the Manor, indeed is fit; but for their evidences, as their copies and leases, the lord hath the Court-rolls[100] of the one, and counterpains of the other; and for freeholders' deeds, their Land is their own, and whether they may be compelled to shew them or not, I cannot tell.

Surveyor   These are frivolous doubts that some have formerly made, but they have been answered to their cost, for the law hath compelled them to shew their evidence.[101] For, admit the Lord of the Manor have the rolls wherein the Copies are Recorded: May not Copies be abused after their entries, or counterfeited in some things prejudicial to the Lord, as may also the Lease, as hath been found often times, names and lives of men, parcels of lands, dates of years, and such like, razed, inserted, or altered? And is it not fit therefore that they be seen and entered together, that without search of so many Court-rolls the Lord may be satisfied, and the Tenants justified?[102] And what prejudiceth it the Tenant, to have his evidences truly recorded, if he mean plainly, be it Copy, Lease, or free deed?[103] He may think it a confirmation of his estate, what casualty soever come to the same, he may be the better assured that such a record will witness with him; whereas, if none such appear, his interest will be the more suspicious; and therefore such as are wise and discreet, will not only consent to this good course, but be thankful unto the Surveyor as behooveth. If it be just and right, that the Lord should know his own, and who should manifest it, but the Tenant himself? And how should he do it, but by his evidence? And most unjust it is in that Tenant, that by any willful or sinister means or covert practice, doth either detract his fellow Tenants from the service or concealeth anything that may further the same.

---

[99]   'What [Tenants] should do in the Lord's Survey'.

[100]   *Court-rolls*   the written record of the Court baron, or manorial court, which included documentation of all land transactions.

[101]   'View of Evidences necessary'.

[102]   'Entry of Deeds convenient for the Tenant'.

[103]   On the distinctions of freehold, copyhold, and leasehold, see the Introduction (pp. xxi and ff.). All three forms of tenure were secured through written deeds entered into the Court-roll.

Farmer   This I cannot deny, although indeed some busy fellows will dissuade, and breed a doubt herein; but I see it is to good purpose, and for our better security, to do all things requisite in this business,[104] and that all the Tenants within the Manor should conjoin in one, and every one for himself, and all for one, and one for all, should seek, examine and declare the uttermost truth of every thing, towards the exact performance of this service, and that the Surveyor should know the quantities, qualities, and indifferent values of every man's tenement and Lands, their rents, services, custom, works, and whatsoever the Tenant is in Law or conscience bound to yield and perform to his Lord. And indeed thus much have I heard given in charge at a Court of Survey, with many other articles, which are now out of my mind, all which may be done by Tenants with a good conscience, both by relation in Courts, and in the perambulation; but the concealing of these cannot stand with an honest mind, in mine opinion: for these things, of themselves, cannot prejudice the Tenants,[105] but the misconceiving, misentering by the Surveyor, may be erroneous, and the overracking, urging and overburdening the Tenants by the Lord, may be extortious.[106] These things may fall out by means of an unjust and unskillful Surveyor, and a covetous Landlord. And the fear of this maketh the Tenants to extenuate the values, and to smother the truth of things, to their souls' danger: therefore happy are those Tenants, that have a gracious Lord, and an honest Surveyor; for then there cannot be but an equal and upright course held between them;[107] then cannot the Tenants but be faithful and loving to their Lords, and their Lords favorable to them; so should the Tenants be defended by their Lords, and the Lords fortified by their Tenants, which were the two principal causes of the original foundation of Manors, as I have heard.

Surveyor   You say rightly, and I am glad to hear you conceive so well of this apparent necessity; for, so may I say, that it is of necessity that the Lord should know the full and absolute estate of his Manor, and of every particular thereof.[108] For howsoever of late days Tenants stand in higher conceits of their freedom than in former times, if they look a little back into antiquity, they shall see that Tenants (for the most part) of every Manor in England, have been more servile unto their Lords, and are in greater bondage than now they are, whom the favorable hand of time hath much enfranchised, and it cannot be altogether everywhere forgotten, because they may see as in a glass,[109] the picture of their servitude in many ancient custom rolls, and in the copies of their own ancestors, and many servile works have been due and done by them, and in many places yet are, though the most are now turned into money; but neither their

---

[104] 'The Tenant's duty'.

[105] 'What things are evil in a Survey'.

[106] *extortious*   extortionate.

[107] 'The principal causes of instituting Manors'.

[108] 'Tenants are now in conceit more free than in former times'.

[109] 'Ancient bondage'. Norden discusses the history of villeinage, or bond-servitude, in Book 2 (pp. 72–4).

enfranchisements, nor the conversion of works into rents, do so far free them, but that they still owe services unto their Lords, in respect of their tenures, as well freeholders as customary Tenants, as both in most of their copies and deeds is expressed in these words, *Pro reditu et servitiis inde prius debit, et de jure consuet.*[110] Which proveth their tenures in a sort to be conditional:[111] which condition, if it be willfully broken by the obstinate carriage of any such Tenant, he endangereth his estate.

Farmer   It were hard, if for not doing some small service unto his Lord, a man should forfeit his living.

Surveyor   And it were very foolishness in a Tenant, for willful refusal thereof, to endanger the same; for if the Lord be in law tied to maintain the right of his Tenant, and to defend him against any other that shall pretend a false title unto his land, the Tenant is again bound to perform all such services, and to pay all such duties as of right he ought unto his Lord.[112] And it is expedient that the Lord should see these duties continued, and it hath been and is daily observed, that the neglect thereof extinguisheth the remembrance of them, and so the Lord loseth his inheritance; for every service of the Tenant is parcel of the same, and the remissness of looking into these tenures, hath brought it to pass, that infinite within this kingdom, that hold in fee, quillets[113] of land, and some Manors, know not how or of whom they hold;[114] so that hereby Lords of Manors, of whom these quillets were heretofore known to hold, have lost their tenures and services, and such as hold the land by unknown tenures, are cast into the danger, to hold to them and their posterities further hurt.

Farmer   If Tenants will be willfully obstinate, and refuse to do and continue their uttermost services unto their Lords, as bound by their tenures, being (as you say) parcel of the Lord's inheritance, they are worthy to be attached of disobedience, and to pay for their contempts; and if Lords will be so negligent, as they will not look into their own, they are worthy to lose their right; and therefore I hold it discretion in the one to do his duty, and providence in the other to continue what is due;[115] and if by age or impotency the Tenant be disabled in person to perform his service, to crave dispensation, or to do it by another; and if the Lord be far off and cannot be present, to substitute one to receive it for him. But Sir, in all your discourse, I have observed, you have pleaded (as it were) for the Lord, against the Tenants, exacting sundry duties from them to their Lords, but I have not heard you speak much against the Lords, in favor of the Tenants, and yet I know there is a kind of reciprocal bond of duty each to the other, and may be broken of either side.

---

[110] *Pro … consuet* ['by the rent and services owed, and of customary right'].

[111] 'Every inferior estate is conditional'.

[112] 'The Tenant's service is parcel of the Lord's inheritance'.

[113] *quillets*   small plot or narrow strip of land.

[114] 'Discontinuance of service hurtful to the Lord'.

[115] 'Service of the Tenant'.

Surveyor   It is very true: for as children are bound to their parents, by the bond of obedience, so are the parents bound to their children by the bond of education; and as servants are bound to their Masters in the bond of true service, so are the Masters bound to their servants in the bond of reward.[116] In like manner, Tenants being bound unto their Lords in the bond of duty, so are Lords bound unto their Tenants in the bond of love; and though I have said little at this time of the duty of Lords to their Tenants, the occasion hath not been offered at this time.

Farmer   I trust you have said enough concerning the duty of Tenants, for they can but pay rent, and do service; more cannot be exacted.

Surveyor   Yet rent and services are divers and diversely answered and done, which I could be content to shew you more at large, but that yonder comes a Gentleman that will interrupt us: Know you what he is?

Farmer   I will tell you by and by as he comes near. Oh, Sir, it is my Landlord, a man of great possessions, Lord of many Manors, and owner of divers Farms, who hath been inquisitive for a man of your profession; but to tell you truly, I altogether dissuaded him before this time, but now having heard your reasons, I will solicit him for your employment, and I would wish you might undertake first the Manor wherein I dwell.

Surveyor   At his disposition and pleasure be it; and so for this time I leave you.

The end of the first Book.

---

[116]   'Lords and Tenants are bound each to other'.

THE SURVEYOR'S DIALOGUE, BETWEEN the LORD of a Manor, and a SURVEYOR:

Wherein, is entreated of the state of a Manor, of the parts and profits thereunto belonging: and how the LORD of a Manor ought to deal with his Tenants.

THE SECOND BOOK.

Lord   Friend, of late I met with a Tenant of mine, who told me you are a Surveyor of Land.

Surveyor   I have been, and am sometimes employed in that kind of service.

Lord   I have at this time some occasion to use the aid of one of your Faculty; and I have heard by my Tenant, that your skill and diligence may satisfy my desire therein.

Surveyor   I shall do mine endeavor wherein you please to command me.

Lord   There be many, I know, that bear the name of *Surveyors*, but when they are put to it, they come far short of some principal points required in the absolute performance of the work,[1] and either leave it half done, or so shuffle it up, as the Lord is abused, and the Tenants wronged, by the blind and uncertain returns of the Surveyor's travails; for a Lord of a Manor knoweth not, but by such as he useth therein, the estate of things, and how the particulars stand between the Lord and his Tenants.[2] If the Lord of the Manor have never so good a mind to deal well with his Tenants, and the Tenants be never so inclinable to do true duty to their Lord, they may be both misled by an unskillful Surveyor, to the unjust condemnation or suspicion of both. And therefore I think it behooveth men of worth, that have use of such as you are, to be well assured of the skill and ability which you pretend to have in your

---

[1]   'All that profess it are not Surveyors'.
[2]   'Ignorance in Surveyors dangerous'.

Profession; and because I have no further experience of you than the bare report of my Tenant, I must entreat you to discourse unto me a little of your knowledge, of such particulars as are to be considered in the absolute Survey of a Manor.

Surveyor   Sir, you seem to oppose me far, and the thing you demand, will require a longer time, and a larger Discourse, than either my leisure, or peradventure my present memory of every particular will readily permit.[3] And it may be, that you that pretend little knowledge in the Art, may apprehend both the truth of the thing, and an error committed in the performance, as well as he that assumeth the Title of a Surveyor, although neither your leisure nor your quality may in reason permit you the travail in it; for I know many Gentlemen of good worth, that have the Speculative parts of the whole, and the [practice][4] of the deepest, and yet they will not be seen to tread that path that a Surveyor is forced to do in the whole business. You have the matter and subject whereon a Surveyor worketh, and without which a Surveyor loseth both Art and Name, and therefore you cannot be altogether ignorant of the things required in the business: as the Master of a feast cannot dress the dainties, but the Cook, yet can the Master reprove the Cook if he do not his duty therein.

Lord   Thou sayest true in thy comparison; but for my part, although indeed I have Land, and I know how many Manors I have, their names, and where they lie, and the most of my Tenants, and their rents, and if you should err in these, it may be I might be able to reprove you; yet for matters of further search, I assume not to be skillful, for then I needed not your service, as of quantities, qualities, values, validities[5] of estates, tenures, customs, and other things incident to a Manor, which are not in all Manors alike, the true discovery whereof belongeth to a Surveyor's office, yet none but such as are truly skillful, can sufficiently discharge the duty herein required; and therefore by your leave, you shall briefly (I will not be tedious) relate unto me what you can say of the definition of a Manor, whereof it consisteth, how, when, and by whom it was erected with other such things as shall be expedient for the Lord of a Manor to know, the particulars whereof I will leave to your relation; and first tell me what a Manor is.

Surveyor   Sith you will needs dive into my poor skill, by your opposal, and sith indeed I do in some measure profess the Art,[6] wherein I think no man is or hath been so exquisite, but he might err in some point or part, much or little, as in other arts, yet to answer your demands, I will as briefly as I can satisfy your desire. And first, where you demand what a Manor is:[7] *a Manor in substance is*

---

3   'Some not having the name of Surveyors may have the skill'.

4   *practice*   practical knowledge.

5   *validities*   capacities.

6   'A man may err in whatsoever Art'.

7   'What a Manor is'.

of Lands, Wood, Meadow, Pasture, and Arable;[8] *it is compounded of demesnes*[9] *and services of long continuance.*[10] As touching the beginning of a Manor, and the institution thereof, the beginning of Manors was, when the King gave lands unto his followers, in such quantity, as did exceed the proportion of a man's manurance and occupation, as a thousand, two thousand Acres, more or less; which quantity of Land being at that time as it were in a lump or *Chaos*, without any distinction of parts, or qualities of Land, he to whom such land was given, to hold to him and his heirs for ever, enfeoffed[11] some others in parts thereof, as one in ten, another in twenty, and some in more, some in less Acres, and in consideration of such feoffments, every of these were to do the feoffer some kind of service, as he and they agreed upon, reserving such a part unto himself, as he might conveniently occupy in his own hands; and by this means the Land thus given by the King, and thus proportioned out to others by the *Donee*,[12] became to be called a Manor.[13] And he that was thus invested in this Land by the King, was in respect of such as he enfeoffed, called the Lord, and such as were enfeoffed, were called Tenants: Lord, in respect of government and command; and Tenants, in respect of their tenures, and manner of holding under the Lord, whom they were to obey.

Lord But when, or about what time, was this erection of Manors?

Surveyor As I take it, and as it seemeth, in the time of the Normans;[14] for among the Saxons was no such name as the name Manor, yet the thing even in substance was then, for they had *Demesnes*, and services in substance, but the *Demesnes* they called *Inlandt*,[15] and the services *Utlandt*,[16] so that it differeth only in name, but in jurisdiction little or nothing at all.

Lord Whereof is it called a Manor?

Surveyor There is some difference of opinions whence the word Manor should be derived: it is in Latin called *Manerium*,[17] yet a word not used among the Romans

---

8   'Perkins fo. 127'. Norden is citing John Perkins, *Incipit perutilis tractatus* (London, 1545), first published in 1528 and known in later English editions as *A profitable booke ... of the lawes of England.*

9   *demesnes*   those lands retained by a Lord and not rented to Tenants.

10   'The beginning of Manors'.

11   *enfeoffed*   the transfer of land in exchange for service.

12   *Donee*   gift.

13   'Lords and Tenants why so called'.

14   'When Manors began'.

15   'Inlands'. The central part of an estate, especially the land surrounding the Lord's manor house.

16   'Utlands'. Outlying areas of a manor, especially lands worked by Tenants.

17   'Whence a Manor taketh name'.

or ancient Latins, and therefore to find the *etymon*[18] by it, cannot be; for the word is used among our Lawyers, as many other made words are, which have been terms raised by our Laws, and are not elsewhere in use; and therefore the nearest way to find the signification of the word, is by the quality of the thing, so that some hold it should proceed of the Latin verb, *Manere*, which signifieth to abide, or remain in a place, as the Lord and his Tenants did in this, whereof the head house, or the Lord's seat was called *Berrye*,[19] which signifieth in the Saxon tongue, a dwelling place; which continueth yet still in Hertfordshire, and in divers other places, and is also taken sometimes *pro castro*,[20] which was also the seat of the Lord of some Manors. Manor houses were also, and yet are called in some places, Halls,[21] as in Essex, and Northward, Courts and Courthouses Westward,[22] as in Somerset, Devon, &c., as also Manor places: all which are places of the Lord's own abode, and therefore it may not unjustly be said, to take name of abiding or dwelling. Some think, and not improperly, that it taketh name of the French word *Manemirer*, which signifieth to till and manure the ground; and of the two, I take this latter to be the most proper derivation of the word Manor, for thereof are many chief houses of tillage called *predia*,[23] Granges, [or *fermes*,[24] which word *farm* is taken of the *Saxon* word *feormion*, which signifieth to seed or yield victual]; for in ancient time their reservations were as well in victual as in money, until at length they were turned into money, and some Farm rents do yet continue in victual. [Furthermore a Manor may take name of *Mainer*,][25] to govern and guide, because the Lord of the Manor had the managing and direction of all his Tenants within the limits of his jurisdiction. Of these derivations *qualem mavis accipe*: necessity ties to neither.

Lord   These significations of the word may stand all with sense, and much material it is not whence the word ariseth, but the likeliest is indeed that which most agreeth with the property of the thing. But I have within my Manor's sundry mesuages:[26] whence is the name derived?

Surveyor   Of *Meisus*, or *mesuager*,[27] which is as much to say, as *familium*

---

[18]   *Etymon*   etymology.

[19]   'Berrye, quid'. The Anglo Saxon *burh* refers generally to any enclosed dwelling place or fortress.

[20]   *castro*   castle.

[21]   'Halls'.

[22]   'Courts'.

[23]   'Predia'. Another term for 'farm'.

[24]   *fermes*   farms.

[25]   *Mainer* or *maner*   rule and government over Tenants (John Cowell, *The Interpreter* [Cambridge, 1607], sig. Ttt2v).

[26]   *mesuages*   a dwelling-house, often including adjoining land.

[27]   '[Mesuage], whence it taketh Name'.

administrare, to govern a household: for every of the Tenants had his family, and of divers of them and of the Lord's family did a Manor consist.

Lord   Then no doubt, if a man have a thousand Acres of Land more or less, to him and his heirs, which lieth in one entire piece, not yet divided, if may be divided into parts, as a portion for the Lord himself, and some parcels to erect such mesuages for Tenants to do him service, as he may make a Manor where none was before.

Surveyor   No, Sir, for although a man have a competent quantity of Land in his manurance,[28] and would convert it to the end you speak of, were it never so great, and could establish many mesuages, and could erect whatsoever services, this would not become a Manor, because all these must have long continuance, which cannot at this day be confirmed by any private man, but by the King only; but he may have thereby a kind of *seigniory*, a Lordship or government in gross over his Tenants by contract or covenant, but no Manor. No man at this day can create a service or a tenure, or by any means raise or erect a Manor: for there must be very Lord and very Tenant in Fee simple,[29] and that of ancient commencement and continuance, or else it can inure no Manor. For a man may have demesnes to occupy, and Tenants to do him services, and that of continuance, and yet no Manor. As if a man that had land, did give part of this land in former time to some others in tail[30] to do him services: here are demesnes in the donor, and services in the donees, and a tenure; yet because there be not very Tenants in Fee simple, it maketh no Manor.

Lord   Whether are all lands holden of a Manor, parcel of the same Manor?

Surveyor   No, Lands may be holden of a Manor by certain services, the service may be parcel of the Manor, and yet the Lands not.

Lord   But may not this Land be made parcel of the Manor at this day?

Surveyor   By no other means but by *escheat*;[31] for if the land fall unto the Lord by escheat, then it comes parcel of the Manor: for then is the service extinguished, and the Land cometh in place of it.

---

[28]   'A Manor may not be made at this day'. The legal right to create a Manor was withdrawn in the thirteenth century. In the early modern period, landlords who tried to establish their own manors were subject to legal prosecution because these local efforts usurped the state's authority over collecting tax revenue (Eric Kerridge, *Agrarian Problems in the Sixteenth Century and After* [London, 1969], p. 18).

[29]   *Fee simple*   'An estate in land, etc. belonging to the owner and his heirs forever, without limitation to any particular class or heirs' (*OED*).

[30]   *tail*   conferral of property to tenant and his heirs.

[31]   *escheat*   Norden's discusses this topic at length later in Book 2: see pp. 62–3.

Lord   May not a man purchase Land that lieth near his Manor, and annex the same, and make it parcel of the Manor, though it held not of the Manor before?

Surveyor   Foreign Land newly purchased, though it lie within the precinct and bounds of the Manor, cannot be annexed, though the Tenant thereof be willing to do his services there; for this is in nature of a new creation of a tenure, which at this day the law will not admit, only the King by his prerogative may.

Lord   What if it were tied unto the Lord of a Manor for the payment of an annuity: Is not the annuity then parcel of the Manor? And if that Land be purchased by the Lord, and thereby extinguish the annuity, doth not that Land come in place of the annuity, and so become parcel of the Manor, as the Land you spake of before, which by the escheat ran in place of the service?

Surveyor   The case is not alike; for the annuity was not parcel of the Manor,[32] neither can it be by such means as you propound by the way of Mortgage. But in another sort it may: as if a Manor be to be divided into sundry parts, and because the parts fall out unequal in value,[33] there must a rent or annuity be apportioned to make up the value, which rent becomes parcel of the Manor.

Lord   If the Manor be divided, as you say, and a Rent allotted to one part, how can the Rent be parcel of the Manor? For as much as in my understanding, the Manor becometh by this partition, to be no Manor; for if there can be no addition to a Manor, there can be no division of a Manor, and yet the Manor to continue still a Manor.

Surveyor   Yes, Sir, of one Manor may be made divers at this day.

Lord   How, I pray you?

Surveyor   If a Manor descend to divers partners, and they make partition,[34] and every one hath Demesnes and services, every one hath a Manor, and every one may keep a Court baron.[35]

---

[32]   '22 Edward IV, c. 44'.

[33]   '22 Lib. Ass. 53'. The reference is to John Rastell's *Liber Assisarum* (ca. 1514), published as *Le Liver des Assises et Plees del Corone* (London, 1561, republished in 1580 and 1606), a printed list of the proceedings of the Court of Assizes during the reign of Edward III.

[34]   '26 Henry VIII, c. 4'.

[35]   *Court baron*   The manorial court that held jurisdiction over the civil affairs of freehold tenants. Cases were presented by the steward and tried before a jury of freeholders. Land purchases were also registered at the court by being entered into the Court-roll (Kerridge, *Agrarian Problems*, p. 24). For discussion, see pp. 82–4.

Lord What if a man make a Feoffment upon condition of parcel of his Manor, or do grant a Lease to another for life of part, or do Entail[36] part: Are not these parts still parcels of the Manor?

Surveyor If parcels of a Manor be once thus severed, they immediately become no parcels thereof; yet may they all revert and become parcels of the Manor again, as if the condition of the Feoffment be broken, if the Tenant for life die, or the limitation of the Entail discontinue for want of heirs.

Lord Then a man may say, that though such Land be not, yet the reversions are parcels of the Manors.

Surveyor So it is intended.

Lord Well, you have reasonably well satisfied me in these points, yet would I gladly have some further satisfaction of some other matters, touching the state and profits of a Manor.

Surveyor I would be willing to do my best to content you, but you partly hinder me of other business. What else would you know? I wish brevity.

Lord It shall be so, neither shall you lose your labor; for I mean to use you, if my future satisfaction be answerable to this former: May every Manor keep a Court baron?

Surveyor Every Manor in the beginning, no doubt, might keep a Court baron,[37] and so it may at this day, unless the Manor be so dismembered, as it wanteth that which may warrant the keeping thereof; for if all the Freeholders of a Manor do Escheat, or all but one, the Manor is then disabled to keep a Court baron, for the Court cannot be kept without suitors, which are the Freeholders.[38]

Lord Then, methinks, the Manor loseth the name of a Manor;[39] for if it lose the quality, it is not the thing, no more [than] a Log that had fire, can be said a fire Log, when the fire is extinct.

---

[36] *Entail* also known as Fee tail, property that could not be sold or transferred and had to pass on to the owner's heirs.

[37] 'Every Manor may keep a Court baron'.

[38] '35 Henry VIII'.

[39] 'A Manor may lose the property, and so the name. Fitz., [c. 3]'. The citation is to Fitzherbert's *The Boke of Surueyinge*; see n. 67, p. 30.

Surveyor   It is true, it becomes no Manor, but a *Seigniory*,[40] having no power to keep a Court baron.

Lord   An ignorant Surveyor, I see, may be easily deceived, in terming that which is no manor a manor, and that no manor, which indeed is a manor. But satisfy me in this one thing: A man having two Manors lying together, and the one of them is decayed, and hath lost his power to keep a Court baron; and the Lord is willing to have the Tenants of both these Manors to do their suits and services to one Court, namely, to that which standeth yet in force, and that methinks were good for the Tenants to ease them; and it would preserve the Lord's right without prejudice to any, for then one homage would serve both, and both serve as one, one Bailiff, and other officers, as if it were an entire Manor.

Surveyor   Yet this cannot be, for this union of the Manors cannot extinguish their several distinctions, for they will be still two in nature, howsoever the Lord covet to make them one in name; and the more powerful Manor hath no warrant to call the Tenants of the decayed *Seigniory*, but every act done in one to punish an offender, in the other is traversable; and, therefore, it is but lost labor to practice any such union. If it be considered by such as are forced to service in this kind, they may refuse it; yet if they will voluntarily submit themselves to such a novation,[41] and the same be continued without contraction, time may make this union perfect,[42] and of two distinct Manors in nature, make one in name and use; and I do not think but such there are.

Lord   Then is there, as it seemeth, no mean to annex two Manors in one, howsoever necessary it were both for the Lord and Tenants.

Surveyor   Yes, Sir, two Manors may become as one, if one Manor do hold of another, and it escheat to the Lord, the escheated Manor may be annexed, and united, and of two distinct Manors become one, if the Lord will, in use.

Lord   I am answered in this point, and it standeth with more reason indeed than the former: Now, I pray you, tell me what things do properly belong to a Manor.

Surveyor   There do belong to a Manor: Lands, tenements, rents, and services, as I shewed you before in part, which are a parcel in *demesnes*, and parcel in service.

---

[40]   'A Seigniory'. The term designates a Manor that no longer possessed a court system.

[41]   *Novation*   a legal term for the replacement of one agreement with another that has been voluntarily agreed upon by all parties.

[42]   'How two distinct Manors may be made one'.

Lord   But speak, I pray you, something more at large of every of these, and first tell me what demesnes are.

Surveyor   *Demesnes* are all such Lands, as have been time out of the memory of man, used and occupied in the Lord's own hands and manurance, as the site of the Manor-house, Meadows, Pastures, Woods, and arable land, that were reserved for the maintenance of the Lord's house from the beginning.

Lord   This, then, is that you call parcel in demesnes: What is that you call parcel in service?[43]

Surveyor   All those lands, tenements, and hereditaments,[44] which yield rents of assizes, as rents of freehold, copyhold, or customary land; all which are parcel of the Manor, yet no *demesnes*.

Lord   But is not all customary land, copyhold land? Why then make you a distinction between copy and customary?[45]

Surveyor   All copyhold land is commonly customary, but all customary is not copyhold; for in some places of this Realm, Tenants have no copies at all of their lands or tenements, or anything to shew for that they hold, but there is an entry made in the Court book, and that is their evidence, and this especially of the ancient Duchy land of Cornwall,[46] and other places.

Lord   These Tenants then may be called Tenants by Court-roll, according to the custom of the Manor, but not Tenants by copy of Court-roll.

Surveyor   It is true, but they are held only a kind of conventionary Tenants,[47] whom the custom of the Manor doth only call to do their services at the Court, as other customary Tenants do.

---

[43]   'Parcel in service'.

[44]   *hereditaments*   inherited property.

[45]   'Copy and customary Land, and their difference'.

[46]   *Duchy of Cornwall*   Norden was extremely familiar with the crown's land holdings in Cornwall, having been appointed as Surveyor of Duchy lands in 1605, a post he would resume in 1616. His maps of Cornwall, intended as part of his *Speculum Britanniae* series, were not published until 1728: see *Speculi Britanniae Pars: A Topographical and Historical Description of Cornwall* (London, 1728), and a modern edition, *John Norden's Manuscript Maps of Cornwall and its Nine Hundreds*, William Ravenhill (ed.) (Exeter, 1972).

[47]   'Conventionary Tenants'.

Lord   The word *convenire*,[48] whereof they be called conventionary, doth, as I conceive, import as much as to call together, or convent[, although some would have the word *conventionary* to come of *conventum*, of covenant, namely, to be *Tenants by covenant*; but the former is more probable]. But what say you to the rents of Assize? What mean you by Assize?

Surveyor   Truly, for my part I take it to signify, set in certainty; for these kind of rents are as in the beginning, neither risen nor fallen, but do continue always one and the same, and only they and none else can be properly called rents of Assize.[49]

Lord   I think you take it rightly: And are all rents of one kind?

Surveyor   No, there are properly three kinds,[50] as rent-service, rent-seck, and rent-charge.

Lord   These terms are strange to me, though I be Lord of many Manors, and, no doubt, I receive rents of every of these kinds; but how to distinguish them, I cannot tell. And whether I have been abused by mine officers or no, I know not; for they never told me of these many kinds of rents: and, therefore, let me entreat you, for my satisfaction, a little to explain their several natures?

Surveyor   These several rents are paid upon several considerations,[51] and have several grounds and commencements, and are diversely to be levied and recovered if they be denied. That which is called Rent-service, is so called because it is knit to the tenure, and is as it were a service, whereby a man holdeth his Lands, or tenements. As, where the Tenant holdeth his lands, by fealty and certain rent, or by homage, fealty, and certain rent, or by any other service and certain rent, the rent is called rent service; for, as the service followeth a tenure, so the rent followeth the service. And if this rent be behind, the Lord of Common right may enter and distrain[52] [for it]. [And if the Lord cannot find a distress in two years upon the land of rent-service, he may have a Writ called *Cessavit per biennium* (*Statute*

---

    [48]   *Convenire*   Norden offers a more moderate etymology for conventionary tenants, preferring the sense designating 'to meet or gather' rather than the definition associated with 'covenant', a term often employed by political and religious radicals in the early modern period.

    [49]   'Rents of Assize, why so called'. *Rents of assize* were rents for freeholders and copyholders that remained at stable and established rates; by contrast, *rack-rent* (see n. 186, p. 75) could be adjusted and raised according to a tenement's maximum market value.

    [50]   'Three kinds of Rents'.

    [51]   'How every kind of rent is to be paid'.

    [52]   *distrain*   seizing goods as payment of debt.

de Westminster 2, c. 21),[53] and recover the Land.] The rent-charge is so called, because when a man granteth any land, whether it be in Fee simple, Fee tail, for life, for years, or at will, and in his deed reserveth a rent, with clause of distress for non-payment, by virtue of this clause, the land is charged with payment of the rent, by express words, and by force of it the Lord may distrain for his rent behind. [And it is to be noted that if a man grant Land under a rent-charge and after taketh to himself some of the Land, he extinguisheth the rent. Otherwise it is in a rent-service, for there the rent shall be apportioned.]

Lord This kind of rent is at this day, I think most common;[54] for few will grant Land, but they will make such provision, that the land shall stand charged with the rent.

Surveyor It is true, for at this day, there can be no rent-service raised, because it cannot be without a tenure, which cannot be at this day created.

Lord What is that you call Rent-seck?[55]

Surveyor It is a bare rent, reserved upon a grant, wherein there is no mention made of charging the land by distress, and it signifieth *redditum siccum*, a dry rent, for the recovery whereof the land is not charged, and so no distress lieth against it; but being once seized of the rent[, and being after detained, he may have an assize, otherwise he hath no remedy].

Lord Few such rents are nowadays, for a man had need to make all the provision he can to secure his rent, and yet he may be driven to try his uttermost means to recover it. But you have satisfied me also touching these rents: now let me entreat you to shew somewhat of other things incident unto a Manor, by which the Lord receiveth profit or prerogative.

Surveyor Profits may rise by infinite means and ways out of a Manor to the Lord, but all Manors yield not profits or commodities alike, neither in nature, or value.[56]

Lord If think indeed all Manors are not alike profitable to the Lord, neither hath every Manor like means; yet I desire to know for my experience sake, what may

---

[53] *Cessavit per biennium* This clause of the Statute of Gloucester (1278, rev. 1285) allowed landlords to terminate the leases of tenants who had failed to pay rent or otherwise fulfill the conditions of their tenures over the previous two years (*Statutes of the Realm*, vol. 1, pp. 82–3).

[54] 'Rent charge most common at this day'.

[55] 'Rent-seck'.

[56] 'Profits of Manors are infinite, and in all Manors different'.

grow out of a Manor, that I may the better look into the natures and qualities of such as are under my power and command.

Surveyor   If you have a Manor or Manors, there is (as I said before) *a Court baron* at the least incident thereunto,[57] and to some *a Leet, or Law-day*,[58] which is called the *view of frankpledge*,[59] by which Courts do grow many and divers *perquisites* and *casualties*, as *fines of Land, Amercements*,[60] *heriots*,[61] *reliefs*,[62] *waifs*,[63] *strays*,[64] *forfeitures, escheats*, profits growing by *pleas in Court*, and such like.

Lord   You may do well to shew me, though briefly, what every of these former things do properly import; for to tell me the names, and not the natures of the things, is, as if I should know there is a Sun but whether he give light and heat, to be ignorant. Therefore, before you pass further in any discourse, shew me how fines of Land do arise unto the lord, and what Amercements are, and the rest.

Surveyor   Fines of Land are of sundry kinds,[65] and yet properly and most especially they arise of Copyhold, or Customary Lands and tenements, which are in divers Manors of divers kinds: for there are Customary Lands, which are called Copyhold of Inheritance, and they are such as a man holdeth to him and his Heirs, according to the custom of the Manor, at the will of the Lord. When such a Tenant dieth, and the Heir cometh to be admitted (if the custom of the Manor bear a Fine certain), he giveth but the accustomed Fine; if it be uncertain and arbitrable, he agreeth and compoundeth with the Lord, or Surveyor, or Steward, for the Fine. Some hold Customary Land for lives, as for one, two, or three lives, whereof the Fine is always at the Lord's will, as is also the Fine for years. There are also Fines for licenses of Surrenders of Customary Land, and for Alienation also of freehold Land, and these are called Fines, which signifieth as much as a final composition;[66] and when the Fine, which is the end of the contract, is answered, all but the yearly Rent during the term agreed upon is paid. These and such like sums of money raised at a Court baron are parcel of the *Perquisites* of the Court, as

---

[57]   'Profits of Court'.

[58]   *Leet*   a manorial court, known as Court leet or Law-day, which was periodically held to deal with minor offences and property disputes.

[59]   *frankpledge*   the division of tenants into groups of ten householders, or tithings, who assumed a policing authority over their fellow tenants.

[60]   *Amercements*   fines paid by tenants to manorial courts.

[61]   *heriots*   payment, often of livestock, due to the landlord at a tenant's death.

[62]   *relief*   a fee that tenants paid to landlords upon succeeding to lands; an inheritance tax.

[63]   *waifs*   abandoned goods, to be seized by the Lord of the Manor.

[64]   *strays*   right to have livestock graze on common lands.

[65]   'Fines of Land'.

[66]   'Fine, why so called'.

are all *Amercements*, which are sums of money imposed upon the Tenants by the Steward, Surveyor by Oath, and presentment of the Homage, for default of doing suit, or other misdemeanors punishable by the same Court, infinite in number and quality.

Lord   Whence taketh the word *Amercement* name?

Surveyor   Of being in the Lord's mercy,[67] to be punished, more or less, crumenally,[68] at the Lord's pleasure and will. It is, no doubt, a borrowed word, as many other words used in our Common laws are: for he that is Amerced, is said to be *In Misericordia*, that is, in the mercy of some body.

Lord   These words may be understood by use, and by the [manner] of the use of things; but he that should seek the *Etymon*, among the Latins, of the Substantive *Amerciamentum*, and the Adjective *Amerciatus*, might seek long, and be never the [nearer]. But, I perceive, we must take it as our Fathers first framed it and left it: I understand what it meaneth in our common sense, and that sufficeth.

Surveyor   Other words, not a few, in like sort to be understood, we find in use amongst us, which doubtless the Romans never knew: and yet they that have to do with the things wherein they are used, understand the meaning, although their derivations be strange, as amongst others it is questionable, whence the name of a *Heriot* may be derived.

Lord   That would I be glad to learn, for I have to do sometimes with *Heriots*.[69] But because I know not why they are so called, what they be, how, where, when, by whom, and for what they should be answered, I do fear I am sometimes abused.

Surveyor   I may tell you as I have heard, and of myself conjectured, whence the word cometh; but I have no certain Authority for it. It may be said, and most likely it is, that it should come of the word *Herus*, a Lord and Master, and *Heriotus*, belonging to the Lord. And it was in the beginning a thing for the Wars, as the best Horse a man that died had at the time of his death.[70] And the Saxon word *Newges*[71] had the same signification that the word *Heriotus* hath, and importeth a thing pertaining to the Wars, which was a Horse trapped, or a Spear, or Armor, or a Sword, or some such Military weapon, which was parcel of the Tenant's service due to his Lord; and if such a Tenant had been slain in the Wars in the company of the Lord, he had paid no Heriot. *Si quis in exercitu, sive in regno, sive extra,*

---

[67]   'Amercements'.

[68]   *crumenally*   monetarily.

[69]   'Heriots'.

[70]   'Heriots, whence so called'.

[71]   *Newges*   Norden's reference is unclear; the Saxon term for heriot is *heregeatu*.

pugnans coram Domino, mortem oppeterit, ei condonatur et remittitur Heriotus.[72] Whereby it seemeth, that his service in the Wars belonged unto the Lord, and Death being the uttermost end of his service, he had done as much as his service bound him to perform; and after his death, his horse and furniture came in place of the service due unto the Lord, and thereof called a *Heriot*, being due unto the Lord, *De Jure*, after his death, and the remission was of any further *Heriot* of his goods, than that which he left behind him at his death in the Field, which of right the Lord might seize, as it seemeth by these words, *Si quis in Curia, sive morte repentina fuerit intestatus mortuus, Dominus tamen nullam rerum suarum partem, praeter eam quae jure debetur, Herioti nomine, sibi assumitur.* So that it appeareth, that at the death of every Tenant, there was due unto the Lord of the Manor of right this *Heriotus*, a thing appertaining to the Lord.

Lord   It seemeth by the quality of the thing thus due unto the Lord, that indeed the name comes as you say of *herus*, as proper or belonging to the Lord; but howsoever the things continue due and answerable to the Lord at this day, I think Tenants are not bound to like attendance on their Lords as in times past; and, therefore, whether are not these *heriots* something altered in their kind, or do they continue as in the beginning?

Surveyor   Tenants are not freed of their service, nor *heriots* altered, but they are by their tenures bound as at the beginning, to attend their Lords in the wars;[73] but that the manner of the proceeding to set forth and to press men to the wars, is not alike; and therefore the discontinuance of the form of the general performance of this kind of military service, hath bred a kind of confusion of these petty and inferior services between Lords and their Tenants, yet not taken away the right of their service.[74] Before the Conquest, *heriots* were paid according to every man's ability, and so are they now,[75] as the best horse, Ox, Cow, or such like, sometimes in money, and sometimes the best implement of the house of him that died.

Lord   A heriot is never paid, but after the death of a Tenant.

Surveyor   Yes, in some places, if the Tenant surrender, [forfeit,] or will voluntarily depart from his customary tenement or lands, he shall pay to the Lord his best

---

[72]   'Of a man slain in the Wars in company of his Lord, left his Horse and Armor for Heriot. 19 Henry VII, c. 15'. See *Statutes of the Realm*, vol. 2, p. 660.

[73]   'Tenants are bound to attend their Lords, by force of their service, to this day'.

[74]   In an example of how feudal terms of military service were preserved in the Elizabethan period, tenants and retainers of aristocratic landlords comprised one-third of the militia that was mustered to repel the Spanish Armada (Samuel E. Finer, 'State- and Nation-Building in Europe: The Role of the Military', Charles Tilly [ed.], *The Formation of National States in Europe* [Princeton, 1975], p. 119).

[75]   'In what things Heriots are paid'.

quick good,[76] in the name of a *heriot*, and in some places a piece of money, in the name of a farewell[, or farelife].

Lord   It falleth out in a Manor of mine, that divers customary tenements heriotable, are dismembered, and such tenements as in former times could yield unto the Lord a good Horse, Ox, or Cow, cannot now yield any quick good at all, because the Lands are sold from the tenement, and I lose my right: What remedy have I?

Surveyor   You must take such a *heriot*, as the Tenant deceased hath at his death.

Lord   But the Land which [belonged] sometimes unto the tenement whereof he died seized, is severed so, as there is no entire parcel in any other man's tenure, above one or two Acres: Is there nothing due for that at the death of the chief Tenant?

Surveyor   No, surely; for the Lands being lawfully surrendered, whereof the Lord cannot but always take knowledge (for it cannot be done without his consent), he cannot pretend to have wrong therein; yet this benefit remaineth to you that are the present Lord.[77] You may take the advantage of any quick, or dead goods, which any of the Tenants have at their deaths, that hold any of the parcels of the Land lately belonging to this heriotable *meese place*.[78] And if a Tenant have but half an Acre thereof, and have elsewhere more land, within, or without the Manor whereupon he keepeth, any kind of Cattle of whatsoever value, though holden of another Manor, the best is yours, wheresoever you can lawfully seize it after his death,[79] yea, although it be upon his freehold, as some say.

Lord   I like that well; yet I promise you, it is more than I thought I might have done, and I have lost much by mine ignorance. But may I not compound with all such Tenants as have these parcels, to give for every Acre so much money, *nomine herioti*? And may not that agreement bind them and their heirs forever, being recorded in the Court-roll?

Surveyor   No, Sir: You cannot make any new custom, although all the Tenants consent willingly thereunto;[80] yet if such a composition were made and continued, without any contradiction of posterities, time might create a new custom, by prescription, and be good.

---

[76]   'A farewell paid in money'.

[77]   'A small parcel of heriotable land draweth a Heriot'.

[78]   'Whence a Heriot may be seized'. A *meese place* is an uninhabited tenement.

[79]   '27 Lib. Ass. 24'. This abbreviation refers to John Rastell's *Liber Assisarum*, a compilation of assize records from the reign of Edward III; see n. 33, p. 46.

[80]   'A composition to raise a new Custom, cannot stand'.

Lord   What if a Tenant have several heriotable tenements, and die? Whether shall he pay one or more heriots?

Surveyor   He shall pay as many as he hath tenements heriotable.[81]

Lord   But there comes a thing into my mind; I pray thee, if thou canst, resolve me. Whether is the *heriot* paid in respect of him that is dead, or in respect of him that is to possess the land after him?

Surveyor   In respect of him that is dead, plainly: for it is not said, it shall be the best good of him that shall inherit, but of him that died; and whatsoever Legacies he gave by his Testament, the Lord will have his due, howsoever they be answered, and may seize it though it be sold.

Lord   It stands, indeed, by reason. But is there but one sort of *heriots*?

Surveyor   There are two sorts:[82] the one called *heriot custom*, the other *heriot service*. It is held of some, that Tenants in Fee simple only pay *heriot service*, and not a Tenant for life; and this kind of heriot is commonly expressed in the grant, or deed, and the Land is charged with the payment, and therefore the Lord may distrain, or may seize it; and if the Tenant bring his action for the taking, the Lord may avow, as for other services. *Heriot custom* is of another nature,[83] for it is held to be *de gratia*, a mere benevolence, given to the Lord by his Tenant at the time of his death;[84] and now hath custom confirmed it as a debt due, recoverable by force of justice. Some say, it was first given by Villains and Bondmen.

Lord   That needed not; for if the Villain and all that he had, were the Lord's, of common right, as I have heard it was, what needed the Lord to take a benevolence, when he might have taken all at his pleasure?

Surveyor   You say truly, yet it might be given as a continual future gratification,[85] upon their enfranchisements and manumission, to be yielded at the death of every such Tenant. Divers customs of divers places make divers kinds of yielding *heriots*.

Lord   I know that well; for custom, as is said, is above the law. Now I pray you, say something touching Reliefs, for, I take it, that was the next branch of your division of the profits rising of a Manor. But first, whence comes the word?

---

[81]   'Many heriots after the death of one'.

[82]   'Two sorts of Heriots'.

[83]   'Heriot custom'.

[84]   'Bracton'. Henry de Bracton, eleventh-century author of *De Legibus et consuetidinibus Angliae* (London, 1569).

[85]   'Divers places have different Customs'.

Surveyor   *Relief*,[86] in French, is as much as *relevatio*, in Latin, which is derived of *relevo*, the verb, which is, to raise and set up again; and therefore *M. Bracton* saith, *Relevatur haereditas, quae fuit jacens per mortem antecessoris*.[87] Whereby it appeareth, that the heir payeth this relief,[88] as a consideration and recompense unto the Lord, to be raised unto the possessions of his deceased ancestors; for this is all the benefit that the Lord hath after the death of his former Tenant, having neither the custody of the land, or body of the heir, as in some cases the Lord hath of both.

Lord   The difference, then, as I gather, between an *heriot* and *relief* is,[89] that the *heriot* is paid in the name of the Tenant deceased, and the *relief* in respect of the heir that is to become Tenant after the death of his ancestor to his possessions: but whether of these is the most ancient?

Surveyor   Surely, the *heriot*; for that was given in the Saxons' time, as is proved before, and that especially of things pertaining to war; but the *relief* came since, by the Normans. And where these matters of war are continued and paid in kind, it is under the name of *heriot*; but where the Normans made composition, and took money for all, it is called *relief*:[90] so that it seemeth, that both these in the beginning were one, but now become two distinct things, both in name and nature.

Lord   You have before told me how the *heriot* is; now tell me how the *relief* is paid.

Surveyor   The *relief* is paid after the death, change, or alienation of every freeholder, or of a Tenant in ancient *demesne*.[91] And the *relief* in some places is the whole year's rent, [in some Manors two years,] and in some places half a year's rent, as the custom of the place permitteth:[92] [in Cornwall, in many Manors they pay for *relief* for every penny five pence;] and if the relief be not paid, the Lord may distrain of common right. And if a freeholder hold of the Lord by Knight's service, and die, his heir of full age, the Lord shall have of the heir, for every Knight's fee, a hundred shillings for *relief*; and if the land be more or less, the *relief* is to be apportioned according to that rate.

Lord   What quantity of land is a Knight's fee?

---

[86]   'Relief'.

[87]   *Relevatur ... antecessoris* ['the inheritance is taken up, which had fallen by the death of the ancestor']; from Bracton, *De Legibus*, Lib. II, Cap. 36, item 3, fol. 84v.

[88]   'The Heir payeth relief'.

[89]   'The difference between a Heriot and Relief'.

[90]   'Heriot and Relief supposed sometimes one'.

[91]   '19 Henry VII, c. 15'. See *Statutes of the Realm*, vol. 2, p. 660, as well as n. 72, p. 54, above.

[92]   'How a Relief is paid'.

Surveyor   There is some difference of the quantity of a Knight's fee, as the custom of the places do differ in measure of land:[93] for in the *Duchy of Lancaster*, *a Knight's fee* containeth four hides of land, every hide four plough lands,[94] called in Latin, *Carucata terrae*,[95] and that is, *quantum aratrum arare potest in aestivo tempore*;[96] and that is (as I take it) which is in the North parts called an Oxgang.[97] And every *plough land* or *carve*, is four yard land, which in Latin is called *quatrona terrae*; every yard land thirty Acres; [half a yard land in some places in the West, is called a *Cosset*; half a *Cosset* is a *Mese*, which containeth about 7-1/2 Acres.[98] I find in an old Record of certain Lands sometimes the Earl of *Richmond's*, namely, *Denton* and *Riswick*, that one *Robert Tortmayns* did hold there *duodecem carucat terrae, quae faciunt feod. unius militis, quarum caruca et dimid. sex bouat. terrae tenentur*.[99] So that there is some difference in these computations, according to the custom of the Country.] [But commonly] a *carve* or *plow-land*[100] *containeth a [hundred] and 20 Acres, every hide of land 480 Acres, and every Knight's fee 1,920 Acres. But after some computation, a Knight's fee containeth five hides* of land, every hide four yard land, and every yard land 24 Acres, after the common account. [In *Shippon*[101] in Berkshire they have a hide of Meadow, and that contains 10 Acres.]

Lord   [So a man may be mistaken in a hide of land. But I see] there is then great difference between a Knight's fee in the Duchy of Lancaster, [the Earldom of Richmond,] and the common account of England, as it appeareth. But, seeing we have gone so far, how many Knight's fees make a Barony?

---

[93]   'The quantity of land of a Knight's fee'. A plot equal in size to 1,920 Acres. The term derives from the amount of land given to a knight in exchange for military service.

[94]   'Hila terrae'. Also known as a *hide*, or 480 Acres.

[95]   'Carucata terrae'. Or 'carucate', approximately 120 Acres. The term refers to the amount of land that could be tilled by a single plow in a year. Also known as *carve* or *plough land*.

[96]   *quantum ... tempore* ['as much as it is possible to plow in the summer'].

[97]   *Oxgang* or *bovate*   15 Acres in size; the term designates a plot that could be plowed by a team of oxen.

[98]   To summarize the land units mentioned by Norden: A *mese* is 7-1/2 Acres, an *oxgang* (or *bovate*) 15 Acres, a *yard land* (or *virgate*) 30 Acres, a *plough land* (also known as *carucate* or *carve*) 120 Acres, a *hide* (or *hila terra*) 480 Acres, a *knight's fee* 1,920 Acres, a *cantred* 3,840 Acres, a *barony* 25,600 Acres, and an *earldom* 38,400 Acres.

[99]   *old record ... tenentur*   An example of Norden's consultation of medieval documents; here he refers to records from estates of the Earls of Richmond in the North Riding of Yorkshire in order to illustrate the variable sizes that had been assigned to plough lands and oxgangs.

[100]   'Quatrona, sive virgata terra'. ['A *Virgate* is one-fourth of a plough land'.]

[101]   *Shippon*   Norden conducted surveys of Shippon in 1616 and 1620 (Frank Kitchen, 'Cosmo-Choro-Polygrapher: An Analytic Account of the Life and Work of John Norden, 1547–1625' [unpublished D. Phil. Dissertation, University of Sussex, 1992], pp. 396, 402).

Surveyor Two *Knight's fees* make one *Cantred*,[102] which, after the first computation, amounteth to 3,840 Acres. Six *Cantreds* 11/26 maketh a *Barony*, 25,600 Acres, whose relief is 100 Marks.[103] One *Barony* and a half make an *Earldom*,[104] 38,400 Acres, whose relief is 100 pound.

Lord Do these proportions of Land always hold with their titles of honor?

Surveyor Surely, no, for we may observe, they are increased and diminished, as men are in disposition to spend, or save, to add to, or to dismember their patrimonies. But these were the proportions at the first institution of these particular allotments, and the denominations do hold, though the quantities of the land be more or less: the lesser parts we see, as *yard-lands, plow-lands, &c.* Place, lands, and their parts differ, as the custom of every Country, drawn by time, doth at this day hold and allow them; but that is no prejudice to the first purpose, which allotted a certainty to every part, and a certain relief to be paid, according to the first institution of every part, and the payment followeth the title, not the quantity.

Lord You have said enough of *reliefs*, now speak of the rest; and, as I remember, the next after reliefs was *waifs*: What are they?

Surveyor *Waifs*, or *waived goods*,[105] are goods or chattels of what nature soever, stolen, and in the fugacy[106] of the thief, he leaves them behind him for want of convenient carriage, or conveyance, being pursued; and wheresoever such goods are, they are the Lords of that Manor or liberty wherein they are found, if the prerogative of the Manor will bear it; for every Manor will not carry them, but such as have it by grant from the King.

Lord Whence cometh the word *Waif*?

Surveyor The goods thus stolen and left behind the thief, are called in Latin *Bona*, or *catalla waviata*:[107] a word which our common Lawyers only use, and the signification is gathered by the use; for I think, none that is a stranger to the terms of our common Laws, be he never so well seen in tongues, can say this word signifies the thing for which it is now taken.

---

[102] *Cantred* typically called a 'hundred' in the early modern period; an area containing one hundred townships, or 3,840 Acres.

[103] 'The quantity of land of a Barony. Magna Carta, Cap. [2]'. The Magna Carta limited the size of reliefs (inheritance taxes) that English monarchs could impose on aristocrats succeeding to baronies to 100 marks (*Statutes at Large* [London, 1587], p. 1).

[104] 'An Earldom'. The term refers to a plot 38,400 Acres in size.

[105] 'Waifs, or waived goods'.

[106] *Fugacy* flight, as of a fugitive slave.

[107] 'Waif, whence derived'. The term *catalla* refers to 'chattels'.

Lord   Well then, as long as we understand the meaning by the use, it sufficeth, without further examination or disputation about the word itself. But how is it to be proved stolen goods? For it may be as well casually lost as feloniously stolen.

Surveyor   Therefore when any such thing is found within a Manor,[108] the Bailiff, or other the Lord's officer, seizeth it to the Lord's use, as a thing wherein at the instant no man claimeth property. And if it be not evident by the pursuit of the thief, that it was stolen, it is proclaimed and presented the next Court, and found by the Jury of what nature it is, and that the property is in the Lord: and because these and *Estrays*[109] are spoken of at large at every Court baron by the Steward, no man can pretend ignorance of them; therefore I will omit to speak any more of them. But a little of *forfeitures*;[110] though, no doubt, you being Lord of many Manors, know right well what they are, and how they grow, and the Tenants, no doubt, could wish you and other Lords knew less than generally you do, how and when they happen.

Lord   Tush, if there were no penalties, men would commit offences without fear,[111] and if there were no forfeitures for abuses done against Lords of Manors, Tenants would too boldly make wastes and spoils of the Lord's inheritance, without regard of law, love, or humanity; and, therefore, let me hear your opinion what forfeitures are, and for what causes Lords of careless Tenants may take advantage of forfeitures, who may omit and forgive as they see cause.

Surveyor   I know many Lords too forward in taking advantage of forfeitures upon small occasions, and if manifest cause be given them, they shew little compassion: And if I knew you were a man desirous to take advantage in this kind, I would be sparing to discover anything tending to that liberty; for, I well conceive, that the law did not so much provide, to enrich the Lords of Manors, by their Tenants' forfeitures,[112] as to keep Tenants in good order, and to restrain them (with fear of losing their tenements) from rash and willful abuses; [as the statutes of the Realm, we see have heavy penalties, but seldom *summo jure*[113] exacted]. And, therefore, in all forfeitures, there are divers circumstances to be considered, as whether the Tenant did it ignorantly, negligently, or as constrained through necessity. In these cases, whatsoever law in extreme justice alloweth, a good conscience forbiddeth to take advantage, though the second be worthy to suffer some smart; for negligence cannot be excused: for nature itself teacheth beasts, and they, in their manner of living, use a kind of providence. But if the forfeiture be committed willfully or

---

108   'How to prove waived goods'.
109   *Estrays*   stray animals or livestock.
110   'Forfeitures'.
111   'Forfeitures fit to curb offenders'.
112   'The chief end of forfeitures'.
113   *summo jure* ['to the full extent of the law'].

maliciously, it deserveth in the first, little, and, in the second, less pity. Yet where a good mind is, there lodgeth no revenge or covetous desire. And where neither of these are, there all extremities die. Yet I wish, that in these last two cases, the offenders should be punished more *in terrorem*, for example's sake, than to satisfy the greedy desire of a covetous Landlord, who (though he may say, he doth no more than the law warrenteth) doth yet strain a point of Christian charity,[114] by which men are bound to measure all men's cases by a true consideration of their own. So shall he that is Lord of much, and of many Manors, looking into the law of the great Lord, of whom he hath received, and holdeth whatsoever he hath, find, that himself hath committed a forfeiture of all, if this high Lord should take advantage of all the trespasses and wrongs he hath done against him.

Lord   You are out of the matter, whereof your talk consisteth. I desire you not to tell me how far I may take a forfeiture by a good conscience, but what a forfeiture is, and refer the taking and leaving the advantage, unto such as have the power to punish or forgive.

Surveyor   So must I when I have spoken all I can.[115] But I hold it not the part of an honest mind in a Surveyor to be an instigator of the Lord's extremities towards his Tenants; though I confess he ought to do his uttermost endeavor to advance the Lord's benefit in all things fit and expedient, yet ought his counsel and advice to tend no further than may maintain obedience in the Tenants towards their Lords, and love and favor of the Lords towards their Tenants, which being on all sides unfeigned, neither of them shall have just cause to complain of, or to use rigor to the other; for it is not the actor himself of any extremity, that is only to be reproved, but the abettor thereunto; and if I wished that any Lord, who shall require the use of my poor travails, would expect more at my hands, than the performance of my duty with a good conscience, I had rather leave than take the reward for such a travail. Neither do I find that you, howsoever you reason of this point, will commit any act toward any Tenant you have, that may not be justified by the law of love: therefore I leave further to persuade or dissuade you herein. And, as touching the matter and manner of forfeitures,[116] I pray you understand, that they be of divers kinds, and divers ways committed; for in some Manors it is lawful to do that which in others incurs a *forfeiture*. *Forfeitures* grow either by breach of a custom, as in Customary or copyhold land, or of a condition or promise in a Lease or grant: of which last, the Tenant cannot say he did not think it was so, because the meaning is expressed in his deed; but of the former, silly men may be in some sort ignorant, if they have not a Custom-roll among them to lead them.[117] But for the most part, causes of forfeitures are apparent, and known of all within a Manor: *as non payment of their*

---

[114] 'A good mean to make Landlords sparing to take Forfeitures'.

[115] 'The part of a good Surveyor'.

[116] 'Forfeitures divers in divers Manors'.

[117] 'A Custom-roll necessary'.

rent; not doing his service; felling of trees upon his customary land,[118] where custom inhibits it; *letting his customary tenement to fall down; alienating his copyhold land without the Lord's license; committing waste*; and such like, which, as I said before, are not alike in all places; and therefore it is most convenient that the customs of every Manor were known, and the Tenants made acquainted with them, that when question groweth for any cause of forfeiture, they may not say they knew it not; for Lords commonly know better how to take advantages of such casualties, than the Tenants know how to avoid them.

Lord   You speak that is reason, I confess. But may a Lord enter immediately upon a forfeiture?

Surveyor   The forfeiture must be first presented by the homage at the next Court holden for the Manor, and there found and recorded,[119] and then hath the Lord power to shew justice or mercy. It were inconvenient, that the Lord should be judge in his own cause, and his present carver of things doubtful. And therefore hath the law ordained, in all controversies, even in these inferior Courts, a just manner of trial by jury.

Lord   May none but copyhold Tenants forfeit their Land?

Surveyor   I shewed you before, that Tenants by deed indented for life or years may forfeit their estates, but that is by covenant or condition expressed in the deed, according to the prescript agreement made, and interchangeably confirmed between the Lord and his Tenant.

Lord   What is an *escheat*? For, as I remember, that followeth in your formerly recited *perquisites of Court.*

Surveyor   *Escheat*[120] is where a freeholder of a Manor commiteth felony, the Lord, of whom his land is holden, shall have his land, and that kind of forfeiture is called *escheat.*

Lord   The Lord may then enter immediately into this Land, because the law having tried the felony, it casteth the Land upon the Lord.

Surveyor   The King hath [the use and waste thereof] for a year and a day, and then cometh it unto the Lord and his heirs forever.

Lord   Is this all the causes of *Escheats*?

---

[118] 'Causes of Forfeitures'.
[119] 'How and when a Lord may enter after a Forfeiture'.
[120] 'What Escheats [are]'.

Surveyor   *Escheat* may also be where a freeholder, Tenant in ancient *demesne*, and a customary Tenant of inheritance, dieth without heir general or special,[121] and none of the blood coming to claim the same, it falleth unto the Lord by way of *escheat*.

Lord   This then is immediately the Lord's, and the King hath no part or time therein, and without any further ceremony, he may enter and dispose of it at his pleasure.

Surveyor   It must be also first found and presented by the homage of the Manor whereof it is holden,[122] and after proclamation made to give notice unto the world, that if any man come and justly claim it, he shall be received; the homage then finding it clear, doth entitle the Lord thereof, as a thing escheated for want of an heir.

Lord   You speak of an heir general or special: What difference is there?

Surveyor   The heir general, is of the body of the deceased, and the special, of his blood or kin.

Lord   So have you satisfied me thus far: now what say you to the *pleas of Court*? For I remember it is part of that you before spake of.

Surveyor   It is true; they are parcel of the *perquisites* of Court.[123]

Lord   Whereof cometh the word *perquisites*?

Surveyor   Of the word *perquiro* (as I take it), which signifieth to search for, or to enquire diligently, as also, to get or obtain.

Lord   It may well be so; for these things before rehearsed under the name of *perquisites*, are all casual, and not at all times alike; and therefore may be called *perquisita*, things gotten by diligent inquiry. And to that end, so many things are given by the Steward to the Jury of a *Court baron*, and *Leet* in charge, that they should diligently inquire of them, find them, and present them;[124] and yet scarcely one of 40, of the several things, wherewith they are charged, are found by the Jury. And some things happen at one Court, that happen not again in 20 Courts after; and, therefore, are also called *Casualties*, as happening now and then, as I conceive it, having little experience in them.

Surveyor   Yes, it seems you have the better part of experience, namely, the receiving the profits that any way happen within the Manor; some know the same,

---

[121] 'Escheat for want of heir'.
[122] 'How Escheats [are] found'.
[123] 'Perquisites of Courts'.
[124] 'Perquisite, why so called'.

but as appertaining to others, not to themselves. Of this nature also are the profits that arise by *Pleas of Court*, which because they are divers, and do diversely arise, there needs no long relation of them.

Lord   Are there no other *Perquisites* of Court, but such as you have already remembered, nor other profits arising to a Lord of a Manor?

Surveyor   There be many other profits that may grow also unto a Lord of a Manor; yet they not certain, nor in all Manors alike.

Lord   Then are they also casual, and may be called also *Perquisites of Courts*.

Surveyor   Casual, but not *Perquisites of Court*; yet some of them may be called *Perquisita*, in some sense,[125] because they be gotten by search and inquiry, as those that are hidden in the earth: Treasures, which as long as they lie unknown, benefit not the Lord; but when they are found they are called *Treasure trove*,[126] as *Silver, Gold, Plate, Jewels*, and such like, before time hidden, which appertain unto the Lord. So do *Minerals* of *Lead, Tin, Copper*, and such like; and *Quarries* of stone, *Free-stone*,[127] *Slate-stones, Marking stones*,[128] and all such, which may lie long undiscovered. As may also *Coal, Lime, Chalk*, and such like, for which, search being made, are happily found; yet because the benefit is uncertain upon the present, and what continuance and vent it may afford, they may pass under the name of *Perquisites* and *Casualties*;[129] as may also *Fishing* and *Fowling*, unless the Lord can bring the same to be of a certain continuing rent; then are they no more casual during the grant, but are in nature of other rents certain. And of these kinds, are infinite other things, incident to some Manors, but not to all. As the profits of *Fairs*, and *Markets, Wood sales, sales of heath, flags*,[130] and *Turbary*,[131] *pannage*,[132] and such like. All which are in themselves uncertain, as touching the value, unless they be turned into a rent certain.

Lord   That I take is the surest way for the Lord, for he that commits the dispensation of these uncertain things to Bailiffs, unless they be very honest indeed, may make their Bailiffs rich, and raise little profit unto themselves, as I am taught by experience, especially dwelling a far off from my Manors.

Surveyor   Yet the Lord must be wary how he lets these casual things, before he know

---

[125] 'Perquisites, but not perquisites of Court'.

[126] 'Treasure trove'.

[127] *Free-stone*   sandstone or limestone used for construction.

[128] *Marking stones*   chalk used to mark cattle.

[129] 'How casualties may become certain'.

[130] *flags*   rocks used for flagstones or pavement.

[131] *Turbary*   a peat-bog.

[132] *pannage*   the right to pasture pigs.

what they are, how they rise, and what profit they may yield, how they will continue, and to whom, and upon what conditions he grants them. Otherwise he may be overtaken and much abused; for a Secret benefit once let, cannot be revoked at pleasure.

Lord　You may indeed call these things Secrets, because their validities are not suddenly apprehended or found, being in themselves Novelties, which sometimes come short, sometimes exceed the hope a man hath in the value which may grow by them.

Surveyor　Therefore I say, it behooveth the Lord, to whom such casualties shall befall, first to make due and diligent trial by men, both of trust and experience, what may be made of any such thing by the year. For such is the wary dealing of some, that have the guiding of things of this casual nature,[133] that they will observe the conditions and qualities, circumstances and value to themselves, and disable the thing, and extenuate the value to the Lord, to bring him out of conceit with the goodness and validity thereof, to the end they may obtain a grant; as hath fallen out in many things, and to many men, whose future profit of the things thus achieved have approved the Lord to be much abused. This I know by experience, in the grant of a *Coal-mine*, which as long as it was in the Lord's hands, it yielded a small yearly revenue, until he that managed the same, got a grant of the Lord, and then the profit was twice quadrupled by the Lessee's own confession. The like of a *Salmon-fishing*, wherein the Lord lost two parts in three, and yet at the time of the letting, made to believe it was hardly worth the Rent. Yet would I wish the Lords of Manors in these casual things to be contented, after true trial made, to grant the same for a reasonable rent, though the lessee gain; for the travail and hazard in these uncertain things deserve some favor; for in receiving a rent, is little toil, and as little danger, but in these kinds of things is uncertain of profit, and assured care and labor.

Lord　I observe by your discourse, that you seem very indifferent between the Lord and Tenant: I mislike it not so you stand firm to the Lord that employeth you, as right and equity requireth.

Surveyor　Every profession, Sir, hath his defects:[134] if they be voluntary or willful, they are utterly intolerable, for they be either for affection or lucre. Negligent defects cannot be excused, for they proceed of the want of heed and careful industry. But for my part, I will endeavor to discharge my duty truly, and will wade in the business, both mine eyes opened; but when I consider the Lord and the Tenants, I will shut them both.

Lord　Will you so? Is that all the care you will have of the Lord's benefit, that payeth you for your [travail]? And shall the Tenant be as well respected as he? I think you will hardly prove a fit Surveyor for me.

---

[133]　'Policy in Bailiffs, and Overseers'.

[134]　'Every profession hath defects'.

Surveyor   If you require other than an upright course between your Tenants and you, I reverence your person, but desire not your service. For, know you this, I pray you, that as the land and the profits of it is yours, and your revenues grow by the rents, labor, and service of your Tenants, your Tenants have as good interest in their tenements for their rent and doing their service, as you (under your correction) have in the Manor, according to the quality of the tenures; and that being saved to them, and a good conscience to me, I shall do what you will require.

Lord   It is as much as I desire; for that which I crave of you, is but to observe and report every particular thing, within the compass of your Survey, whereby I may apprehend truly the full estate of my Manor,[135] as behooveth, and what commodities do arise, or may by any means lawfully be raised in the same.

Surveyor   If a painter should draw your picture, Sir, and you having a blemish in your face, or defect in your [lineaments of body], would you think he dealt truly with you if he omitted the blemish, and made your [parts] perfect and straight, being deformed and crooked?

Lord   I know your meaning; I like no such flattery, neither would I he should make a straight leg crooked, but true conformity in all parts.

Surveyor   So will I as near as I can; for neither in quantity, quality, or value, will I, for I ought not to be partial;[136] for these are the things wherein injury may be done to the Tenants : neither will I, for I ought not conceal or counterfeit their estates, terms of years, lives, covenants or conditions, rents, services, forfeitures or offences; neither whatsoever profits, emoluments, or commodities that may any ways arise or grow unto the Lord. For a partial eye seduceth the heart, and the heart the hand, and the hand the pen, which cannot but witness against a corrupt entry of these collections, many years after the Surveyor is in his grave.

Lord   Thou speakest as an honest man, and I mislike thee not, if thy words and thy works agree. And seeing we are grown thus far, I pray thee make an end of thy whole discourse, and tell me what else appertaineth to a Manor.

Surveyor   I have already declared the most. But Manors much differ in their profits. For a Manor of small quantity of Land, and few Tenants, may be more beneficial to the Lord, than a far greater.

Lord   How may that be?

Surveyor   Divers Lordships yield extraordinary commodities, some under the

---

[135] 'What a Lord may justly challenge of his Surveyor'.

[136] 'A Surveyor should be equal between Lord and Tenant'.

earth,[137] some of the earth, some above the earth: as *Tin, lead, copper, coal, stones, millstones*, and such like, found under the earth, which every Manor hath not.

Lord   But these are chargeable commodities to get.

Surveyor   So is the Lord of a Manor at no cost in planting, plowing, setting, or sowing them.

Lord   That is true, but commonly the Land is barren where these things are found. And therefore it is a great work of divine providence,[138] to yield such a commodity from under the barrenest soil, to supply the want thereof in places more fertile, of other things most behooveful for the relief of man. And yet in many of these barren places, groweth by the diligent man, corn in abundance, as the Psalmist saith: *A handful of corn shall be sown upon the top of the Mountain, and the fruit thereof shall shake like the trees of Lebanon.*[139]

Surveyor   Where diligence is and the fear of God, there, no doubt, God blesseth the labors of men, and *Waters even the highest Mountains, from his chambers.*[140] For when Israel turned to God from their Idolatry, he promised by *Ezekiel*, that their desolate places, and high Mountains, should be tilled and sowed.[141] *But he maketh a fruitful land barren, for the sins of them that dwell therein.*[142] So that, whether God send his blessings under the earth, upon the Mountains, or in the Valleys, whether in grass for Cattle, in herbs for the use of men, whether in Wheat, Oil, or Vines, he truly entitleth none unto them, but such as fear to offend him, and shew thankfulness for them.

Lord   Though these words digress from our present matter in hand somewhat,[143] yet it is good, that both Lords and Tenants should know and acknowledge indeed,

---

[137] 'Commodities under the earth'.

[138] 'The wisdom of Nature'.

[139] 'Psalm 70:16' (Psalm 72:16). Norden gives a different—but similarly incorrect—verse number for this passage when he later cites it in Book 5 (n. 231, p. 192).

[140] 'Psalm 104:13'.

[141] 'Ezekiel 36:9' (Ezekiel 36:10).

[142] 'Psalm 109:[34]' (Psalm 107:34).

[143] The Lord dismisses the inclusion of religiously inflected language as a digression. Earlier in the text (p. 61), the Surveyor had drawn on scripture in order to critique landlords' excessive enforcement of forfeiture, which may explain the Lord's interest in getting the discussion back on track and away from any potentially dangerous application of religious ideals. Despite the fact that Norden maintained a thriving second career as a writer of homiletic devotional texts—composing 24 of these works, several of which were best-sellers—these passages are the only examples of a polemical use of scripture in *The Surveyor's Dialogue*. (See p. xxxi.)

from whom all these good things do proceed.[144] For although they come, some from under the earth, some of the earth, and some above the earth, they be not yet the gifts of the earth, but of God, that hath provided the earth to bring them forth to our use. But what mean you by the things of the earth? Come not these of the earth?

Surveyor   Yes, I confess it; but some things are more perfect of themselves than [others]. But such as, by an extraordinary working of man's art, are made of the earth, I term things of the earth, and they also rest to the benefit of the Lord of that Manor where such earth is found: as the earth whereof *Alum, Copperas,*[145] *Saltpeter, Glass*, or other such is made,[146] together also with *Fuller's earth,*[147] *Brick, Tile, and Potter's clay*, which are not common.

Lord   Is there any other thing material, incident to a Manor?

Surveyor   Yea, and amongst all the rest of the privileges which the Lords of Manors have to raise their further benefits by, are two not yet mentioned, wherein if they be not very precise and circumspect how they bestow them, and in what sort they dispose of them, there will follow a fearful account, when the great Lord of all Lords shall take survey of the things done by the Lords of the earth.

Lord   What are these things, I pray you, that you make such scruple to utter them?

Surveyor   Things of themselves lawful by the laws of the Land, where they be judiciously and carefully handled, as they are by the laws intended, and by the chief disposers meant:[148] namely, [the education and] the marriages of *Wards*, and disposition of their lands in their minorities, and the presentations of Benefices in the gifts of private men.[149]

Lord   For the first, I have not yet occasion to make proof how or what they are; but the second I have had some power to bestow, wherein I was not so remiss, as that I presented such as were not fit for the function, which I think is your meaning; and therefore let that pass awhile, and learn me what a ward is, and how he and his land is to be disposed by the law, that I may learn it against the time I may have use, to dispose both the Ward and his land.

Surveyor   The word *Ward* is as much as *Guard*,[150] which signifieth tuition or

---

144   'Lords and Tenants must acknowledge all to come from God'.
145   *Copperas*   a sulfate of iron.
146   'Things made of the earth'.
147   *Fuller's earth*   a watery silicate of aluminum, used to clean cloth.
148   'Wards'.
149   'Presentations'.
150   'The word Ward, whence taken'.

defense, and he that is in ward, is under some man's government and keeping; and the word hath a passive signification, as it is used in our common speech, and yet the same word is also used in the active sense, as they that watch or attend for the defense of any are called the Ward or Guard of that person or thing they do protect. But the Wards whereof we are now to speak of, are the sons or daughters, heirs to some person,[151] that held his land either of the King in chief, or of some inferior person by Knight's service, whose heir male being under the age of 21 years, and the female within the age of 14 years, the Lord shall have the Ward, Guard, or custody of the body and of the lands so holden of him, to his own use, until they come to these ages, without making account to the heir when he or she comes to age, as law books will tell you.

Lord   Then, methinks, the word as it is commonly used is improper, namely, to call such an heir a *Ward*; it is more proper to say, he is in *ward*, and not a *Ward*.

Surveyor   I take it as you do.

Lord   But what is the reason that the Lord should have the land to his own use? Why rather do not the profits redound to the use of the heir in his minority.

Surveyor   This kind of warship had some reason for it in the beginning. For you must understand, that he whose son or daughter is to be thus guarded, and his land to be disposed by the Lord, was in his lifetime bound, by the tenure of his land, to do manly and actual service in person, in the time of war, or to keep a Castle, with some kind of warlike weapon, in the time of war and peace. And these kinds of capital services, were called either tenures *in capite*,[152] as holden of the King, who is the chief, Escuage[153] uncertain, grand serjeanty,[154] or some other like service, and was called *servitium militare*, service of a Soldier, now called Knight's service; for the title of Knighthood came first by military service, and *Miles*, signifying a Soldier, signifieth also a Knight: though every Knight now be not a Soldier by profession, yet every approved Soldier is a Knight by imputation. For he that holdeth by these services, though he be not a Knight, yet the service is called Knight's service. And these services were not to be discontinued, for to that end, were the lands first given by the King, and other inferior Lords of Manors, that they might have the continual service of their Tenants.[155] And therefore whensoever the Tenant of such a tenure died, having none to supply the place of like manly service, the heir being under age, and not of power, the Lord was and is supposed to be bound for the defense of the Realm, to perform the service by a person, for whom he must answer in the heir's minority. And because the charge

---

[151] 'Wards, what they are'.

[152] 'What tenure draws Wardship'.

[153] *Escuage*   or shield-service, obligation of 40 days' military service per year.

[154] *grand serjeanty*   military service.

[155] 'The cause'.

was in former times great and dangerous, and the land given only for that cause, the Lord was to keep the heir, and to see him trained up, and to be made fit for the same service; and for his maintenance and supply of the service, to have the use and profit of his Land, until he became able to perform the service himself in person; [and so far] I hold the heir hath no wrong in law nor conscience.

Lord   I think this to stand with great reason; for if it had not been thought reasonable, the laws would not have provided in that case as they have done, as it appeareth by your relation.

Surveyor   Many Statutes indeed have been made touching *Wards*: Magna Carta, cap. 4, 7, and 28; Mary 1, cap. 6, 7, 8 &c.; Westminster 1; Westminster 2; and many Statutes since, to which I refer you, too long here to relate.[156]

Lord   What needed you then to give such a strict caveat touching *Wards*?

Surveyor   Truly, to put Lords and others (into whose hands they often happen) in mind to be careful of their education and disposing, because many inconveniences follow, if their Guarders be not faithful and provident for their well bestowing.

Lord   How, in bestowing?

Surveyor   In marriage.[157] For the Lords have the marriage, both of the Male and Female, if they be unmarried at the time of their ancestor's decease. And it falleth out many times, that partly for their land, and partly for their marriage, they are bought and sold, and married young, and sometimes to such as they fancy not, and when they come to riper judgment, they bewray their dislikes too late, and there grows disparagements. And sometimes their education is so slenderly regarded, that when they come to govern themselves, and their families, their estates and patrimonies, they discover what their education was, good or evil.

Lord   There be three especial ends whereunto the good education of such an Infant should tend, as I suppose.[158] The first and principal, is *fear of God*, in true Religion; the second is, the benefit that the *Commonwealth* shall reap, by his virtue's sufficiency; the third and last, the ability by which he may govern his family, and manage his patrimony, for his best maintenance. But what can you now say, touching the second of these chief points? Namely, the presenting of Clerks into Ecclesiastical livings, and how it cometh to pass, that our Layman

---

[156] 'Statutes for the confirmation of Wardships'. On the Court of Wards, see H.E. Bell, *An Introduction to the History and Records of the Court of Wards and Liveries* (Cambridge, 1953).

[157] 'Marriage of Wards'.

[158] 'Three ends whereunto the good education of Wards tendeth'.

(as he is called) may nominate and present a Clerk, to a Parsonage, Vicarage, or free Chapel, whose function is high and divine.

Surveyor The reason why these *Lay-lords* of Manors do present,[159] as aforesaid, is in right of the *Parsonage, Vicarage,* or *free Chapel,* belonging to their Manors, and where the Lord of the Manor is very and undoubted Patron of such an Ecclesiastical gift, he may make his choice of the Parson or Vicar. Always provided, by divine ordinance and human institutions, he must be *Idoneous,*[160] fit for the place.

Lord But lieth it in the Lord's power, only to nominate and present such a one? And is it then sufficient if he deem the party fit?

Surveyor No, he must be approved fit by his *Ordinary,* the Bishop of the Diocese, by whom he must be instituted and inducted.

Lord Then is the Lord in his nomination and presentation cleared of offence to the Church, if the party prove after insufficient.

Surveyor He is in some sort. But he is bound in conscience to be very circumspect in his choice. For if any carnal consideration moved him to the party, he standeth not clear before God, into whose stead he intrudeth himself after a sort in this case. But if he do it in a godly zeal of the good of God's Church, he will aim only to the virtues of the man, and not to any human respect.[161] For, although the party have an higher probation, namely, by the *Bishop,* that is specially of his *literative,*[162] which is easily found by examination, but his qualities, conditions, and conversation, by time and experience, and that must the presenter have good trial of,[163] before he either name him or present him. For he is as it were the hand that reacheth him forth to be received of the Church. A matter far higher, and of greater moment, than every man that covets *advowsons*[164] for such presentations' sake, can reach unto by their rashness. For if they weighed the matter in the balance of divine judgment, they should find their understandings far too light to perform it as they ought. For if he prove unprofitable, or scandalous to the Church, as too many do, he that presented him so unadvisedly will fearfully answer it in time to come.

Lord Now surely, although peradventure some may think these things digress much from matters of Survey, yet I hold thy words within the compass of it, for these are necessary observations and admonitions to us that are Lords of Manors,

---

[159] 'Why Lords of Manors do present Clerks'.

[160] *Idoneous* suitable.

[161] 'No carnal consideration must move a Lord to present a Clerk'.

[162] *literative* literacy, educational qualifications.

[163] 'What a Patron must consider in his choice'.

[164] *advowsons* a patron's right to present candidates for benefices.

and to whose lot it often falleth to perform this work. And I hold thou hast in this done no more than an honest Surveyor should in advising men to be wary how they dispose of this part of their patrimony.

Surveyor   Sir, I hold it neither part of their Patrimony, nor part of a Manor,[165] neither a thing unto them of any advantage to their person; the greatest benefit is, that he may upon the vacation, appoint a worthy man to teach himself, and his Tenants, which as I conceive it, is a sweet gain, for by the godly Minister, he and they may gain heavenly riches.

Lord   As thou sayest, it is a great benefit, nay, it is a high blessing, to have a godly teacher of the people; and it is the blessing of God on him, that having a godly care, findeth, nameth and presenteth such a one; and woe to him, that negligently or willfully the contrary. But what say you to impropriations?[166] For they also are within the compass of a Survey, where the Lord takes the *tithes*, and nominates a *Minister*, *Vicar*, or other *hireling*, and he (often times) unworthy the turn, as is commonly discerned in too many places of this Realm.

Surveyor   I know too many such, the more to be lamented, and that in Manors of great value and parishes very populous, whose continued ignorance of divine duties, bewrayeth the original to proceed, first from that *Satanical beast*,[167] to foster monastical idleness. And as a matter too high for me, to aim at the means of reformation, I reverently leave to their discretions, who have authority to reprove it and power to reform it.

Lord   You say well: What else is there to be considered, touching the things incident to a Manor?

Surveyor   Nothing, Sir, that I now remember, but a matter almost out of use, a tenure called *Villainage*:[168] that is, where the Tenants of a Manor were *Bond-men*

---

[165] 'A Parsonage or Vicarage no part of a Manor'.

[166] 'Impropriations'. The term refers to the seizure of a benefice's revenues.

[167] *Satanical beast*   A reference to Revelation 13:1, a passage often cited in anti-Catholic polemic.

[168] 'Tenure in Villainage'. (I have retained Norden's spelling, 'villainage', throughout the text.) Villeinage refers to the feudal forms of tenure that gradually became codified as copyhold in the late medieval period. Villeins, denied security of tenure and protection from eviction, were also obligated to perform feudal terms of service for their Lords. Despite the precariousness of their legal status, and the servile associations tied to the name, villeins often amassed a relatively large amount of wealth. It is more accurate to see villeins as an intermediate class situated between freeholders, on the one hand, and cottagers and other wage-laborers on the other. For further discussion, see especially Paul Vinogradoff, *Villainage in England* (1923; New York: Russell & Russell, 1967) and Martin, *Feudalism to Capitalism*, pp. 36–45.

and *Bond-women*, the men were called *Villains* and the women *Neifes*.[169]

Lord   It hath a base title: a *Villain* is an opprobrious name, howsoever it took beginning.

Surveyor   As the word is now used and taken, it is indeed a word of great dishonor; but the time hath been, the word hath been of no such disgrace. And it is now but as the thing is meant by the speaker, and taken by him to whom it is spoken; although some say, that a villain is [*quasi servus*],[170] which name indeed is of a more tolerable construction in our common sense, than is now the name of *Villain*, which is indeed no more than *villanus*,[171] a Rustic or Countryman, which word is in sense contrary to *Cives* or *Oppidanus*,[172] but that since the Conquest by the *Normans*, these *villani* became [*mancipii*,][173] bondmen;[174] for where the Conqueror came and prevailed by force, there the Country-people became *Captives* and *Slaves*. But *Kent*, which was not subdued by the sword, but by composition, retained their freedom still, as did also many *Cities*.

Lord   When then should the name *Villain* be so odious, if it signify but a Countryman, for there are many civil and wealthy Countrymen.

Surveyor   Because [many of them] endured under that name, many kinds of servitude and slavish labors under their Lords, as did the *Israelites* in *Egypt*. [In Suffolk and other places, there is land called *major tenura*, and the Tenants of this tenure did all kinds of servile works the Lord would impose; and another, called *Minor tenura*,[175] which were not altogether so subject to servitude, yet had the name bondmen. There is also a tenure, called *Backner-land*,[176] which had a peculiar custom, to do works in harvest, for hire of a penny *per diem*, finding themselves, or a halfpenny having meat]; and whatsoever they possessed, was not theirs, but the Lord's[, before their enfranchisement].

---

[169]   *Neifes*   bondwomen.

[170]   *quasi servus*   a kind of servant, as opposed to a bond-slave.

[171]   'Villain, quid'.

[172]   *Oppidanus*   provincial; from a city other than Rome.

[173]   *mancipii*   under Roman law, the status of non-free dependents, as distinguished from slaves.

[174]   'Villains came by Conquest bondmen'.

[175]   *minor tenura*   This term typically designates the conditions of tenure for wards (Cowell, *The Interpreter*, sig. Ttt1v); Norden is using it to refer more broadly to mitigated terms of bond-servitude.

[176]   *Backner-land*   land whose title reverted back to the Lord upon a tenant's death. In addition, whereas a feudal tenant often owed service of one day per week to the Lord, this duty—or 'boon-work'—increased to three days during harvest-time. For further discussion, see Vinogradoff, *Villainage*, pp. 174, 297, 308.

Lord   I blame not any man, then, to take exceptions at the name, for he that would call me *Villain*, and I were not, I think meant to bring me into like thralldom; but I think there be not many under this kind of servitude at this day.

Surveyor   There are not; yet there be as many *Villani* as in times past, in that sense, from which this word was first derived,[177] which, as I said, was from the place of their inhabiting the Country, and Country-villages and out-farms. And a man may be called *Villanus* without offence, unless it be spoken in opprobrious sense; for if a man should ask a Scholar how he would call, or what adjunct he would give unto a man, dwelling in a Country village or house, he would say he were *Villanus*, or *Villaticus*, a man belonging to a village, or to some Country house or Farm: for *Villa* signifieth a village, a Farm or a house out of a town. *Cuius ego villam contemplans*, saith *Cicero*:[178] whose Manor or Farm I beholding.[179] So in Cornwall, and some part of Devon, a house in the Country is called a Town. This I produce, to shew whence the word *Villain* was first derived. But the word at this day needs not to be so carped at, unless the party do the service of that *base tenure*, which upon the Conquest was imposed upon the Country people[; as Solomon made all the *Amorites, Hittites, Hivites* and *Jebusites* bondman, upon whom he imposed what tax of good, or labor of body he listed, 1 *Kings* 9:20, 21]. Which kind of service and slavery, thanks be to God, is in most places of this Realm quite abolished, and worn out of memory; yet some bear the mark, both in their ancient and new Copies, by this word *tenens nativus*, which signifieth a bond Tenant, or born of the blood, and yet it may be their ancestors were manumised[180] long ago. And it were not amiss, that Stewards of such Courts, wherein such Copies are made, would be careful in making their copies upon Surrender of such a Tenant, whose ancestors evermore possessed the thing he surrenders; for when a free man shall take such a copy, under the name of *tenens nativus*, he hath wrong,[181] and I think it little material, if the word were generally omitted, where there hath been an enfranchisement; for the greatest argument for the continuance is, to maintain the antiquity of the Manor, and methinks it were better that such an odious brand were clean wiped and razed out of every man's inheritance; although (no doubt) there are yet some within this

---

[177] 'Many Villani at this day'. Confirming his observation, Norden had himself come across bondmen tenants while conducting a survey at Falmer in 1607. But the number of villein tenants was declining in the early modern period as tenants purchased their manumission through the payment of fines. Landlords often abused this process, extracting excessive cash payments in exchange for the nominal enfranchisement of their erstwhile villeins (Kerridge, *Agrarian Problems*, p. 91; also see Tawney, *Agrarian Problem*, pp. 41–6, 52–4).

[178] *Cuius ... contemplans* ['as I gaze upon his country house']; Cicero's admiration for Manius Curius's villa, from his *Cato Maior de Senectute* [*Cato the Elder on Old Age*], XVI.55 (*De Senectute, De Amiticia, De Divinatione*, William Armistead Falconer [trans.], Loeb Classical Library [Cambridge, MA, 1923], pp. 66–7).

[179] 'Villa signifieth a house, or Farm in the Country'.

[180] *manumised*   manumitted, freed.

[181] 'tenens nativus, in a Copy, a badge of bondage'.

Realm without manumission: few known, but some concealed, and some (no doubt) have been by the act of their Lord freed, and neither their Lords witting of it, nor the Tenants taking present advantage; for if the Lord buy or sell with his bond Tenant, it is an immediate enfranchisement of the Tenant and his posterity. And some have voluntarily released their Tenants of such a slavery: an act of charity.

Lord   Truly, I think it is a Christian part so to do; for seeing we be now all as the *children of one father, the servants of one God, and the subjects to one King*, it is very uncharitable to retain our brethren in bondage, sith, *when we were all bond, Christ did make us free*.[182] I fear we are now most in bondage to pride, covetousness, gluttony, lasciviousness, drunkenness, and such; if men could free them from these, they might say they were indeed manumised and truly enfranchised. [But for their abuses, God threatens to give a people into the hands of some tyrant, that may make us bondmen again, which God forbid.]

Surveyor   You say well, and I wish that all men would but truly desire that manumission, and that you that are Lords would be conformed to a moderate course of exaction upon your Tenants bond or free, that you that are Lords may live of your lands, and your Tenants by their labors in such a measure, as you Lords should not be too strict in taking, nor they too backward in duty, but in a mutual manner, you to be helpful unto them, and they loving unto you.[183] And by this means, should your strengths increase far more by their love, than by your lucre, and their comfort grow as much by your favor, as doth now their groans under your greediness.

Lord   Methinks you conclude more sharply against Landlords than is cause, for I am of opinion, there is little cause why Tenants should so much grudge, as some of them do.[184] If they say their rents are raised, or complain of the greatness of their fines, let them enter into consideration how they vent their commodities, and they shall find as great inequality of the prices of things now and in times past, as is between rents and fines now and in times past.[185] And as far as I can perceive, an observing and painful husband liveth, fareth, and thriveth as well upon his Farm of racked rent[186] as many do that are called Freeholders or that have Leases of great value for small rent.

---

[182]   'Charity, to free bondmen'. Norden paraphrases 1 Corinthians 12:13: 'For by one Spirit are we all baptized into one Bodie, whether we be Iewes or Grecians, whether we be bonde, or fre [*sic*].'

[183]   'A mutual course between Lords and Tenants'.

[184]   'Prices, Rents, and Fines in times past and present, not much unequal'.

[185]   On the rising prices of agricultural commodities in the sixteenth century, see n. 30, p. 23.

[186]   *Racked rent*   Rent calculated according to the maximum market value of a property, in contrast to *rents of assize* (see n. 49, p. 50). The practice of landlords raising tenants' rents at steadily climbing rates was a frequent complaint throughout the sixteenth century. Some economic historians have explained this practice as a response to market conditions: because rents were at historic lows while the prices of agricultural commodities continued

Surveyor   There is some reason for it,[187] which every man either seeth not, or seeing it, doth not consider it, or considering it, hath no will or power to reform it. Some Freeholders, and the Lessees of great things of small rent, bring up their children too nicely, and must needs, forsooth, Gentlelize them; and the eldest son of a mean man must be a young master:[188] he must not labor, nor lay hand on the plough (take heed of his disgrace); he shall have enough to maintain him like, and in the society of Gentlemen, not like a drudge. And when this young Gentleman comes to his land, (long he thinks) he hath no leisure to labor, for Hawking, Hunting, or Bowling, or Ordinaries, or some vain or lascivious, or wanton course or other, leaving plough and seed, and harvest, and sale to some ordinary hireling, who may do what he list, if the poor wife be as careless at home as husband is abroad. And at his elbow he hath perchance some vain persons, that dissuades from covetousness, and from too much frugality, and that he needs not to care for getting more: he hath no rent to pay, but some to receive which will maintain him, and when he is gone, all is gone; spending is easier than getting. And thus by little and little roweth himself and the hope of his posterity under water, in the calm Sunshine of his pleasures. Whereas he, that hath a rent to pay,[189] is not idle, neither in heart nor hand: he considers the rent day will come, and in true labor and diligence provides for it, and by his honest endeavors, and dutiful regard, gets to pay rent to his Lord, duties to the King, relief to the poor, and maintains his estate more pleasing to God, more obedient to the King, more profitable for the Commonwealth, and more truly contented in mind, than sometimes his thriftless Landlord. I infer not yet by this, Sir, that because they sometimes thrive well that live upon racked rents, therefore you Landlords should impose the greater rent or fine: that were to do evil that good might come of it, nay, rather to do evil that more evil may follow; for if there be not a mean in burdens, the back of the strongest *Elephant* may be broken. And the best and most careful, and most laborious and industrious husband, may be overcharged with the rent of his land.[190] Happy therefore is that Tenant that meeteth with a considerate Landlord, and happy is that Landlord that may see his Tenants prosper and thrive and himself have his due with love. And, on the contrary, I think it will be very unpleasant to a good mind, to see his Tenant to be overcharged and be forced to full under the burthen of an overheavy imposition.

Lord   Well, I have heard all thy discourse with patience, and indeed my desire was to hear thee in these things; and I mislike not anything in thy whole relations, and thy conclusion is not amiss: though perchance some young novices of the world

---

to rise, rack-renting was a kind of 'market adjustment' (Richard Lachmann, *Capitalists in Spite of Themselves* [Oxford, 2000], p. 175).

[187] 'The reason why some Farmers live as well as some Freeholders'.

[188] 'Young Gentlemen, Yeomen'.

[189] 'The Farmer cares to pay his Rent, and labors for it'.

[190] 'Happy is the Tenant that hath a good Landlord'.

might censure thee, reason will not but allow what thou hast said. And I wish that all the Tenants that I have may live under me with comfort; for, to tell the truth, I had rather buy a [smile] and a good report of my faithful Tenants, something to my loss, than to get their frowns to my gain.[191] For there is no comfort in a discontented people, though some have said *Rustica gens, optima flens, pessima gaudens*,[192] [as if *gens rustica* did *pungere ungentem* and *ungere pungentem*, namely, did abuse them that used them well and were subject to them that used them most hardly] which may hold among *Infidels* and under *Tyrants* but not among *Christians* that should not grieve one another.

Surveyor   I am right glad, Sir, you are of so qualified a disposition: your example may do good to others; if not, it will give evidence against the contrary minded in time to come. And so for this time I must entreat you, I may take my leave of you. I will attend your other occasions forthwith.

Lord   That is my will. But who comes yonder?

Surveyor   I take it, it is your Tenant that lately departed from us.

Lord   So it is. I will leave you two together; fare you well: You know the places where mine occasions will draw you, and in the meantime I will make you a warrant to go in hand with it.

The end of the second Book.

---

[191]   'A good resolution in a Landlord'.

[192]   *Rustica ... gaudens*   a medieval Latin proverb; as Fynes Moryson translates it, commenting on the early modern Irish, 'the country clowns are best when they do weep, and worst when they in plenty laugh and sleep' (Charles Hughes [ed.], *Shakespeare's Europe ... Unpublished Chapters of Fynes Moryson's Itinerary* [New York, 1967], p. 314).

THE SURVEYOR'S DIALOGUE, BETWEEN The FARMER and SURVEYOR: Wherein is shewed the manner and method of keeping a Court of Survey, with the substance of the Charge, and the Articles to be inquired of, how to Enroll Copies, Leases and Deeds, and how to take the Plot of a Manor.

THE THIRD BOOK.

Farmer   You are happily met here again, Sir: Have you ever since had conference with my Landlord?

Surveyor   Yea.

Farmer   He is a man of good understanding, and very inquisitive of things of profit. And yet, to tell you truly, he is a good man to his Tenants .

Surveyor   Love him then, for such deserve love.[1]

Farmer   He is beloved of his Tenants indeed, for they will go, and ride, and fight for him.

Surveyor   It is the part of good Tenants, and an argument of a good Landlord. But fare you well, I cannot now stay; I have been long letted by your Landlord and you, and I have present business.

Farmer   Are you presently to undertake the survey of my Landlord's Lordships?

Surveyor   I am now going about it.

---

[1]   'Good Landlords deserve love'.

Farmer   I think it be in your choice where to begin: Let me therefore entreat you to begin with *Beauland*, a Manor of his here at hand, whereof I am both Tenant and Bailiff; and therefore I will and must attend you, and yield you my best aid, both by my travail, information, and records of the Manor.

Surveyor   Keep you the Lord's records?

*Bailiff*²   The key is in my keeping that leads to the Chest, but the key of the Chest is in my Lord's keeping; but I will send for it, that you may have the full view of the evidence.

Surveyor   So it behooveth. [For a Manor can never be aptly or truly surveyed without the view of the *Evidence*, which discover from whence the original interest is derived, how it is holden, by what *tenure*, the *Customs*, and other such necessary points, as not being known, the survey (though in some things may be perfect) cannot be absolute.

Bailiff   But I remember some of the *Evidences* of this Manor are in *French*, and some in *Latin*, so ancient as few can read them.

Surveyor   They are so much the more certain, by how much the more ancient. And it is a great defect in a Surveyor, if he cannot understand the French deeds, nor read, nor understand the most ancient Records.

Bailiff   Indeed it is necessary a *Surveyor* should be able to understand them, though I think few of them do.

Surveyor   No doubt many do, and all ought, but some Lords are too curious in suffering the *Surveyor* to peruse them, wherein they prejudice themselves; for if they will not trust a *Surveyor* to see the Evidence, let them never permit him to survey their lands.]³ Is this a large Manor?

Bailiff   It is spacious in circuit, and of great appearance of Tenants: full of divers commodities, both under and above the earth, as also of fishing, and fowling, and beareth not the name for nought, for the Manor is fair, and very commodious.

Surveyor   Be you then my guide: Is yonder it, with the fair house by the wood's side?

Bailiff   That is it, and a stately house it is indeed.

---

²   As discussed in the Introduction (p. xxvii), the Farmer's speech-prefix changes at this point, as his professional identity—as Bailiff—replaces his customary role as tenant.

³   'A Surveyor ought to see the Lord's evidence'.

Surveyor   It seems to be a large and lofty cage, if the bird be answerable.

Bailiff   What mean you by that?

Surveyor   I mean, that a *Titmouse* may harbor a *Peacock's* cage, and yet the cage maketh her not a *Peacock*, but will be a *Titmouse*, notwithstanding the greatness of the cage;[4] so it this lofty Pile be not equalized by the estate and revenues of the builder, it is as if *Paul's steeple* should serve *Pancras* Church for a belfry.

Bailiff   I think my Landlord sent you not, instead of surveying his Land, to deride his house.

Surveyor   The house is beautiful and fair; I deride it not—you do yourself wrong in attaching[5] me— neither discommend I the builder. For he that hath gold enough, let him build a house of gold with *Nero*, who made unto it a pond *Maris instar*[6] *and woods full of all kind of wild beasts.*[7] *Publius Clodius*, whom *Milo* slew, bought a house which cost him 147,000 *Sesterties*.[8] Let Princes have their Palaces, and great men their pleasant seats: for the poorest will please his fancy, as far as he may. But to tell thee by the way, (for this is but idle communication) that I have observed in nothing more sudden and serious repentance, than for building:[9] I could point out places and persons [too] with my finger, but what needs that? I wish their repentance could redeem the thing repented of, but it can no more do it than *Quintus Curtius*[10] could redeem himself out of the devouring gulf. We have in our days many and great buildings, a comely ornament it is to the face of the earth. And were it not that the smoke of vainglory did raise so many dusky clouds

---

[4]   'Great houses with small revenues, cannot suit well'.

[5]   *attaching*   accusing.

[6]   *Maris instar*   'a pond like the sea'; from Suetonius's description of Nero's gardens in *Vita Neronis* [Life of Nero], CXX (*Suetonius, II*, J.C. Rolfe [trans.], Loeb Classical Library [Cambridge, MA, 1914], p. 136).

[7]   'Martial lib.2'. The reference is to the second stanza of Martial's *Liber de Spectaculis* [Book of the Games] (*Epigrams*, Walter C.A. Ker [trans.], Loeb Classical Library [Cambridge, MA, 1961], pp. 2–5). Martial's satirical image of Nero's palace looming over the poor of Rome is a stark contrast to Suetonius's homage to the Emperor. Norden's citation of this passage demonstrates his use of classical allusions as a way of registering the effects of agrarian change. On this issue, see the Introduction (p. xxxix), as well as his citation of Ovid in Book 5, below (p. 104 and n. 112).

[8]   'Great houses fit for great men'. *Publius Clodius*, first-century BCE Roman tribune, was killed in a street brawl between his followers and those of his rival Titus Annius Milo.

[9]   'Building often repented'.

[10]   *Quintus Curtius*   the reference is to the legend of a fourth-century CE Roman named Marcus Curtius, who leapt into the gulf opened up by an earthquake in order to rescue the city. This figure is often confused with Quintus Curtius Rufus, the first-century CE Roman biographer of Alexander the Great, an error that Norden is repeating.

[of ambition],[11] to hinder the heat and light of the sun [of good hospitality from the poor], it were more tolerable and more profitable.

Bailiff   [The fire] is made most in the kitchen.

Surveyor   Then it besmoketh not the hall, as old worthy houses did, whose kitchens' smoke sent forth clouds of good meat and showers of drink for the poor[, as filled many hungry bellies].

Bailiff   Yea, Sir, that was a comfortable smoke. But *Tempora mutantur, et* [*nos mutamur*] *in illis*: no earthly thing continueth constant, but hath his change. Lo, Sir, now you are come to the house itself.

Surveyor   Truly, here is a pleasant ascent, neither too steep nor too flat, and of a good length.[12] And now we are come to the top of the hill: here is a goodly prospect and pleasant. And these springs I like well. For a house without lively water, is maimed; and the water is well conveyed, that it cannot annoy the foundation of the house, and yet serveth the most necessary offices very commodiously; and I see the conducts are made of earthen pipes,[13] which I like far better than them of Lead, both for sweetness and continuance under the ground. The trees are well placed about the walks, but that they are somewhat too near together, their branches confound one the other; they are but twenty foot, and I like better thirty. It standeth warm, and comfortable towards the Southeast, to which the best lights are made fitly to serve; but if the ground would have served, I like plain South the better point, for the comfort of the Sun at all times of the year. And nature hath planted this wood most commodiously in the North side of the house. And it is delicately advanced upon the edge of the hill: it is not possible to seat a house more delightfully, for winter and summer, in mine opinion; [especially], if upon view of the demesnes, and the rest of the parts, it be not found like unto a child born in *Cheshire*, with a head bigger than the [body.] Now to our business: You are Bailiff; take this Precept, and summon the Tenants to make their appearance, according to the purport of the same.[14]

---

[11]   'Many chimneys, little fires'. Demonstrating the stronger political commentary found in the 1618 edition, Norden substitutes 'of ambition' for the 1610 edition's 'in the air', and makes a more explicit reference to the decline in hospitality to the rural poor: see the Textual Notes.

[12]   'The best situation of a house'.

[13]   'Earthen Conducts'.

[14]   A number of early modern texts offered detailed instructions for calling a Court baron: see, for example, Anon., *The Maner of Kepynge a courte baron and a lete* (London, 1538); [Sir Anthony Fitzherbert], *The boke for a Iustice of Peace ... that teacheth to kepe a courte Baron, or a lete* (London, 1539); John Kitchin, *Le Covrt Leete, et Court baron* (London, 1580); Jonas Adames, *The Order of keeping a Court Leete, and Court baron* (London, 1593); John Wilkinson, *A treatise collected ovt of the statvtes of this Kingdom, ...*

The Form of the Precept.

These are to will, and in the name and behalf of [*A.B.*], the Lord of this Manor,[15] to require you to give notice and warning unto all and singular the Tenants of the same Manor, that they[, and every of them,] make their personal appearance on Monday next, being the tenth of this instant June, at the place where the Lord's Courts of this Manor are usually kept. And also to warn them, and every of them, to bring with them all such Deeds, Copies, Leases, and other evidences, whereby they, or any of them do hold, or claim to hold of the Lord of this Manor any Land, tenements, or Hereditaments. And that they then and there shew, or cause the same to be shewed unto the Lord's Surveyor, at the Court then, and there to be holden for that purpose; and to give their further attendance, as occasion of the service shall require. Whereof fail you not, &c. Dated the 3 of June, in the fourth year of the reign of our Sovereign Lord, James by the grace of God, King of great Britain, France, and Ireland, &c.

Per J.N. Supervis.

To the Bailiff of the Manor of Beauland, or
to his Deputy.

Commonly the Lords of Manors do direct their [own letters] of warrant unto the Tenants, unless the Surveyor be a known *Surveyor* by patent,[16] and performeth the service when and where he thinketh most fit for the Lord's use.

The order of a Court baron being performed (for a Surveyor hath not power to administer an oath *ex officio*, unless he be a Surveyor by patent, or by commission out of the *Chancery* or *Exchequer, Duchy Court, Court of Wards*, or such like) by a particular *Steward*, or by the *Surveyor*, who for the time may supply the *Steward's* office; and the charge of the *Court baron* ended, the *Surveyor* may proceed to his admonition and charge, to the effect following:

First, taking note of the names of every Tenant, both *Freeholder, Copyholder, Lessee*, and *Tenant at will*, in a paper, and a Jury for the Survey being impaneled,[17]

---

for the keeping of a Court Leet, Court baron, and Hundred Court (London, 1618). All of these guides went through several editions.

[15] 'Beauland Manerium'.

[16] *Surveyor by patent* a Surveyor commissioned by an authority outside the manor— including the Courts of Chancery, Exchequer, Duchy Court, and Court of Wards. These Surveyors would be able to call a Court of Survey into session without the assistance of a Bailiff or Steward (A.W. Richeson, *English Land Measuring to 1800: Instruments and Practices* [Cambridge, MA, 1966], p. 93).

[17] ['It is to be noted, that it is fit all the Tenants be impaneled for the Court of Survey, for that every of them is to answer for his own Lands'.]

(after they be sworn) the Surveyor may premonish[18] them to the effect following[, in words according to his own discretion]:

You that have been here presently sworn to perform your uttermost duties, in all the things that are and shall be given to you in charge, do, or at least you may conceive, that as the *Court baron* (the charge whereof you have already heard) is with you ordinarily twice a year, and (if the Lord will) every three weeks: this kind of Court, which I have now to admonish you in, tending to the survey of the Manor, hapneth not (perchance) in the time of man's age, though the Lord hath power, and (no doubt) occasion to keep it oftener. You must therefore shew yourselves so much the more diligent in this, [by how much] more seldom you are troubled therewith. And it behooveth you to call to mind, what by oath you have assumed to perform, namely, all that shall be given you in charge, whereof part hath been delivered unto you already: which being so ordinary amongst you, it must needs be more familiar than the things you have seldom heard of. And for that this business of *Survey* stretcheth a little further than the *Court baron*, let your due attention and examination, and faithful presentments witness your true affections to the persons and ends to which the purpose of our present meeting at this time tendeth. The *particulars* inquirable are many and of many kinds, but the persons and ends few. The first is God, in whose presence we all stand: *who loveth truth from the inward parts*,[19] that is, when the *action* and the *will* concur, and hateth dissimulation. The second is the King, whose we all are, under God, whose laws we are to follow, as well in this business, as in any other; for that it tendeth to the seeking and settling of *truth* (the mother of true *peace*) between you and your Lord, in giving both to you and him, what is equal and just. The third, is the *Lord of the Manor*, whose you are under *God* and the *King*, and therefore requireth at your hands at this time equal dealing, neither to discover for malice nor to conceal anything for favor to either party. The fourth, is yourselves, whom you can in no better sort befriend in this action than to keep your hearts and lips pure, in concealing or uttering; for there is as great a danger in concealing truth, as in uttering a falsehood. And there is no such burden, as the burden of a guilty conscience, which is laid on no man, but [by] himself. And lastly, the persons to be considered in this business, are your *posterities*, whom your true or false relations will either help or hurt. The ends whereunto it aimeth, are first, to explain unto the Lord of the Manor, what is his by the examination of your *Estates, Rents* and *Customs*, and to establish you in all things that are rightly yours; both which being truly found, and duly recorded, cannot but preserve amity between you and your Lord, which should be the principal end of all endeavors. And sith *God is the first and the last*,[20] and will be present in the beginning, in the middle, and in the end of all your consultations, and will be a witness for you or against you, even in your most secret counsels, set him before the eyes of your hearts: so shall you tremble

---

[18] *premonish*   advise.
[19] *who .. parts*   Psalm 51:6.
[20] *God ... last*   Revelation 22:13.

to conceal *truth*, or utter *falsity*, whether it be with, or against yourselves or dearest friends, yea, or the Lord of the Manor himself; whose purpose in this service is, that the manifest truth might be confirmed, the hidden revealed, and errors abandoned. And all this lieth in you, and at your hands it is required to search, and by searching and examination to find out; and found, to deliver and present the whole, and not a part of your sincere knowledges. For from your mouths must be taken and had, which must be recorded for the direction of your *posterities*, as a perpetual glass, wherein the estates of all the particulars within this Manor, may be at all times seen and confirmed: wherein you shall discharge your duty to *God*, who commands and commends *truth*; to the *King*, who by the *sword of his Justice*, maintains *truth*; to your *Landlord*, who desireth only to know, and have his own; to yourselves, who by this means shall *possess your own in peace*;[21] and to your posterities, who by this your [travail], diligence and true information, shall partake of your sincere and faithful service, being enrolled, and recorded under your names, to your perpetual commendation. Whereas if you delude me, and abuse the Lord of the Manor that hath sent me, I, by your sinister information, may commit error, and leave it to your posterities by record; yet shall I be free of the wrong, and you shall answer it. And if you should frame any defense against the service, and plead either ignorance or shew obstinacy, pretending thereby to stand dispensed of your oath, because you do it not, you deceive yourselves; for the service is so inseparably knit to your tenures, and your tenures to the Lord of the Manor, as deny or refuse to do the one, you forfeit the other; howsoever some may say, that they are *freeholders*, and they are *customary Tenants of inheritance*, which in their conceit implieth a kind of freedom, let them not deceive themselves; their estates are conditional, as, both by their *deeds* and *copies*, they may be easily resolved by these words: *Habendum sibi et haeredibus suis* (in the deed); *ad voluntatem Domini, secundum consuetudinem manerii* (in the copy); in both, *pro reditu et servitiis inde prius debit, et de jure consuet.* And because some of you do not (perchance) understand the meaning of these words, [of your own Evidences,] thus they signify, that you are to hold your tenements, to you and your heirs, &c., [being of inheritance], for such rent, and doing such services, as have been heretofore due, and of right accustomed. Is not this a condition? For if you pay not the rent, [or if you deny] the service, you are at the Lord's mercy to be compelled. I do not think therefore that any of you, of any discretion, will adventure the loss of his interest, for not performing a service so just and reasonable at his Lord's command, that tendeth also to his own benefit, and to no prejudice at all [to himself or his posterity].

The end therefore of all mine admonition is to move you (being a thing of common right) to shew yourselves like unto yourselves, true and faithful Tenants unto the Lord, concurring all in one mind, to do the Lord this service in love, and the Lord, no doubt, will recompense it with like favor, although there be no recompense due for that which duty bindeth to be done. By this means you shall confirm your own strengths, by gaining and retaining the Lord's kind countenance;

---

[21] *possess ... peace* Deuteronomy 25:19.

and he again shall be the more fortified, by your true affections towards him: for what a joyful thing is it, for Lord and Tenant to dwell together in unity? Now having thus prepared you to attention unto the matters of your charge, I will here read and explain unto you such *Articles* as shall be for your instruction, and leave them with you in writing for your better memory; for I know, and have often found, that a bare delivery of many words, and of divers things (as in the charges commonly given in *Courts Baron* and *Leet*) even to ears well prepared, may be little effectual, less to him that heareth and regardeth not, but least of all to him that will not regard or hear at all. Such hearers there are of divine things, but many more of human, of this kind; but were they masters of carnal pleasure and delight, they would be both heard and practiced: And therefore I the more move you to attend unto the things which I now am to deliver unto you.

The Substance of the Charge of a Court of Survey, Contained in the Articles Following.

First, as no doubt you all know, that *A.B.*, Knight, the reputed Lord of this Manor,[22] is the true and undoubted *owner* of the same, and of all the Lands, Meadows, Pastures, and other hereditaments within and belonging to the same;[23] and that you, and every of you do hold your Lands belonging unto this Manor of him: if not, who hath the interest and right of the same, to your knowledges?

2. You shall duly and diligently set down, or shew unto the Surveyor in his perambulation of the Manor, all the *circuit, butts, bounds*, and *limits* of the same,[24] and upon what, and whose Manors, Lordships, Lands, and Parishes it bordereth on all parts. And whether any confining Lord or his Tenants, do anywhere intrude or encroach upon this Manor, where is it, by whom, and how much is so encroached.

As for the bounding of the Manor, it is fittest to be delivered unto the Surveyor, when he treads the circuit, and that the best experienced Tenants accompany him for information, and some of the youth, that they may learn to know the bounds in time to come.[25]

3. Whether there be any other Manor or Manors lying within the limits or circuit,[26] or extending in part into this Manor: what are the names of the Manors,

---

[22]   'Beauland Manerium'.

[23]   'Owner of the Manor'.

[24]   'Bounds of the Manor'.

[25]   In walking a circuit around the manor, the surveyor retains earlier customary practices such as the rogationtide ceremony, in which young parishioners would trace the boundaries of the parish, but adapts them to a professional, market-driven context. For discussion of these customary rituals, see Garrett A. Sullivan, *The Drama of Landscape: Land, Property, and Social Relations on the Early Modern Stage* (Stanford, 1998), pp. 44–5.

[26]   'Manors intermixed'.

and who are owners of them, and how are they distinguished from this Manor. And whether this Manor do any way extend into, or lie within any other Manor.

It is often seen, that one Manor lieth within another, and intermixed one with another, in such sort, as the true Circuits, Butts, and Bounds, become confounded; necessary therefore it is, that their distinctions should be carefully observed and recorded, for often times one is devoured, or otherwise injured by the other, when Lords are remiss, and Tenants careless, to bring that to certainty, which is, or may become doubtful. And especially where many Manors lie intermixed, and one man holdeth Land copy or free of them all, there often times groweth confusion, unless each part be well butted and bounded; for though he can say how many Acres he holdeth of either Manor, yet he cannot distinguish the land, whereby some of the Lords cannot but be abused, or the Tenants wronged[, as it is commonly seen and found, where one Tenant holdeth confining Lands of divers Manors].

4. What Freeholders there are within,[27] or do belong unto, and hold their land of this Manor: what are their names, what Land hold they, what Rent pay they, by what tenure do they hold, and what services owe they to the Lord?

[*Freeholders* are of divers kinds, of divers tenures and services. And] the negligence of Lords in the due continuance of the substance of this Article, hath bred prejudice to many; for where Freeholders dwell out of the Manors whereof they hold and pay unto their Lords but a small acknowledgement, as a rose, a pepper corn, or lilyflower, or some such trifle, or are to do some service at times, whereof in many years hath been no use, as Knight's-service, Serjeanty,[28] or the like, to be done in the time of wars, they have not been looked for, neither have their suits been continued for long time, in so much as they and their tenures have grown out of memory, and their services out of use, and other Lords have entitled themselves to the Land, and the right Lord lost all possibilities of estate, wards, marriage, &c.[29] As common experience maketh more plain, by the daily questions and suits which rise, when profits apparent may grow by any of the former casualties.

And therefore it is most necessary to have always a true Suit-roll,[30] whereby the Steward should every Court call the Free suitors by name, and to express what rent he should pay, and what services he ought to do; and that at the death of every suitor, his heir with the land, rent, tenure, and services, would be inserted in his stead. The profit that will hereby grow unto the Lord and Tenants is manifest,

---

[27] 'Freeholders'.

[28] *Serjeanty* obligation to contribute to a military campaign, often in terms of monetary support rather than personal service; *grand serjeanty* (n. 154, p. 69), by contrast, entailed conscription.

[29] ['Littleton, *Tenures*, Title Socage, cap. 5'.] Sir Thomas Littleton (d. 1481) wrote *Les tenures de Monsieur Littleton*, known as *Littleton's tenures* in its English translations, the authoritative text on property law that was republished dozens of times throughout the early modern period. Norden cites Littleton's discussion of the replacement of feudal service with socage (rent payment), which appears as the fifth chapter of Book II (sections 117–32): see *Littleton's tenures in English*, ed. Eugene Wambaugh (Washington, 1903), pp. 58–65.

[30] *Suit-roll* document listing names of those to appear at the manorial court.

[namely, to the Lord, the possibility of escheat, Ward, Marriage, relief, &c., and to the Tenant, a certainty of whom and how he holdeth;] and this roll is to be made by the Surveyor, and to be indented,[31] the one for the Lord, the other for the Tenants, upon view of every Freeholder's evidence and land.

5. Whether any Freeholder within or belonging to this Manor, hath committed any felony or treason,[32] and hath been thereof convicted, the Lord not yet having the benefit of the forfeiture, or whether hath any such Tenant died without heir general or special. If so, who hath the present use and possession of the Land, and by what right: what land is it, where lieth it, how much in quantity, and of what value?

It is a great defect in the Survey of a Manor, which remaineth to posterities, being enrolled or engrossed for perpetual memory, when the Surveyor doth superficially pass over the observation of the lands of every Freeholder, their tenures, quantity of land, the place where it lieth, the rent and services. For upon sundry necessary occasions, the Lord is to seek in every of these, and some are worthy, because they love not to be at charge to find out and continue that which is not presently profitable.

6. Whether doth any bastard hold any land belonging to this Manor,[33] as heir unto any: what is his name, what land is it, and where lieth it, and what is it yearly worth?

A Bastard though he be known to be the son of that father that leaveth him the land, cannot inherit *jure haereditario*, but by conveyance. Neither, if he purchase land in his own name, can any inherit it after him of his supposed blood, unless he be married, and have children lawfully begotten to inherit, because it is *contra formam ecclesiae*,[34] as appeareth more at large: Merton, cap. 9.[35] For a Bastard is no man's or every man's son [or daughter. Yet if a man take a wife that is with child by another man, that was not her husband, after the child is born it shall be reputed *Mulier*,[36] and no bastard, though it be not the son of the husband].

7. What *demesne lands*[37] hath the Lord within or belonging to this Manor, what and how much woods, underwoods, Meadow, pasture, arable, moors, marshes, heaths, wastes, and sheep walks. And what is every kind worth yearly by acre, how many sheep may the Lord keep upon his walk winter and summer, and what is a sheep-gate worth by year, and what is every acre of wood worth to be sold?

---

31   *indented*   drawn up in duplicate.

32   'Felony, Treason'.

33   'Bastard'.

34   *contra formam ecclesiae* ['against the strictures of the Church'].

35   *Merton*   Norden refers to 'The Provisions of Merton', 20 Henry III, cap. 9 (c. 1235–6). See *Statutes of the Realm*, vol. 1, p. 4.

36   *Mulier*   for couples who had produced an illegitimate child but later married, their subsequent, legitimate children were classified as 'mulier puisne' (or 'since born'). See *Littleton's tenures*, section 399 and ff. (pp. 190–91).

37   'Demesnes'.

Although this Article, and sundry other hereafter mentioned, be in substance enacted by a Statute made Anno. 3 Edward I, called *extenta Manerii*,[38] to be inquired of by the Tenants, yet it is the part and office of a Surveyor, to see, examine, and judge by his own experience and knowledge, every particular, comparing the Jury's presentment with his own opinion; so shall he more truly attain to the true understand of the things he seeketh, and the more, if he discreetly feel the minds of foreign inhabitants that are ignorant of the cause of his inquisition.

8. What *demesne lands* hath the Lord lying in the *common fields* of the Manor,[39] how much in every field, and every furlong, and what is an acre of ordinary field arable land worth by the year? The like you are to present touching demesne meadow, lying in any common meadow within the Manor.

9. Also you are to present the names of all your common fields, and how many furlongs are in every field and their names, and the common meadows and their names.[40] And what beasts and sheep, every Tenant ought to keep upon the same, when the corn and hay is off, and what a beast-gate and sheep-gate is worth by year; also, at what time your fields and common meadows are laid open, and how are they, or ought to be used. And whether is it lawful for the Tenants, to enclose any part of their common fields or meadows, without the license of the Lord and consent of the Tenants.

This article is duly to be considered, first in setting down in certainty, what every man is to keep upon the fields and common meadows; because injury is daily done by some of greatest ability to the meaner sort, in oppressing the fields with a greater number of Cattle than according to a true proportion will fall unto their share, which is very extortion, and a punishment is to be inflicted upon the offenders.

Also enclosers of common fields, or meadows in part, by such as are most powerful and mighty, without the Lord's license and the Tenants' assents, is more than may be permitted; the reason is, that the rest of the Tenants have as much right to every herb and grass within the same, when the corn is off, as he hath that encloseth the same.

Bailiff But, Sir, if they lay it open at Lammas,[41] or at such time as custom requireth, I think he doth neither Lord nor Tenants wrong.

Surveyor Yes; for first, he depriveth them both of the feed, of as much as his hedges, ditches, and enclosures take; besides, whether is it as convenient for pass and repass of Cattle at one little gap or two, as when there is no estoppel[42] at all?

---

[38] *extenta Manerii* the statute, from 1276, which first established the procedures for conducting manorial surveys; see also n. 66, p. 30.

[39] 'Demesnes in common Fields'.

[40] 'Common Fields, and common Meadows'.

[41] *Lammas* The 1 of August, which celebrated the first wheat harvest of the year.

[42] *estoppel* obstruction to the flow of water.

Bailiff   You like not enclosures then.

Surveyor   I do, and I think it the most beneficial course that Tenants can take, to increase their abilities; for one acre enclosed is worth one and a half in Common, if the ground be fitting thereto. [But that Lords] should not depopulate by usurping enclosures: a thing hateful to God and offensive to men. [But if the wastes and unprofitable commons in England were enclosed and proportionately allotted, it would feed more people by good manurance than any one shire in England.]

10. What *Commons* are there within the Lordship,[43] which do properly belong to the Lord and Tenants of this Manor, and how are the Tenants stinted,[44] whether by the yard land, plough land, oxgang,[45] Acres, or rent: how many may every Tenant keep, after either proportion or rate?

In this the like consideration is to be had as of the former; but that this kind of pasture is called in the statute of *extenta Manerii, 3 Edward I., Pastura forinseca,*[46] foreign herbage or pasture, because no part of it is proper in any sort to any peculiar Tenant, no not to the Lord himself, as are the common fields and common meadows. This kind of Common, or *pastura forinseca*, is in three sorts: the one is where a Manor or Township having and holding their land in severalty, have by consent limited a certain parcel of ground, to lie common among them, and from the beginning have stinted every man according to a proportion between them agreed, and that is commonly by the acre, which the pasture containeth.

Another manner of such kind of Common pasture is where certain waste grounds, one, two, or more lie within the Manor or Township, and the *Herd* of the whole Town is guided and kept by one appointed by the Tenants, and at their general charge, to follow their Cattle; in which kind of pasture, there is also a limitation or stint both of the number and kinds of Cattle, and this most in the north parts.

A third kind of this pasture, or common feeding, is in the Lord's own woods that lie common to the Tenants, as also common Moors or heaths that were never arable.

In all the former commons of pasture, there should be a certain stint and allotment, both to the Lord and his Tenants; but in this latter, it seemeth that the Lord should not be limited, because all these latter commons are supposed his own, and the Tenants have no certain parcel thereof laid to their holdings, but only bit of mouth with their Cattle. But the Tenants ought to be stinted in all sorts of common, lest, as I said before, the rich devour the poor: for the one can provide sheep and other Cattle for the summer, and have enclosed pasture for the winter, or can sell again when the foreign pasture is gone; but the poor cannot do so.

---

[43]   'Commons'.

[44]   *Stinted*   setting of boundaries of land.

[45]   A *yard land* was 30 Acres in size, a *plough land* 120 Acres, and an *oxgang* 15 Acres; the terms derived from the amount of land that could be ploughed in one year: see n. 98, p. 58.

[46]   *Pastura forinseca*   foreign pasture, commons.

[*Commons* again may be distinguished into *Commons in gross, Common appendant, Common appurtenant*, and *Common by way of neighborhood. Common in gross* is where a man by deed granteth unto another common of pasture.

Common appendant is where a man is seized of land, to the which he hath common for such beasts as serve for composting of his land, wherein Geese, Goats, and Hogs are exempted; and this kind of common is by prescription as an appendix or addition only to arable land, and not to any other.

Common appurtenant is in the same nature, but with greater liberty, because it is for all kind of cattle, hogs, goats, &c. as for other kinds. And this common may be made at this day, and may be severed from the land to which it is appurtenant, and so cannot common appendant be.[47]

Common by neighborhood is where the Tenants of two Lords, or more, adjoining, do enter common either upon other with all commonable cattle. But one may not put his cattle upon other's commons; if they do, an action of trespass lies.]

11. Whether hath any man to your knowledges encroached any part of *the Lord's waste*[48] *by enclosure, or adding any part thereof to his own land; present who hath so done, where, how much, and how long it hath continued.*

This kind of encroachment is not rare, especially where great wastes and mountainous grounds are, where the Lord nor his officers walk not often, and where Tenants, for favor or affection, will wink at evil doers; or, for their own private lucre, commit the same error themselves, with hedges, ditches, pales,[49] walls, sheds, &c.

12. *Whether hath the Lord any Park*, or *demesne wood*,[50] which by stocking may turn to the Lord's better benefit, by *pasture, arable*, or *meadow*; and what is an Acre worth, one with another the stocking; and how many Acres is the Wood; and what will an Acre of the Wood be worth; and what will an Acre of Land be worth by the year to be let, when the ground is stocked and cleared.

Although it be the part of the Jury to yield their opinions in this case, yet it behooveth the Surveyor to have so much judgment in every of these points, as he may be able to satisfy himself and his Lord by sufficient reasons, lest he be deceived and the Lord abused, either through ignorance or partiality. And above all it behooveth the Surveyor to look into the nature of the soil of the Wood; for there are some Wood-grounds that are good for no other use, as a dry or cold gravelly ground, whose virtue and disposition may be easily observed by the herbage.

---

[47] *Common appendant*   allowed a tenant to keep animals used for plowing on wastes or commons; *common appurtenant* extended this right to all livestock (E.P. Thompson, 'Custom, Law and Common Right', *Customs in Common: Studies in Traditional Popular Culture* [New York, 1993], pp. 130–31).

[48] 'Encroaching the Lord's waste'.

[49] *pales*   fences.

[50] 'Park, demesne woods'.

13. Also you must present the names of all *customary Tenants*, within or belonging unto the Manor; what Mesuages,[51] Tenements, or Lands they hold, and what every Mesuage or Tenement is called; what Rent it payeth; and what profit ariseth to the Lord, by the death of any such customary Tenant, or by the death of any Freeholder, by Fine, Heriot, or Relief,[52] by the custom of the Manor.

Commonly these customary Tenants,[53] upon death and alienation do pay a fine, which in some places is certain, and in some, even in the most, they are at the Lord's will; and in most places they are also heriotable.

Bailiff   In this Manor there be some customary Tenants heriotable, and some not: How comes that? Can there be two customs in one Manor?

Surveyor   There may be so. And the reason may grow by the escheating of a Manor, that had in this point a contrary custom to the Manor to which it was escheated and annexed; and so the customs of either may hold under one Court.

Bailiff   Your reason is good; and I take it, it may also be, that these that pay no heriots are tenements of a newer erection, and so upon their first grants, the heriots were omitted.

Surveyor   That is not so likely; for that if any such new erections were, they were granted in such form as other tenements, with these words—*Habendum, &c. ad voluntatem domini secundum consuetudinem Manerii*[54]—which words do imply all duties and services, which the most ancient tenements are bound unto.

There is also a Copyhold estate, called *ancient demesne*, and the Tenants, *Sokemans*,[55] whereof some are of frank-tenement, and some of base tenure. Tenants of Base tenure are they that hold by verge, at the will of the Lord, and the frank tenement thereof is in the Lord.[56]

It is to be noted, that Copyhold lands are very ancient, before the Conquest, in the Saxons' time, who called this kind of land, *Folkland*, and their Charter lands were called *Bookland*.[57]

---

[51]   *Mesuages*   dwelling-houses.

[52]   *Relief*   for Norden's discussion of these terms, see Book 2 (pp. 52 and ff.).

[53]   'Customary Tenants'.

[54]   *Habendum ... Manerii* ['Transfer of right to property in exchange for annual payments according to the custom of the manor'].

[55]   'Briton fo. 165'. Norden cites the compilation of English law (ca. 1290) attributed to John le Breton and first published as *Britton cum priuilegio regali* (London, 1533). *Sokemans* were Tenants holding their lands by socage, or payment, rather than feudal service.

[56]   *frank tenure* (or free tenure) was analogous to freehold, while *base tenure*, like copyhold, was secured through Court-roll and entailed duties of service to the Lord of the Manor.

[57]   Under Saxon law, *bookland* referred to property held by written grant or charter, while *folkland* consisted of land inherited by common law: on this issue, see Theodore F.T.

14. How doth the customary land of this Manor, by your custom, descend after the death of an Ancestor to the younger or elder son?[58] And whether will the custom of the Manor allow an entail[59] by copy; and whether doth it bear widow's estate, or whether may she have it during [her] life, though she marry; and whether may a man hold by the [courtesy,[60] or as long as he holds himself widower].

Sundry differences there are in sundry Manors, touching the substance of this Article.

The custom of some Manors is, that the youngest son shall inherit, as in *Borough-English*,[61] if he have not a son his youngest brother, as at *Edmonton* in Middlesex. [In *Ottery Saint Mary* in Devon, the Land which is customary of inheritance, descends to the youngest Son or youngest Daughter.

In the same Manor, a man that holds that kind of Land in right of his Wife, and she die, the Husband living, he shall enjoy the Land as long as he lives unmarried, though he have no issue by her. The like custom is there in a tenure called *Five acre land*, and descends likewise to the youngest Son or Daughter.

In the same Manor, there is a tenure called *old Burton Land*, which descendeth to the eldest Son or Daughter, and the wife of such a tenement shall hold, during her life, though she marry. And the husband of a wife inheritrix of that land, shall hold after the death of his wife, as long as he is unmarried.]

The custom of some Manors is, that all the sons and all the daughters shall inherit alike,[62] as in [*Gavelkind*].[63]

The custom of some Manors is, that if the Tenants die seized of five Acres or under, then the youngest son shall inherit; but if above, then all the sons shall [inherit.]

The custom of some Manors is, that neither the wife shall have dowry, neither the husband hold by Courtesy. And the custom of some other Manor is, that she

---

Plucknett, 'Revisions in Economic History: III. Bookland and Folkland', *The Economic History Review* 6 (1935): 64–72.

[58]   'Descent of Customary Land'.

[59]   *entail*   Also known as 'Fee tail', a stipulation that land could not be sold or transferred but must pass on to the owner's heirs.

[60]   *courtesy*   a tenure allowing a husband to lay claim to his wife's inherited property after her death.

[61]   *Borough-English* or ultimogeniture, a system of inheritance that conferred property to the youngest son or daughter; the rare instances of this practice have been found among medieval copyhold tenants. See *Littleton's tenures*, sections 211, 603, and 735 (pp. 35, 272, 331). *Five acre land* and *old Burton Land* refer to varieties of ultimogeniture: the former, for instance, enabled a younger unmarried daughter to inherit property from her father provided that she partitioned five of every 20 Acres to her married sisters (*Littleton's tenures*, section 268, pp. 123–4.).

[62]   'Heir'.

[63]   *Gavelkind*   a form of tenure allowing a tenant's land to be equally divided among his sons; associated most especially with the county of Kent.

shall have the third part of the rent, as at Bushey in Middlesex, and no part of the land in dowry.[64]

In some Manors, the wife being a virgin at the time of her marriage, shall have all the Copyhold land for her frank bank,[65] whereof her husband died seized. And many such. At Kilmersdon in Somersetshire, the wife hath widow's estate, and if she marry she loseth the land; but if she be found incontinent, and come into the next Court riding astride upon a Ram,[66] and in open Court do say unto the Lord, if he be present, or to his Steward, these, or words to this effect:

> For mine arse's fault I take this pain,
> therefore my Lord let me have my land again.

She is by the custom to be restored unto it without further Fine, doing this penance: [the like hath been in Sunning in Berkshire, and in many other Manors. In the Manor of Cheltenham in Gloucestershire, there is a custom, that a man cannot marry his daughter to any man, neither can a widow marry without the Lord's license; and if a man by his wife have never so many children, and die, his widow may marry another man, and he shall carry away all the land after the death of his wife, from all the former children; and he may marry again be he 100 years old, with a girl of six or seven years, and she shall carry away the land from all the heirs.

Bailiff These are foolish and unreasonable customs.]

[*Surveyor*] 15. Whether are there any *Customary tenements* that are *heriotable*, dismembered and divided into parcels,[67] to the weakening of the tenement; and who be they that have these heriotable parcels; and what quantity hath every of them?

Although there be no immediate profit can accrue unto the Lord, by the presentment of the substance of this Article, yet it behooveth the Lord to know, who be the Tenants to any part of the land belonging to an heriotable tenement, because every part continueth heriotable, and draweth unto the Lord the best beast of the tenement of such land deceasing, though the land, in regard whereof he payeth it, be but an acre, and he have

---

[64] *dowry* Norden relegates consideration of the property and inheritance rights of women solely to one heading, a stark contrast to the extended discussions found in his legal sources such as Littleton's *Tenures*. He seems to ignore these rights because he associates them with other customary practices that impede the workings of the market. Book 6's dialogue with the Purchaser of Land, for instance, advocates shorter term leases as a way of inducing thriftiness in male heirs, and does not even refer to the property rights of wives, widows, and daughters.

[65] *frank bank* or 'free bench', copyhold lands that revert to a widow at the death of her husband, provided that she was a virgin at the time of marriage.

[66] *Ram* a reference to the use of public shaming rituals for punishing transgressions of sexual and domestic norms. For discussion, see especially David Underdown, *Revel, Riot, and Rebellion: Popular Politics and Culture in England 1603–1660* (Oxford, 1985).

[67] 'Heriotable tenements dismembered'.

elsewhere free or copy, that maintaineth horse or other cattle of great value, the Lord may seize the best for his heriot[, due for that acre].

16. Whether are not the *Fines for admittances*[68] of a new customary Tenant, being heir, or coming in by purchase, or upon Surrender, at the will of the Lord, or are the fines always certain?

This is an Article, whereat [many Tenants seem] to stagger, being the nature of all men to favor themselves, and their posterities, and to work so, as they may (if it be possible) make the Fines certain, by looking back into time's past, wherein they have found by old Records, and by report of Tenants before, that the Fines have been certain; and so they may be in some places, though in few at this day. And it may be, former times did afford such favor, until land became of more value; but of late years, that course hath been broken, and Fines become arbitrable. Wherein I wish, that Lords and their ministers would use a mean in exacting.

17. How, and by what means, may a *customary Tenant forfeit his Copyhold tenement*?[69] Whether for felling of timber trees, plowing up ley[70] grounds, or meadows never tilled before, or for suffering his houses to decay, or for pulling down any houses, or for committing any other willful waste, or devising his customary tenement or lands, for longer term than the custom of the Manor will bear; or for committing any other act, contrary to the custom of the Manor. And whether hath any Tenant of the Manor offended in any of the former things, who is it, and wherein is any such offence committed.

Divers Acts there be, whereby a Tenant in one Manor may forfeit his Copyhold tenement, which act is no forfeiture in another Manor. For customs are very different in divers Manors; for in some Manors a man may cut down wood and timber trees upon his Copyhold land, and fell them at his pleasure, which in some Manors is a forfeiture.

Some Manors do allow the Customary Tenants of the same, to let their land for three years, some for more, without the Lord's license; and in some Manors to let the same above a year is a forfeiture[; wherein is admitted an intolerable error in many places, namely, a Tenant having let his land for a year, lets it a second, a third, &c., which is a mere deceit; for he ought to let it one year, and unless he have license, he is to take it into his hands one whole year before he let it again.]

In some Manors a man may let fall all his customary houses, which in some other Manors is a forfeiture.

In some Manors a man may not plow up or sow his Copyhold Meadow, or ley ground, that hath not been used to be tilled; in some Manors contrary.

So that these kinds of forfeitures are according to the custom of every Manor, which yet Tenants will endeavor to wrest.

---

[68] 'Fines'.

[69] 'Forfeiture of Copyhold'.

[70] *ley*   fallow, unplowed.

18. What are the customs of the Manor in general,[71] both in the behalf of the Lord, to perform or suffer to the benefit of his Tenants, and of the Tenants to perform to the service of the Lord.

In the beginning of every Manor, there was a mutual respect of assistance between the Lord—who gave parcels of land, whether in fee, or to hold at will, or upon other conditions—and the Tenants of every nature, for aiding, strengthening, and defending each other; the continuance of which first proposed course, hath bred that which is now called custom, by the favor of time. And thereby that which at the beginning came *ex gratia Domini*, is now maintained by strong hand against the Lord, and what came of a voluntary consent of service of the Tenant to the Lord, the Lord may exact of his Tenants by law; and either, in right of the custom due to other, constraineth each other to do that which in the beginning was of either part voluntary.

Customs are of divers kinds, and diversely to be performed. Some in the course of inheriting the land, some in the way of women's dowries, some in the estates of land, some in matters of forfeitures, some in works, some in rents, some in fines, some of the Lord's benevolence in allowing his Tenants meat, drink, money, &c. in time of their works, as these customs in several Manors, severally are allowed.

Manors themselves may have strange commencements and continuance, as the honor of *Rayleigh* in Essex, which hath a Custom Court kept yearly the [Wednesday] next after Saint Michael's day: the Court is kept in the night, and without light, but as the Sky gives, at a little hill without the Town, called the King's hill, where the Steward writes only with coals, and not with ink. And many men, and Manors of great worth hold of the same, and do suit unto this strange Court, where the Steward calls them with as low a voice as possibly he may; giving no notice when he goes to the hill to keep the same Court, and he that attends not is deeply amerced,[72] if the Steward will.

[The title and entry of the Court is as followeth, viz.

Rayleigh Honor.
Curia de *Domino rege*
Dicta, *Sine lege*,
tenta est ibidem,
Per ejusdem consuetudinem
Ante ortum solis
Luceat nisi *Polus*
Senescallus solus,
Scribit nisi colis.
Clamat clam pro *Rege*,
In Curia sine lege.
Et qui non cito venerit
Citius poenitebit,
Si venerit cum lumine
Errat in regimine.

---

[71]   'Customs'.

[72]   *amerced*   fined, payment to manorial court.

Et dum sunt sine lumine
Capti sunt in Crimine,
Curia sine Cura
Jurata de injuria.
>   tenta est die Mercurii,
>   Prox post (festum *St Michaelis*).][73]

But for particular Manors, as the customs of them are many and divers, so it behooveth every Tenant to know whereunto he is bound by custom; if there be no ancient Custom-roll to lead them,[74] it behooveth the Surveyor to renew the same, wherein he is to set down every Tenant's name, his tenements, Lands, Meadows, Pastures, &c., the rent and service due for every of them, and whether works be turned into Rent, and to indent the same, that the Lord may have the one part and the Tenants another. The neglect whereof hath bred many inconveniences, both to Lords and Tenants, by quarrels and suits.

19. Whether is there within this Manor any *Villain or Neife*,[75] namely, any *Bond-man or Bond-woman*: if there be, what are their names, what land do they hold, and what is the same yearly worth[, and what goods possess they].

Although this kind of tenure be in manner worn out of use, yet some there are (no doubt), though concealed in some Manors, never enfranchised or manumised.[76]

20. Whether hath any Tenant or other person within this Manor *stocked up any hedge-row, plowed up any Baulk,*[77] *or land share, removed any Mere-stone,*[78] *land mark,*[79] or other bound between the Lord's demesne and the Tenant's Freehold, or customary land of inheritance, or between his Freehold and customary land, or between this, and another Manor or Lordship: where is any such offence committed, by whom, and where ought the same bound so removed, altered, taken away, or displaced, to stand. [*Solomon* counseleth not to remove the ancient bounds which our fathers have made, *Proverbs 22:28*.]

---

[73] *Rayleigh Honor*   The Honor of Rayleigh, also known as 'The Lawless Court', was an annual custom of ritualistic social inversion during which the manorial court of Rayleigh (near Rochford, Essex) would be held at an 'unlawful' time, before dawn on the Wednesday following Michaelmas. It would feature some of the oddities mentioned by Norden: the court would be conducted in the dark, with the steward and litigants whispering to one another, and proceedings would be recorded in coal instead of ink. The preservation of this tradition, which lasted from the fifteenth until the nineteenth centuries, garnered the interest of other early modern antiquarians along with Norden (H.W. King, 'The Lawless Court of the Honour of Rayleigh', *Essex Archaeological Society* 4 [1891]: 179–95).

[74] 'Custom-roll'.

[75] 'Villains and [Neifes]'.

[76] Norden discusses villein tenure in Book 2: see n. 168 and pp. 72–4.

[77] *Baulk*   ridge, often a burial ground.

[78] *Mere-stone*   boundary marker.

[79] 'Removing of Meres or bounds'.

This is a necessary Article to be duly considered, because that by this means of removing, or taking away *Mere-stones* and *land marks*, the Lord often times incurreth great prejudice; for that when a Lessee of the Lord's demesnes being either a Freeholder, or a customary Tenant of inheritance, hath land of his own adjoining unto the demesnes, or intermixed, and he take away the marks of division, leaveth the matter doubtful which is the Lord's, especially where a long lease or patent is, whereby the Tenant hath time to make alteration; and it is no new or strange thing, to attach[80] some by name and place, that are culpable, and have yielded to reformation, being found out before their intents were fully ripe. And, above all, such are most worthy to be punished, for altering any such known marks, under whatsoever pretence of ease or necessity, which is the common cloak of the mischief, used most in the King's lands, where long patents are granted.

21. What customary Cottages[81] are there within this Lordship, *tofts, crofts,* or *cartilages:*[82] what are the Tenants' names, what Rent pay they, and what services do they.

It is to be understood, *Cotagium,* signifieth as much as *casum,* a little house, or a place of abode only, or a little dwelling, whereunto a little ground belongeth, but an Orchard, garden, or some small toft, croft, or curtilage; but Cottages of themselves are not ancient, as I take it; [a toft is a little piece of land, upon which sometimes was situate a dwelling house, and, in Lincolnshire, a Cottage is called a toft; a croft is a little pitle, pingle,[83] or small plot, near a dwelling house].

22. Whether are there within this Manor, any *new tenements or Cottages, Barns, Walls, Sheds, Hovels, Hedges, Ditches,* or such like erected, set up, or made; or any *Water-courses,* or *Ponds,* digged upon any part of the Lord's waste, without the Lord's license: where is it, and by whom was it done, and by whose license, and upon what consideration?

The overmuch liberty of too many new erections, breedeth sundry inconveniences, not only to a Manor, and the Lord, and Tenants thereof, but to a whole Commonwealth, and therefore not to be permitted without good consideration, although it is most convenient that the poor should have shelter and places to shroud them in, if they be found honest, virtuous, painful, and men of ability to gain their own and their family's relief.

But it is observed in some parts where I have travelled, where great and spacious wastes, Mountains, Woods, Forests, and Heaths are, that many such Cottages are set up,[84] the people given to little or no kind of labor, living very hardly with

---

[80]   *attach*   arrest.

[81]   'Cottages'.

[82]   *croft* a small enclosed field; *toft* a homestead and adjoining land; *curtilage* the enclosed ground and buildings surrounding land.

[83]   *pitle* and *pingle*   terms for a small enclosed plot of land.

[84]   ['New Cottages ought to have four Acres of Land'.] A 1589 Statute (31 Elizabeth, c.7) had prohibited the construction of unlicensed buildings on commons as well as cottages possessing less than four Acres of adjoining land (*Statutes of the Realm,* vol. 4, part 2,

Oatenbread, sour whey, and Goat's milk, dwelling far from any Church or Chapel, and are as ignorant of God, or of any civil course of life, as the very Savages amongst the Infidels, in a manner which is lamentable, and fit to be reformed by the Lord of the Manor.[85]

23. What Tenants are there within this Manor, that do hold any lands or tenements by *Indenture of lease*:[86] what are their names, what land hold they, for what rent, under what conditions and covenants, for what term of years or lives?

This Article is most especially to be observed, touching the covenants by view of the Tenants ' leases, but the Jury is to find the names, and to present them with the land and rent as far as they can learn.

24. Whether hath or doth the Lord employ any land to *justment*,[87] as in taking in cattle to pasture and herbage: who hath the disposing of the same, what quantity of land is so disposed, and how many cattle will it pasture; and what is a Cow, Ox, Horse, or Sheep-gate worth by the year, or by the week, within this Manor?

Much Land is thus used in Yorkshire, and other places Northward, more beneficially than to stock it.

25. Whether hath the Lord of this Manor any customary *Water-mill, Wind-mill, Horse-mill, Grist-mill, Malt-mill, Walk-mill, or Fulling-mill*?[88] Whether is there within this Manor any other Mill, *Iron-mill, Furnace*, or *Hammer, Paper-mill, Sawing-mill, Sheer-mill*, or any other kind of Mill: what is it worth by year, and in whose occupation is it?[89]

Where sufficient rivers, brooks, stagnes,[90] ponds, or Water-courses are, there are commonly some kinds of Mills, or other profitable devices, that human wit and invention hath set up for necessary uses, for the benefit of man, and for the Lord's profit of the Manor, where such devices are erected. And yet all kinds of devices are not convenient in all places: as where no Lead, Tin or Coal is, there is no need of the use of water, to move a wheel, to blow the fire for the melting and trying thereof; yet there may be like use for Iron Ore, and where neither of them is, there may be use of Walk-mills, or Fulling-mills; and where those are not, yet there may be use of Corn-mills, and such like. And in some places the

---

pp. 804–5). This law remained on the statute books until the late eighteenth century (Steve Hindle, *On the Parish? The Micro-Politics of Poor Relief in Rural England, c. 1550–1750* [Oxford, 2004], pp. 302–3).

[85]   For a discussion of the social position of early modern cottagers, see Mark Netzloff, *England's Internal Colonies: Class, Capital, and the Literature of Early Modern English Colonialism* (New York, 2003), pp. 204–10.

[86]   'Indentures'.

[87]   'Justments'. Also known as *gistment* or *agistment*, the leasing of land for grazing animals.

[88]   'Custom Mill'. *Grist-mill*   mill for grinding corn; *Walk-mill*   a horse-driven mill; *Fulling-mill*   a mill producing cloth.

[89]   For a related discussion, see Joan Thirsk, 'Industries in the Countryside', in *The Rural Economy of England: Collected Essays* (London, 1984), pp. 217–33.

[90]   *stagnes*   fish-ponds.

force of Water-courses is used to raise water out of one place into another, where the natural current denyeth the coming and mounting thereof, with infinite other devices, according to the situation of the place and necessity of the thing required. Which, though they be not all Mills to grind corn, yet may they bring profit to the Lord, which is the thing the Surveyor should covet, not only to observe what is already, but must have also some judgment to erect some, if the water-course will conveniently afford the same to increase the Lord's revenues.

To the Corn-mill, which are custom Mills, doth belong a kind of duty from the Tenants, that is, that they are bound to grind their corn at the Lord's Mill: and that kind of custom is called *Socome*.[91]

Bailiff   Must a customary Tenant of a Manor, where such a Mill is, be forced to grind all the corn he spendeth in his house at the Lord's Mill?

Surveyor   Of necessity, if it grow upon the Manor, or else the Lord may amerce him for his default.

Bailiff   What if he be forced to buy it in the Market?

Surveyor   Surely then it is a question, whether he be bound to grind it there or not. But I take it, he is at liberty to grind it where he will, even where he finds himself best served. For there is *bond-Socome*, that is, where the Tenant is bound by custom, and *love-Socome*, where he grindeth of free-will.

Bailiff   We that are Tenants would be glad, if you could tell us, what toll our Milner[92] may take; for we are much abused in it, as we think, and because we be bound by custom, we cannot conveniently leave the Mill, and yet we find no remedy of the Milner's abuses.

Surveyor   As touching *Toll* (which word cometh of the verb *tollo*, to take away, as it seemeth), there are so many differences, by grants made by Lords of Manors, that the certainty in general can hardly be declared. Some Millers take a twentieth, some four and twentieth part; Tenants at will should pay a sixteenth part, and a bond Tenant a twelfth part, and some are toll-free. But howsoever the toll be, fear not, the Milner will be no loser; and for his abuses, you have your remedy in the Lord's Court, or at the common law.

26. Whether hath the Lord of the Manor any *peculiar fishing*[93] within any river, brook, mere, stagne, pond, or other water: where and how far doth it extend, and what it is yearly worth, and who be Farmers thereunto, and what common fishings are therein, and how is the same used?

---

91   'Socome'.
92   *Milner*   Miller.
93   'Fishing'.

As this Article is little needful to be propounded in Manors where no rivers of sufficient waters are for fishing, so it is very necessary to be examined, where such waters are. For it is daily observed, that many abuses are committed against the Lord himself, by such as usurp his peculiar fishing, and against the Commonwealth, in destroying fish, as appeareth by the punishment ordained against offenders therein, *25 Henry VIII, cap. 7 and 31 Henry VIII, cap. 2.*[94] Therefore it behooveth the Surveyor to be more careful in seeking the means how to raise a profit unto the Lord by his fishing, than to find the present abuses which are inquirable and punishable at every Leet; although, if any apparent offenders be found, he is to advertise the Lord for reformation, but not enroll the same in his book of Survey. For nothing is therein to be inserted, but matter of perpetuity, in recommending the present state of the Manor unto posterities, and for the Lord's immediate use; the Court-rolls of the Manor do shew the abuses and punishments in those kinds. And therefore besides the ordinary fishing in small land rivers, brooks and ponds, there must be also remembered what profit may arise by fishing in the Sea, if the Manor be near it, or any creek thereof, in Oysters, Mussels, Cockles, Crabs, Crevishes,[95] and such like.

27. Whether hath the Lord of the Manor any *Fowling* within this Manor,[96] by means of any moors, marshes, waters, brooks, reeds, or such like: as of *Duck, Mallard, Widgeon,*[97] *Teal, Wildgeese, Bustard, Plovers, Bittern, Swans*, or such like fowl; or any woods wherein do breed any *Heronsews, Shovellers, Stork*, or such like; or any *Pebble, Beach*, or *Sea-bank, wherein breed Sea-pies, Olives, Peewits*, or such:[98] who taketh the profit of them, and what are they, or may they be worth by the year, unto the Lord?

These kinds of commodities are not in every Manor; and therefore as in all other things it behooveth the Surveyor to consider of these particulars, and give no more unto the Jury to be enquired of, than he either knoweth to be enquirable, or likely by examination to be found in the Manor he intendeth to Survey, yet not to omit any whereby the Lord's revenues may be increased[, nor to trouble the Jury with needless articles].

28. Whether hath not the Lord of this Manor (time out of mind) had and received all *waifs, estrays,*[99] *felon's goods, treasure found*, within the Manor, and such like profits, and whether hath he been answered of them from time to time

---

[94] The former statute, 25 Henry VIII, cap. 7 (1533), prohibited the killing of young salmon and eels, while the latter, 31 Henry VIII, cap. 2 (1539), banned unlicensed fishing in private ponds (Stuart A. Moore and Hubert Stuart Moore, *The History and Law of Fisheries* [London, 1903], pp. 176–7).

[95] *Crevishes* freshwater crayfish

[96] 'Fowling'.

[97] *Widgeon* wild duck.

[98] *Sea-pie* (like *olive*) a name given to the oystercatcher, a bird found in marsh lands and coastal regions; *Peewit* lapwing.

[99] 'Waifs. Estrays'. Terms referring to stray livestock on commons.

truly, or not, and who is the officer that doth oversee, and take notice of the same to the Lord's use[, and whether they be totally and fully answered].

Although these kinds of profits may redound unto the Lord by prescription, yet most commonly they are confirmed by charter, and therefore the Lord's evidences, together with the use, must be examined[, as also how and by whom these casualties are prized, wherein Lords are often abused].

29. Whether are there within this Manor,[100] any *Tin-mines, Lead-mines, Copper-mines, Coal-mines, Quarries of stone, of Marble, Free-stones, Mill-stones, Lime-stones, Grinding-stones, Marl, or chalk-pits, slimy or moorish earth*, fit for soiling of land, or any *Potter's clay, clay for Brick or Tile*, or any *Fuller's earth*,[101] or any *sand*, or *gravel-pits*, or such kind of commodities, and what is every such kind worth to the Lord, or may be made worth by year.

These are casualties, and seldom or never all happen in any Manor together; and few Manors but have some or one of them, which may be very beneficial to the Lord, if the Surveyor be willing and skillful to advantage the Lord.

30. Whether hath the Lord of the Manor any [*Bushes,*] *Turfs, Peats, Heath, Broom, Furze, Fern*, or *Flag*,[102] which are, or may be yearly sold within the Manor, and what may they yield the Lord by year, if they were improved [to the uttermost value].

These things are not in every country, much less in every Manor: for I think *Essex* can afford little of them, unless it be of Turfs and Peats, if they were sought in some low grounds in some creek of the Sea; *Northumberland, Westmorland* and those wild [fells], yield store of Peats and Turfs; so doth [*Lincolnshire, Cambridgeshire,*] *Yorkshire, Lancashire*, and other places many within this Kingdom, which wold[103] be very profitable, make good fuel, and save much wood.

Bailiff   What mean you by *Turfs* and *Peats*? Are they not heath Turfs you mean?

Surveyor   There are *heath Turfs*, which are also meant in this Article, but the *Turf and Peat* is of another kind: for they are taken in bogs, and such rotten grounds as cattle cannot feed upon. And those that are first cut up, are called *Turfs* of the upper part, and such as are taken downward, are called *Peats*.

Bailiff   How mean you downward?

Surveyor   Under the first cut; for you may cut a spear's length deep in some places in the summer time, and that kind of earth will burn very excellently. And if it be cut never so deep, it will fill again in few years, and then may it be digged again; insomuch that the profit will be continual [to the Lord, and the use to the country].

---

[100] 'Mines. Quarries'.

[101] *Fuller's earth*   a silicate of aluminum.

[102] 'Turfs and Peats'.

[103] *wold*   a plain; open country.

Bailiff   Then it is beneficial ground.

Surveyor   So it is; and I think there be many grounds would serve to this purpose, if they were sought out, where scarcity of other fuel is. But there is no greater enemy to thrift than idleness, and ignorance of things of use not in use. [For in many places such is the scarcity of wood and furze, as they are enforced to burn cow dung.

Bailiff   That is a strange fuel; as for] *Furze*, I take that to be no good fuel, but to brew or bake withal; it maketh only a flame as doth stubble or straw.

Surveyor   Yes, it is good firewood in *Devonshire* and *Cornwall*, where they make great profit in venting it for that use, in many the greatest towns, and in *Exeter* especially.

Bailiff   Then are they better than our ordinary *Furze* about us?

Surveyor   The Country people do call them *French Furze*: they have a very great stalk, and grow very high, and their prickle very strong; but that they grow thick, and the body is commonly bare to the top, where is only a green bush of the tender and small branches, and seldom elsewhere, so that they easily make them into faggots, and so vent them [with great profit].

31. Whether is there within the Manor any *Slate-stones* for tilling, *red* or *black Lead*, or *Ochre* for Marking-stones?[104]

These kind of Slate-stones are full in *Cornwall*, and the Marking-Stones most about *Derbyshire* and those parts Northward, as are also millstones about the Peak.

32. What *Deer* hath the Lord of this Manor in his Park, red or fallow:[105] how many of Antler, and how many rascal;[106] who is Keeper, and what is his Fee by year; whether hath he any *Warren of Conies* or *Hares*? Who is the Keeper of either of them, and what Fee hath he by year, and what is the Warren of conies worth by the year, and what were the Park worth by acre to be let by year, if the Deer were destroyed, and how many Acres is there within the pale?

A Park for Deer is more for the pleasure than for the profit of the Lord or Commonwealth, and yet fit that Princes and men of worth should maintain them at their pleasures; yet not so fit, that every man that listed should maintain that game, for his private pleasure, that depriveth a Commonwealth of more necessary commodities. But men of late are grown more considerate, and have disparked much of this kind of ground, and converted it to better uses. As for Warrens of Conies,[107] they are not unnecessary, and they require no rich ground to feed in, but mean pasture and craggy grounds are fittest for them. It is therefore in the discretion of a good and circumspect Surveyor, to advise his Lord how to dispose

---

[104] 'Slate-stones. Marking-stones'.

[105] 'Deer'.

[106] *Rascal*   young or lean deer.

[107] 'Conies'.

of these things for his best advantage. And in craggy and unprofitable grounds to keep Goats, especially where they may not annoy profitable things.

33. What *pensions, portions, payments*, or *fees*, are or ought to be yearly paid out of this Manor:[108] to whom are they paid, and for what, and what *rent* or *annuity* is there paid, our ought yearly to be paid out of any Manor, or by any person, unto the Lord of this Manor; and whether hath the same been duly paid, or discontinued; what is the annuity or rent, by whom ought it to be paid, for what thing, and how long hath it been discontinued.

These things are very duly to be examined, both which go out of a Manor or be paid to a Manor, although in many places they be much neglected; not in calling for (I confess), but if such payments be denied, the Lord, to whom such things are due, can hardly say or avow, for what, or in consideration whereof they are due. And by that means men lose their right, both of the payment, and sometimes of the land, if it be escheat, yea, whole Manors, sometimes.

34. Whether is there within this Manor any *Market* weekly, or *Fair* at any time of the year kept:[109] on what day or days, who hath the toll and profits of the same, and what is it, or may it be worth unto the Lord by the year, whether in his own hands, or let to farm, and for what rent?

Fairs and Markets are commonly Patent from the King[, and consequently the toll standings and scallages].[110]

35. Whether doth the Lord, or may he, take in any *swine to pawnage*[111] yearly into this Park or woods: what is the *pawnage* worth by year?

Bailiff   Sir, you need little to enquire of that; for *Oaks* and *Beech*, that have been formerly very famous in many parts of this Kingdom, for feeding the Farmer's venison, are fallen to the ground and gone, and their places are scarcely known where they stood. [*Iam seges est ubi quercus erat.*][112]

Surveyor   It is very true; and it is pity, that Lords of Manors have no more care of their posterities. For assuredly there will be greater want of timber in time to come in this Realm, than may be supplied with little charge from any part else whatsoever.

---

[108] 'Reprises and payments'.

[109] 'Fairs. Markets'.

[110] *Scallage*   entry-way, tollbooth.

[111] 'Pawnage'.

[112] *Iam ... erat*   A variation on Ovid's 'iam seges est, ubi Troia fuit' ['Now are fields of corn where Troy once stood'] (*Heroides*, Epistle I, ll. 53–4), with Norden substituting 'oaks' ['quercus'] in place of the fallen city as a way to mark the effects of deforestation (*Heroides and Amores*, Grant Showerman [trans.], Loeb Classical Library [Cambridge, MA, 1958]). Bacon similarly drew on this passage in a 1597 parliamentary speech opposing enclosure: 'And I should be sorry to see within this kingdom that piece of Ovid's verse ring true, "Jam seges est ubi Troja fuit;" so in England, instead of a whole town of people, none but green fields' (*Works*, vol. 9, p. 82). Norden discusses deforestation at length in Book 5 (p. 167). On this issue, also see the Introduction (p. xxxix).

And therefore might Lords and Farmers easily add some supply of future hope, in setting for every 20 Acres of other land, one acre of Acorns, which would come to be good timber in his son's age, especially where there is, and like to be more want.

Bailiff   The course were good, but you prefix too short a time far; for Oaks are slow of growth, and it will be long ere they come to be timber.

Surveyor   I know in *Suffolk*, where in twenty years, Acorns have yielded fruit already, near as high as a steeple of ordinary height.

Bailiff   Truly, it is pity it were not enjoined to men of ability and land to do it. But I think men imagine, there will be timber enough to the end of the world, as many things else presage it cannot stand long.

[*Surveyor*]   [36. Whether hath not the Lord Leet and Law-day within the Manor:[113] what is the extent of the precinct, and whether is there not a court kept within the Manor from three weeks to three weeks,[114] and what sum or value hath the court power to determine?

Bailiff   If Leets and views of Frankpledge[115] were duly kept, and the true meaning of the first creation of them and their powers duly executed, they would reform many abuses in the Commonwealth.

Surveyor   It is true, but the negligence of Lords, and corruption of Stewards, have much impeached both the credit and use of those most necessary Courts.]
    [37]. Whether hath any of you any *Deeds, Evidences, Court-rolls, Rentals, Suit-rolls, Custom-rolls, Books of Survey, Accounts*, or any other escripts,[116] or [muniments],[117] touching or concerning this Manor? If you have any such, produce them at this Court for the Lord's use and service; or, if you know any that have any such, deliver their names, that the Lord may procure them to shew the same.
    Men that have such are nice in delivering them; but if they have them and conceal them, they are no good Tenants in not revealing them[, and without records there can hardly be a good survey].
    [38]. Who hath the *Advowson*,[118] *Nomination, presentation* and *gift of the Parsonage, Vicarage*, or *Free chapel*, whereunto this Manor belongeth; or whether

---

[113]   'Evidences'.

[114]   *three weeks*   that is to say, every three weeks.

[115]   *Frankpledge*   oath holding a group of Tenants liable for each other's actions (also see n. 59, p. 52).

[116]   *escripts*   writs, written decrees.

[117]   *muniments*   documents.

[118]   'Advowsons'. Patronage of the selection of parsons.

is it an *impropriation*[119] belonging to the Lord of this Manor? Who is incumbent of the Parsonage or Vicarage, or who hath the impropriation in use, and what is it worth by year?

Some have taken and set down a Parsonage or Vicarage to be parcel of a Manor, but I take it otherwise; for a matter of spiritual or Ecclesiastical function cannot be parcel of a secular living. But a Manor, as touching the Tithe, may belong to an Ecclesiastical charge; neither do I think that an *Impropriation*, though it belong unto the Lord, yet is it not parcel of his Manor; because that *ab origine*, even from the first institution, it was dedicated to a spiritual office. And although the profits were afterwards disposed to a secular person, yet are not the profits parcel of the Manor.

[39. Whether is there any land concealed, or rent detained within this Manor; and by whom, for what, how much, how long, or whether is any land granted in Mortmain.][120]

[40]. Who is the Lord's *Bailiff*, what is his name, what yearly fee hath he, and whether hath he a Patent for life, or is at the Lord's will; and who is *Steward* of the Lord's Courts:[121] what is his fee, and whether doth he hold it by patent or at will; who is *Woodward*,[122] and what other Officers are there within, or belonging to this Manor, and what are their fees?

Sundry Manors have sundry officers: some of the Lords' election and appointment, and some of the Tenants', among whom they are yearly chosen, as *Hayward, Reeves*, &c.[123]

[41]. Within what *Diocese* and *Deanery*, within what *division and hundred*, lieth this Manor,[124] and to what place are you that are the Tenants, usually called to do your services, to muster, and to shew your Armour and weapons; and what *Beacons* are you appointed to watch and ward at?[125]

It were a simple part of a Surveyor, if his Lord should ask him these questions, and he should answer, I cannot tell; and yet are they things fit for the Lord to be acquainted with, upon sundry occasions.

[42]. What *Market* Towns are nearest unto this Manor,[126] and what commodities are there especially vented at every of them?

This is also necessary to be known of the Lord that dwelleth remote from his Manors, for many reasons. Thus much for the charge.

---

[119] *impropriation*   power to seize a benefice's revenues.

[120] *Mortmain*   right of the Church and other corporations to hold land inalienably.

[121] 'Lord's Bailiff. Steward'.

[122] *Woodward*   officer in charge of manorial forests.

[123] *Hayward*   officer responsible for fences and enclosures; *Reeve*   supervisor of estates, usually subordinate to the Steward.

[124] 'Diocese, hundred, &c'.

[125] Military training as part of the local militia was compulsory after 1558 (John S. Nolan, 'The Militarization of the Elizabethan State', *Journal of Military History* 58 [1994]: 399).

[126] 'Market Towns'.

Every Surveyor is in discretion to order his own business, and none is tied to this method of charge;[127] yet he must take the substance of these Articles, or such and so many of them, as in his conceit (guided by some foreknowledge of the state of the Manor which he is to survey) are fittest to be delivered unto the *Jury*; and, withal, he is to explain unto them the sense and meaning of every Article more at large than he will give them in the letter. And having thus finished the charge, I hold it fit to give the *Articles* in writing unto the Jury, to the end they may answer their knowledges to every of them in writing. And because the *Jury* (perchance) cannot so methodically set down their own plain meanings, as is fit to be engrossed in the Lord's book, the *Surveyor* must correct the form, still keeping himself within the compass of the meaning of the *Jury*, and then to read the same unto them distinctly, that they may allow or disallow the same; and because they shall have sufficient time, to consult and deliberate upon every Article, they may have day given them, until such time as the *Surveyor* doth think he shall finish the Perambulation and view of the Manor in such sort as he intendeth, and then to take their verdict, and accordingly to engross the same, together with his own private necessary observations, touching the same.

Immediately after the charge thus ended, the Surveyor is to make proclamation, in the name of the Lord of the Manor, that every Tenant do presently produce his *deeds, copies, leases*, and other *Evidences*, to the end that the Surveyor and his Clerk may enter them roughly in a book, and afterward enroll them fair in a book of Parchment for continuance.

And if any man make default, he may find it by the Catalogue of the names of the Tenants, which he must take at the beginning of the Court, and cross them as they bring their Evidences to be entered: the manner of which entries doth briefly follow.

Intrationes omnium et singularium Chartarum,[128] copiarum, Identurarum, [omniumque] aliarum Evident. tenetium, ibidem factae tertio die Novemb. Anno Regni Domini nostri Jacobi, Dei gratia, Magnae Britanniae, Franciae et Hiberniae Regis, fidei defensoris, &c. 4.ut sequuntur, viz.

Chartae Liberorum tenentium.[129]

W.P. de F. Com. M. Yeoman, per chartam dat. tertio die Martii, Anno regni Henr.7.secundo, tenet libere sibi & haeredibus suis (if it be entailed, then according to the limitation) ex donat. R.S. unum mesuagium sive tentm. vocat. Whytlocks, situat. in quadam venella vocat. Potters-street, inter mesuag. R.L. ex austr. & quandam viam vocat. Love-lane ex parte Bor. abutton. super magnam communiam vocat. Hownes-Moore in Occiden, & super com. campum vocat. Beggars Bushfield in Orientem, &, continet in longitudine quadragint. pertic.

---

[127] 'Notandum. Every Surveyor is to use his own method'.

[128] 'Beauland Manerium'.

[129] This first Latin extract is a sample deed for a freehold Tenant; Aaron Rathborne's surveying manual provides a similar example in English: see *The Surueyor in Four bookes* (London, 1616), pp. 224–5.

& in latitudine novem pertic. & dimid. unum clm. prati. vocat. Mosse-meadow, cont. per estimat. quinque acr. & quinque acr. prat. jac. in commun. prat. vocat. Colliers-mead, & tres clausur. terrae arabilis insimul jacent. vocat. Bathyes, cont. in se in to. per estimat. decem acr. unum clm. pastur. vocat. Abbots-close, jacent. &c. cont. per estimat. tres acr. Quod quidem mesuagium [praed.] R.S. nuper perquisivit, de quodam A.B. habend, &c. per redd. unius libr. Piperis, & per servic. inde debit. & consuet.[130]

In hac forma [caeterae] omnes irrotulentur chartae, secundum particularia in eisdem specificata.[131]

Copiarum Custumariorum tenentium, intratio.[132]

B.C. per cop. Cur. Dat. nono die Maii An. regni Elizab. 30. tenet exsursum redditione. W.R. unum tentm. jacent. in quodam vico vocat. Church-street, int. &c (according to the buttals) & unam clm. terrae voc. Haywood jac. &c. cont. per estim. duas acr. unum pratum vocat. Deare meade, cont. quinque acr. & decem acr. terr. in com. campis. Habendum sibi & haered. suis ad voluntatem Domini secundum consuetudinem Mannerii, & dedit Domino pro fine 3 pounds, 6 shillings, 8 pence, & reddit per annum.[133]

If the estates be for lives, as in the most Manors in the West, then the entries of the Copies must be according to the words of the copy; and at the foot of the entry of every copy, it is fit to set down the ages of the Tenant in possession, and of them in reversion.

Also it behooveth a Surveyor in the entry of all Deeds and Copies, to set down the names of all mesuages and tenements, and the names of every particular close, and parcel of land, as they are set down in the Copy. And not only the present Tenant's name, but [the former Tenants for] two, three, or four descents, if it be expressed in the copies.

It is a fault in some Stewards, that, in making out Copies, do set only down the name of him that surrenders, and the name of him to whom the surrender is made, without further relation of any former Tenant's name; and do also set down the mesuage, without setting down the particular parcels of land belonging unto it, [the rent or fine,] using only general words, which in all things import incertainty. Whereas, if he did well, he should observe and set down every parcel both in quality and quantity; namely, what is meadow, pasture, arable, wood, &c., with the

---

[130] 'I. Libr. Piperis'. Or 'A pound of pepper', an alternative to cash payment for annual rent.

[131] A deed would typically feature a second component, a detailed description of 'particulars' (houses, fields, and the like) to be included as part of the property; see the example in Rathborne, p. 224.

[132] Norden cites a sample deed for a copyhold tenant; for a comparable example in English, see Rathborne, p. 225.

[133] 'Finis 3 pounds, 6 shillings, 8 pence'; '2 shillings, 6 pence'.

principal butts and bounds, by the Surveyor's book. But for want of true surveys many beneficial things are omitted, and many hurtful admitted.

> *De intratione dimissionum, sive Indenturarum, in quibus ea quae sequuntur,*
> *observanda sunt praecipue.*[134]
> Dies, mensis, et annus.
> Partes, inter quas facta est Indentura.
> Consideratio concessionis.
> Particularia quae per Indenturam traduntur.
> Habendum, cum termino annorum aut vitarum, pro quo aut quibus conceduntur.
> Redditus, et tempora solutionis.
> Clausa districtionis, aut foris facturae.
> Conventiones, et Provisiones breviter, sed distincte.
> Quomodo obligatur ad warrantizandum Concessor, &c.

This sufficeth for the form of the entry of Deeds, Copies, and Leases.

Bailiff   Is this all that is required in the making up of a book of Survey?

Surveyor   Some think it sufficient to come into a Manor and to call the Tenants, and to cause them to shew their evidences, and to enter them, and so to give the Lord a book of the estates, and think they have done a great work; which is as much as if a Cater[135] should provide meat, and the Cook to send it to the table raw for his Lord to eat. The Cater's office doth as much towards the Lord's diet, as the bare knowledge of the estates of a Manor doth towards the performing on an absolute Survey. Yet is the Cater's office a good inducement, and without his provision the Cook can do nothing; and without the knowledge of the estates, a Surveyor's [travail] is to little purpose.

Bailiff   Yet you will enter every man's particular lands again, will you not, notwithstanding the entering of their Evidences?

Surveyor   It must be so, after the view had and made of all the Manor.

Bailiff   What else require you at my hands to be done then at this time? For I perceive you have given the Jury their charge, and limited them a day to bring in

---

[134] *De intratione ... sunt praecipue* ['To register an Indenture of Lease, be sure to follow these particulars']. What follows is Norden's poetic explanation of those features of a deed held by leasehold that a Surveyor should register: the duration of the lease, the parties entering into the agreement, the conditions, rent, provisions, and penalties for forfeiture. See Rathborne's more prosaic example, pp. 221–2.

[135] *Cater*   purchaser of household supplies, or 'cates'. Natasha Korda discusses the relation of household 'kates' to early modern domesticity in *Shakespeare's Domestic Economies: Gender and Property in Early Modern England* (Philadelphia, 2002), pp. 52–75.

their verdict; and you have seen and entered all the Deeds, Copies, and Leases of the Tenants which have appeared. What will you now do in the meantime?

Surveyor   I must now command you (the Lord's Bailiff) to appoint me some sufficient Tenants, to accompany me in the perambulation and description of the Manor.[136]

Bailiff   What, will you make a plot of the Manor?[137]

Surveyor   It is very expedient and necessary for many causes, which I shewed you in our first conference.[138]

[*Bailiff*   Will you do it by instrument?

Surveyor   Yea.

Bailiff   Then you need the less help, for you will use no chain, nor staff, cord or pole, as many do?][139]

Surveyor   I will, and it behooveth to use the chain, notwithstanding the instrument, or some other like measure.

Bailiff   I have heard some of your profession say, they could plot out a Manor, and never use line or chain with the instrument.

Surveyor   A Painter can by his art delineate the proportion of any creature, without using perspective glass or a compass, even by the eye and serious observation; so may a man, having the true use of any topographical instrument by rules geometrical, describe a Manor in a kind of form, without line or chain or other measure. But if he will say he doth, or that he can truly delineate a Manor with all the members—as every street, high-way, lane, river, hedge, ditch, close, and field in form, with true curvings, angles, lengths, and breadths, so that by the plot which he so maketh, a stranger by scale and compass may truly find the quantities of the particulars—I will then say he is a rare [man], and [more] to be admired [for his self-vain opinion than for his skill]; because I must needs speak as I find, that it is a matter both

---

136   'Tenants must accompany the Surveyor in his perambulation'.

137   Significantly, it is only at this late stage in his series of dialogues that Norden first begins to consider the visual, cartographical components of a surveyor's work.

138   'A plot of a Manor necessary'.

139   *chain* a Surveyor's chain, 40 poles (66 feet) long, would be used to measure ground manually, with length determined by moving a brass marker along a series of 100 links. A *staff* refers to the Jacob's staff, or cross-staff, an instrument originally used in navigation that was adapted for field surveying; it consisted of two interlocking, perpendicular poles that were held aloft to determine the angle of the sun.

unnecessary and unprofitable: unnecessary, because it is as if a man should build a house without pin or nail, by ingenious geometrical conclusions, to magnify Art, when with more certainty it may be done by the ordinary aid of pins and nails; and it is unprofitable, because it will require a ten-fold time more than the ordinary course of the instrument or chain. And yet when *curiosity* hath done all that it can in this behalf, he shall find (though the conclusions be true) the work will be false.

Bailiff   Then I perceive, there be some vainglorious of your profession:[140] for some have not stuck of late to write, and some profess, that they can perform it truly. In that manner I have seen one come into a field, and set his instrument in the middle, or in some part thereof, and hath taken upon him immediately to say, 'the content is thus much'.

Surveyor   I have heard one also to say, he can keep all the commandments of God, and err no jot in any.

Bailiff   Fie on him that will assume that power that was peculiar only to Christ.

Surveyor   The like vainglorious is he that so assumeth unto himself admiration, who may be more admired for his presumption than for his truth in performance, for a piece of ground cannot lie in any such form, as he with an instrument at one station can find the quantity, though he may aim at it at two stations; but a piece of land may so lie as he shall err, let him take as many stations as he can, and yet he must measure between his first two stations at the least, and toil himself and his companions, more than if he went the true course of Art and Reason.

Bailiff   What you mean by stations? I am not acquainted, but I hold the plainest way, the truest way in all conclusions, if *Art* and *Reason* be not against them; and sith the chain, I perceive, is necessary to be used with the instrument, I will provide you help, both for your aid in that behalf, and for your information, hoping that you will not be against me to view your [manner] of working; and if I do ask you a question now and then, for my better satisfaction, you will not be curious in advising.

Surveyor   I will not only not be curious, but I will gladly impart my poor skill unto you, if you be willing; and I will bestow demonstration, if you will afford attention and practice.

Bailiff   What call you this instrument?

Surveyor   Some call it the [*Plane*] *Table*.[141]

---

[140]   'Vainglorious Artists'.

[141]   *Plane Table*   As reflected by its early modern spelling, 'plain table', this instrument demanded relatively little technical skill to operate. Placing a large sheet of paper over a flat

Bailiff   Is there no other instrument used in plotting of ground?

Surveyor   Yes, according as men of skill do fancy.

Bailiff   But which do you approve most? For as there be divers, so men diversely affect them.[142]

Surveyor   Affection is often blind, and it may mislead a man, but reason seldom or never; and therefore he that can maintain the credit of that he affecteth, by sound experience and reason, I hold that a fit instrument for his use: there are but two principal instruments fit indeed for the plotting of grounds, and that is this that hath the name of a [*Plane*] *Table*, and the *Theodolite*,[143] which sometimes I use also.

Bailiff   But I have seen many and divers forms of instruments, and are they all comprehended under these two names?

Surveyor   No, they have sundry names, but they are all grounded upon like principles;[144] and as a man may make sundry kinds of clocks, one differing in a kind of form from other, and call them by divers names, yet they are all founded upon one ground; and as every clock bringeth forth like effects, as to strike and distinguish times; so these instruments, though they differ in form and name, yet they produce like effects, if they tend to this part of *Geometry*, which is most principally called *planimetry*:[145] namely, the measuring of the length, and breadth of anything, as of a Manor, and of all sorts and forms of grounds.

---

board that was then mounted on a tripod, the surveyor would use an alidade, a ruler with sights, to mark out angles at a series of stations. Norden's selection of the plane table for his demonstration illustrates how his text is directed to a general audience rather than to professional surveyors. By contrast, other contemporary surveying manuals dismissed the use of the plane table: Ralph Agas saw it as an antiquated device, too inaccurate to measure larger areas, while Aaron Rathborne found it better suited for 'the weake vnderstanding of meanest capacities' (Agas, *A preparative to platting of Landes and tenements for Surueigh* [London, 1596], pp. 3–4; Rathborne, *The Surueyor*, p. 125).

[142] 'As Instruments are divers, so men diversely affect them'.

[143] *Theodolite* This instrument, also known as the simple or azimuth theodolite, had three main features: an outer circle, usually larger than one foot in radius, which was marked by gradations of 360 degrees; two geometrical (or 'shadow') squares, located inside the circle, which would provide ratios to convert the angle of distances to figures for height; and an azimuth, a needle mounted at the center of the circle and protruding from it on two opposite sides, which would be used to read angle measurements from the circle.

[144] 'All instruments have one ground'.

[145] 'Planimetria'. *Planimetry* is the geometry of plane surfaces.

Bailiff But I have heard of an instrument called a *Circumferentor*,[146] which some do use about this business with high commendation.

Surveyor It is true; it is a new name given to the very *Theodolite*, used in a sort otherwise than the *Theodolite*, but not contrary. For as the working upon the *Theodolite* is performed by reducing the needle always upon the point North, as it is marked in the box, the *Index* turning to the degree, and pointing out the line of oppositions, so the *Circumferentor* having his Index fixed, pointeth to the opposite, and the needle falleth at adventure upon some degree marked in the box. And the difference is only in the protraction: for where the one protracteth the work by the degrees found by the fall of the wandering Index, so the other protracteth from the degree whereupon the needle falleth.

Bailiff This differs as much as if the bell should strike the hammer to make it strike, where it is more ordinary that the hammer should strike the bell; but if the sounds be like certain, and sensible, it makes no great matter whether do strike the other. And if either of these instruments will perform the work, let men use whether they list.] But I pray you, let us proceed in our intended business; we have company sufficient both for your instruction of every man's land, and to aid you to carry the chain; as for your instrument, I will carry it. Is it much material where you begin?

Surveyor Truly, no, yet I hold it most fit to begin about the middle of the Manor,[147] and then to take a course as the convenient lying of the land will move us, or at one end or side: all is one.

Bailiff [Then I think here is a convenient place to begin the business: here is a spacious waste, and near about the middle of the Manor.

Surveyor I pray you then set down your instrument there.

Bailiff What will you do with that paper, Sir?

Surveyor I must fasten it upon the Table, that as I go I may cut the form of every particular.

Bailiff But what is that brass ruler that you have taken out of the case?

Surveyor It is the Index of the [Plane] Table.

---

[146] *Circumferentor* a surveying compass in which angles were measured by the position of a magnetic needle on a divided circle. Rathborne provides a detailed description of this instrument in *The Surueyor*, pp. 127–9.

[147] 'Where to begin to describe a Manor'.

Bailiff   Where strike you that line upon the paper, throughout the Table, at adventure?

Surveyor   It is *a meridian line*, upon which, at every station, as you shall see, I lay the Index, observing to lay it always alike, lest I mistake the North point for the South, and the contrary.

Bailiff   Wherefore serveth this great box, and needle upon the middle of the Index?

Surveyor   It directeth to set the Table always precisely upon one point.

Bailiff   Must it stand always one way, and direct always to one point? How then can you find the true curvings of the angles?

Surveyor   When the needle of the index standeth true,[148] as I take it now it doth: look upon it.

Bailiff   Indeed it is right over the line.

Surveyor   Then, I pray you, let me have one to go before me, always to stand with a mark at every angle.[149]

Bailiff   There is one gone.

Surveyor   I see him. Lo, I stir not the Table. Now it is truly rectified, and upon this line I make a prick, which is the very station where the instrument is supposed to stand; and now for this prick, laying the Index hard unto it, I, by the sight of the Index, lay it unto the mark, which is set up in yonder angle; let him not remove it till I come to it; and then as you see, I draw a line from the prick by the Index, as it lieth truly and firmly to the mark. Come on with the line. How many sticks is it?

Bailiff   Sir, it is 25 sticks.[150]

Surveyor   That is 75 pole.[151]

Bailiff   Is your chain three pole?

---

[148] 'The manner of describing'.

[149] *mark ... angle*   the Surveyor determines survey marks by aligning the degrees of angles indicated on the azimuth of the plane table with the figures of his Tenant-assistants standing at a distance in front of him.

[150] *sticks*   an imprecise unit of measurement; in Norden's usage, approximately 50 feet.

[151] *pole*   another term for perch, or 16-1/2 feet.

Surveyor   Yea.

Bailiff   Oh, Sir, what do you now with your compasses, that you first laid to your Index, and after to the paper?

Surveyor   I lay out the true distance, which is from the place where we begun to the place where the mark standeth.

Bailiff   How do you know whether you strike that line too long or too short? Do you aim at it, as a man would divide a thing in divers parts by his eye?

Surveyor   No, there is in all Arts sundry parts, and every part hath his several practice. A man is not presently a Musician, as soon as he can say his [*Gamut*].[152] There are steps and degrees to every perfection. But this little note that you take hold of is not the least of the practice in this faculty.

Bailiff   What call you it? For as Arts have divers parts, so every part hath his several denomination.

Surveyor   And this whereof we are now in hand, is called *the use of the scale*.[153]

Bailiff   I pray you, if I trouble you not too much, let me see your demonstration.

Surveyor   You see in this Index divers inches, diversely divided:[154] one, you see, is divided into 16 equal parts, another into 20, another into 60; these are called scales of ascending, or descending, to a higher or lower computation and extension, according to the number of perches found between station and station. This (as you see) is 75 pole, and the scale or divided inch, which I have chosen, is 20, as you see the inch so divided.

Bailiff   But how can you take 75 out of 20, for that you say is your scale?

Surveyor   I cannot take a greater out of a lesser:[155] therefore you see me apply my compasses to more inches than one; though some of them be divided more or less, I must conceive every inch in the whole Index to be 20. Then I lay the one foot of my compass over 3 inches, which maketh 60, then I lack 15 to make 75. Therefore I set the other foot of my compass into the scale of 20 and reduce it only to 15, which 15 and three inches next adjoining, being imagined 20 apiece, makes 75. And as you see the compass thus spread, I apply it without altering to the line

---

[152]   *Gamut*   in music, a scale of notes.

[153]   'The use of the Scale'.

[154]   'The dividing of the Scale'.

[155]   'How to find the number of perches in the scale'.

which I drew from the first prick; and where the other foot of the compass falleth, there is the second station, namely, the place where this mark standeth.

Bailiff   Truly, Sir, I thank you;] I conceive it well: for I perceive, I must always account the inches, not as they are in themselves divided, but every of them 20. And if it be under 20, then I must refer me to the very scale itself, which is divided 20, and take the number out of it; and if it be above 20, I must take the next inch or inches to the scale, and take the odd out of the scale itself.

Surveyor   If your sudden apprehension have as strong a retention, you will do well; but commonly quickest conceits do soonest forget.[156] Therefore must you often chew it in your mind, and apply it to your memory, and, as we pass in this business, you may make some use of my practice.

Bailiff   Sir, I thank you.

Surveyor   What call you this common?

Bailiff   Ye that are Tenants, and are sworn, inform the Surveyor.

Jury   Sir, it is called Water-hurst Common.

Surveyor   [So, you that carry the mark: I pray, go to the next angle, and set up your mark, and stir it not till I come. *Bailiff*, set down the instrument again, here, where the mark stood.

Bailiff   I perceive you lay the Index upon the line again; and then you turn the Table, till it be by direction of the needle, North and South, as before.

Surveyor   I do so.

Bailiff   But why do you now lay the Index, and by it look back again?[157]

Surveyor   Only to try whether the needle be right; for if the Index from this last prick, do fall truly upon the first station, then may I be bold that I shall make the next angle true.

Bailiff   I have seen some have one to stay always behind at the last place whence you come, and so the Surveyor looks back to make his next angle.

---

[156] 'Quick conceits soon forget'.

[157] *look back again*   As Richeson points out, Norden was the first English writer to recommend backsighting as a way of checking the accuracy of measurements (*English Land Measuring*, p. 94).

Surveyor   Some do so, but it is more troublesome; for by this kind of working by the needle and the meridian line, a man may make the angles right without any back opposite.

Bailiff   It is far the better, more easier, and speedier working, as I take it, now you lay the Index to yonder mark before you, and the line that you have stricken from the last prick is the line that directeth to it; but because you know not yet how many pole it will be, you omit applying your compasses to the scale until you come to the mark and know the number of perches.

Surveyor   I must do so; now come on with the chain. How many pole is it in the whole?

Bailiff   37 pole: I see you take almost 2 inches for this number, namely, one entire inch for 20 and 17 parts of the scale of 20, which in the whole maketh 37. And, I see truly, as 37 is the half almost of 75, so is this last line the answerable half of the first, and the angle falleth out in the paper just alike unto the angle of the field. Surely, this is a perfect way, and I conceive the doing of it very plainly.

Surveyor   Then we may go on the faster, for this doth a little hinder our business; but if you think fit to ask any question, do it freely, and I will answer you willingly.

Bailiff   When I come to any doubt, I will be bold, Sir; now we have gone round about the Common of *Water-hurst*, and you have closed it up as rightly like it in form, as one form may be made like another: Whither will you go next?

Surveyor   Into the next field.] What field call you this?

Jury   Ox Lease.

Surveyor   Whose is it?

Jury   Thomas Turner's.

Surveyor   How doth he hold it?

Jury   He holds it by Copy of Court-roll.

Surveyor   Is it Meadow?

Jury   Yea, as we call it, upland Meadows.

Bailiff   I perceive you write the names of the Commons and closes[158] you take, and the name of the owners and occupiers, and the quality of the ground, and how it is held in every particular close.

Surveyor   I must of necessity do so; for memory may not be trusted to retain so many things, as are to be noted in this business.

Bailiff   I pray you proceed to the rest.

Surveyor   What River call you this?

Bailiff   Will you have the names of the Rivers too?

Surveyor   Yea, and the name of every other particular else whatsoever;[159] for it is very material, whether it be River, Brook, lane, high-way, cross, tree, pond, hill, hedge, corner, gate, stile,[160] gravel, or sand-pit, mere-stones,[161] balks,[162] land-shares,[163] or any matter or thing memorable, because they are often mentioned in records, butts, boundaries, deeds, copies, leases, and to distinguish between land and land, Manor and Manor, Parish and Parish, and such like.

Bailiff   Indeed, I perceive it is very material to remember them all; this river indeed is called *Otter-brook*, and is indeed the bounds between this Manor of *Beauland* and the next Manor.

Surveyor   What call you the next Manor, on the other side the river?

Bailiff   The Manor of *Littleton*. But will you observe the names of all the Manors that border upon this Manor?

Surveyor   Yea, of necessity, and whose Manor it is;[164] for it were a simple part in me, to take the circuit of this Manor, and if the Lord should ask me what Manors lay about it, I should answer, I cannot tell: it is fit the Lord should know who were his neighbor Lords, and what Manors were near him. Whose is the Manor of Littleton?

---

[158] *closes*   enclosed lands.

[159] 'The names of all particulars are to be set down'.

[160] *stile*   steps at a gate, used to fence in livestock.

[161] *mere-stones*   boundary marker.

[162] *balks*   ridges, unplowed land used as barriers.

[163] *land-shares*   lots, property divisions.

[164] 'Confining Manors are to be noted'.

Bailiff   The King's Manor; and, therefore, whether you may boldly set it down, you may be advised.

Surveyor   There is no fear, where is no purpose of offence; and in this, it is not only not offensive, but expedient that the true bounds, meres, and marks of division between Manor and Manor should be observed and set down, that either may know how far his own extendeth.

Bailiff   [It is, I confess, very necessary. But, Sir, how will you do now? Here is a great pond, through which you cannot measure: how can you find the breadth of it, that when you come to the other side you may take the just distance? For, as I conceive, if you should lay it down by your scale, as you call it, too far, or too short, you should bring all the land near it out of rule, making it either too much or too little.

Surveyor   I perceive you understand well, for you say truly. Therefore if you observe what I do, you shall find that I will not commit that error much sensible.

Bailiff   How, I pray you?

Surveyor   You see how the instrument standeth, truly erected as before, and you see a little Mole-hill upon the further bank of the pond: I lay (as you see) the Index upon it, and take it for my mark just in the middle of it; and from this last station I strike a line at adventure, in the extension, but truly upon the mark; then without moving the instrument, I turn the Index from this station, where the instrument stands, unto the staff which the mark-bearer hath set up yonder, and strike likewise a line to it, as you see; now I measure from this station to the staff, and I find it is 16 perches, that you see how I take it with my compasses upon the scale, as I shewed you before; and where the foot of my compass falleth, there is the place where the staff standeth. Now, see, I erect mine instrument again: and then I place my Index upon this place measured unto, and turn the same unto the middle of the former Mole-hill; and, you see, that the index doth cross the first line, and I draw a third from the place of the staff, to the Mole-hill; and it crosseth it, you see, at this place; then I find that the very point of these cross lines is the place of the Mole-hill.[165]

Bailiff   But how know you by this, how far the river or pond is over?

Surveyor   I will tell you presently. Lo, I lay the one foot of the compass upon the first station, and the other upon the prick of the Mole-hill: and now, mark, I lay the

---

[165]   The Surveyor is explaining the principles of triangulation to the Bailiff: he calculates the distance from his current station to the inaccessible Mole-hill by first determining the coordinates between his present location, his prior station, and the spot where his assistant holds a surveyor's mark.

compass, without stirring the feet, unto the scale; and, as you see, it taketh three inches and a half; therefore I lay the compass so, as the one foot may rest upon the scale, which I have chosen, which is the inch divided into twenty parts; and that, you see, is just in the middle of the inch, which is ten perches, and the other three whole inches are twenty a piece; so the whole breadth of the pond is 70 perches, deducting as much on either side, as is between the brink of the pond and the marks on either side, because I could not plant mine instrument so near the water but that some space must be of necessity between.

Bailiff   I understand this well; and I see that by this rule a man may take the distance of a place far off, and never measure to it.

Surveyor   So may you, and to tell how far distant divers things are one from another, though neither of them be near you. But for these things, if you covet more instruction, you may refer you to divers in London, or elsewhere, that are practizers and teachers of these Geometrical conclusions;[166] for now time will not serve us, neither for me to teach, nor you to understand the things at full, which are required in the Mathematics, whereof this is but a part.

Bailiff   I thank you for your present willingness; when better your opportunity and leisure will permit you, I will be bold to trouble you further, and I will be thankful. I will not now let you: I pray you proceed.]

Surveyor   What house is this?

Bailiff   These men of the Jury will tell you better than I; for I am but a stranger here to speak of, and I dare not be too bold to speak either by guess, or by report, of things which must be recorded to posterities.

Surveyor   You do better to forbear, and to be silent indeed,[167] than to speak what may lead us into error, as many busy and forward fellows do, to the hurt sometimes of the Lord, sometimes of the Tenant.[168] And some Surveyor, overcredulous, will take their raw reports for matter of record, and so leave doubts or untruths to them that shall come after. But what say you that have been sworn?

------

[166]   *teachers of these Geometrical conclusions*   Norden may be referring to the activities based at Gresham College, founded in 1597 to disseminate mathematical and geographical knowledge to an urban, mercantile clientele: for discussion, see E.G.R. Taylor, *The Mathematical Practitioners of Tudor and Stuart England* (Cambridge, 1954); Mordechai Feingold, *The Mathematicians' Apprenticeship: Science, Universities and Society in England, 1560–1640* (Cambridge, 1984), pp. 166–89; and Lesley B. Cormack, *Charting an Empire: Geography at the English Universities, 1580–1620* (Chicago, 1997), pp. 203–24.

[167]   'They that inform, must know what they say'.

[168]   'Raw reports without knowledge, are unfit to be recorded'.

Jury   The name of the house is *Fullers*; but why it is so called, we cannot tell.

Surveyor   It is so called (no doubt) of some former Tenant of that name; for houses and farms are often times called [of] sundry names, according to the variety of the Tenants ' names;[169] and it is a good course to set down all the ancient names of a farm, because in ancient records, names are found both of farms and closes, and such like, that are out of knowledge, for want of the continuance of expressing them in their Copies, Deeds, Leases, Rentals, Suit-rolls, and custom Rolls. But whose is the house now?

Jury   It is now in the tenure of *William Sands*.

Surveyor   How doth he hold it?

Jury   By Lease, for 21 years.

Surveyor   When I come to any of the land that belongeth to this house, let me understand it; for it is convenient to mention, in setting down every piece of ground, to what house, farm, or tenement it belongeth.

Bailiff   Here you are now come to the Lord's wood.

Surveyor   What call you this Wood?

Bailiff   I take it, it is called *Frith-wood*.

Surveyor   It is parcel of the Lord's demesnes, is it not?

Jury   It is so, Sir.

Surveyor   Here are good timber trees: we will number them.[170]

Bailiff   Number them? How is it possible to number them: they are so many, and stand so thick?

Surveyor   I confess (especially if it be thick of bushes and underwoods) there is difficulty in [numbering them.][171]

---

[169]   'Houses are called after the names of Tenants'.

[170]   'To number trees'.

[171]   In the only section of the 1610 text cut from the 1618 edition, the Surveyor shows the Bailiff how to estimate the number of trees on a plot of land: see the Textual Notes for this missing portion of the text.

Bailiff   To what end is it? What is the Lord the better, to know the number of the trees?

Surveyor   Howsoever the Lord be pleased to think of the service, a Surveyor ought to know it;[172] that when he shall be demanded of the Lord, what he thinketh the Wood to be worth to be sold, he may be able to answer it, and give a reason for that he saith, and not to speak at [random] or by guess, without some ground of reason or proof. For how can a man value a wood, when he knows not what crop it beareth? For a wood may have an hundred trees in an acre, some woods not twenty, some not five; and, therefore, it were great negligence in a Surveyor that would pass by a wood of the Lord's and would not take note of the trees, yea, and of the reasonable value of them one with another, that he may readily be able to satisfy the Lord, when he shall demand the Surveyor's opinion, though he cannot answer precisely, yet near.

Bailiff   You say truly: But what if there be no trees at all in the wood, as here is a wood adjoining, called *Buck's-grove*, that hath the name of a wood, but hath no trees at all?

Surveyor   Then is it underwood, which must be considered in another kind,[173] for there is difference between timber trees, and underwoods;[174] for an acre of timber trees may be worth forty pounds, and far more, or much less, when an acre of underwoods cannot lightly exceed five pounds, and may not be worth twenty shillings. Therefore must the Surveyor be heedful, I say, to note what trees are among the underwoods, and must also have skill to judge the values of the trees: namely, to judge what a tun of timber, or a load is worth,[175] and how many loads a tree will make. And because this is not alike in all places, he must be careful to observe the plenty or scarcity, the use and little use of timber or fire-wood in the place where he is to deal;[176] and, accordingly, in discretion to judge of the values of that he hath in hand, else may he deceive himself and his Lord much, if he prize wood in the *weald of Sussex* as it is worth about *Salisbury Plain*.

---

[172]   'A Surveyor should seek to know the number of timber trees'.

[173]   Technically, *underwood* consists of small trees and brush. This passage illustrates the Surveyor's difficulties in representing the effects of deforestation; see the Introduction for further analysis of this point (p. xxxix). Demonstrating Norden's personal interest in the subject, he composed two manuscript treatises in 1608 dealing with the condition of crown forests and the renewal of timber stocks (Coote, *DNB*, p. 551). Norden also supplemented his income through the sale of timber on the lands he surveyed (Kitchen, *DNB*, p. 6).

[174]   'Difference between timber trees and underwood'.

[175]   *tun*   a large barrel, a unit of measurement used most often for liquids; *load*   the amount of a material that can be carried at one time.

[176]   'The place to be considered'.

Bailiff Saving your speech, the like is to be considered in the letting and sale of Land.

Surveyor [Some there is, more in opinion than [in deed]; for the difference of prizes of land of like quality cannot be so great in several places; for land that will yield *per acre*, like feeding in pasture, burden of hay, or profit in tilling, will yield like maintenance of families of equal companies; and, therefore, in reason, the difference of yearly values of land of like quality differ not much.

Bailiff In reason, indeed, the difference should not be great, yet it is commonly valued according to the vent of commodities: but let this pass.]

Surveyor [We] have had a good walk between these two stations, and a long discourse. But methinks I see a quarry of very good stone here.

Bailiff Yea, Sir, here is both excellent free stone and good Marble; and, as we shall go, you shall find divers sorts of minerals and earths, which you cannot note upon your plot, because they are things hidden under the earth.

Surveyor Yea, but I will (for so I ought) set down in the plot the place where every of these commodities are found.[177] But for the matter and substance, and the profit and value, I know the Jury will bring in, in their verdict; for they are all given them in charge, and as I shall find in mine own opinion, I will likewise compare with the Jury's, and so set it down for the Lord's instruction.

Bailiff These things are necessarily given in charge. But here is a Mill. Sir, will you take note of it upon your plot?

Surveyor In any case, for it is not the least ornament of a Manor:[178] a fair stream, and a well-conditioned and well-wrought Mill upon the same. In whose use or occupation is this Mill?

Bailiff It is one *G. Johnson's*.

Surveyor By what right?

Bailiff Let them of the Jury speak.

Jury He holdeth it freely for a peppercorn a year. But it was parcel of the Lord's demesnes, but he sold it; and it was a Custom-Mill,[179] very profitable.

---

[177] 'To note special places of profit'.

[178] 'A good Water-mill, an ornament to a Manor'.

[179] *Custom-Mill*   the mill where Tenants were required to grind their corn.

Surveyor   He that persuaded the Lord to sell away his Custom-Mill, had little respect to the Lord's profit or royalty:[180] the profit comes easily, and the custom confirmeth the antiquity of the Manor. And such a member of a Manor, I would wish none to put away. But *humor* and *necessity*, are two opposite Emperors: the one commands, willeth, and doth what he listeth; the other forced to do what it would not.[181] And therefore men that may do what they list, and will do what they may, if they err to their own hurt, are not to be lamented. But they that are constrained to do what they would not to their prejudice, I pity them. But, I take it, we have near trodden the whole Manor.

Bailiff   Almost, indeed. Here are some few closes more, and then an end.

Surveyor   But here are certain cottages, methinks, builded upon the Lord's waste.[182]

Bailiff   Yea, but let them pass: never meddle with them, for they are only shelter for poor people, and yield the Lord little or no commodity; and therefore spare labor of observing them.

Surveyor   Nay, it is a parcel of my task; I must omit nothing that may inform or benefit the Lord.

Bailiff   Be it then as you will.

Surveyor   What, are we now at an end?

Bailiff   Yonder corner is the last; for it is the place where you began, in *Water-hurst* common.

Surveyor   So: then we will retire.

Bailiff   What will you then command to be done?

Surveyor   Cause the Tenants all to appear, and let the Jury bring in their verdict.

Bailiff   The Tenants are at the Court-house, and the Jury ready with their presentment.

Surveyor   I will go with you and take it: make proclamation, and call the Jury by poll.

---

[180]   'Not good for a Lord to alien his Custom-Mill'.

[181]   'Humor and Necessity, two Emperors opposite'.

[182]   'Cottages on the waste'. For discussion of cottagers, see pp. 98–9, above, and the Introduction (pp. xxxvi and ff.).

Bailiff   They all appear.

Surveyor   You sworn-men of the Court of Survey, have you agreed upon the answer of the Articles that were given you in charge, and are you provided with answer unto every of them in writing?

Jury   Yea, Sir: here it is fairly written.

Surveyor   You have well done in your endeavors, though, peradventure, there may be defects in the form of your answers; yet if you have observed the main purpose, which is the seeking out and the delivering truth, you have discharged the parts of honest Tenants, and men fearing God. And because that it may be, some things may be omitted, which you may now instantly call to mind, blush not to declare it here, before you be deprived of that you have written; for this paper I must have, and that under your hands.

Jury   What need we set to our hands?

Surveyor   Because if I err from it, your hands shall testify against me; if you have erred, and I err through you, your hands shall justify me.[183]

Jury   The thing is reasonable; we will subscribe.

Surveyor   Now will I read the Articles of your charge, and to every Article your answer, that you may yet correct or add what shall be thought fit; and therefore, I pray you, listen.

Jury   Read you, Sir.

Surveyor   You agree to all these things willingly, whereunto you have set your hands.

Jury   We do so, and do here confirm it by the delivery thereof, by our fore-man in the name of us all, to the behoof of our Lord. And what you else require at our hands, we are ready to perform.

Surveyor   You do kindly, and like dutiful Tenants; and be you assured that your forwardness herein shall not be concealed from the Lord, but with true report of your endeavors for the furthering of the business, which cannot but draw a kind consideration from the Lord again to you; which, both to gain for you, and to retain it, I will truly do my best; and so, for this time, I will leave to trouble you further, until I have set my other collections, which I have taken in the perambulation of

---

[183] 'The Jury must subscribe their verdict'.

the Manor, in some order; then will I be bold to trouble you again, to the end that you may all approve what is done, whether I have truly set down the particulars: namely, the Lord's demesnes, the free, copy, and leased lands, under their true names and due owners; if not, that by your help I may reform it, before I engross it, to continue to your children. For what we do, will be hereafter a light unto them that shall come after you; and if it should be erroneous, it would be prejudicial to your posterities.

Jury   I pray you, therefore let there be an examination, and we will gladly give both our attendance and best aid to perfect it.

Bailiff   I shall then make an *O yes*,[184] and adjourn the Court, until they have notice again.

Surveyor   Do so.

Bailiff   You will now keep your chamber, until you have made your collections perfect, and cast up the land.

Surveyor   I purpose so.

Bailiff   I would gladly see the manner of your casting up of the Acres, as you do it; for the rest, I shall see when you have done. For the Jury's examination, I will leave you till the morning, and then will I come to your chamber.

Surveyor   Do so.

The end of the third Book.

---

[184] *O yes*   an abbreviation for *oyer and terminer*, the commission used for special legal proceedings such as Courts of Assize or Courts of Survey.

THE SURVEYOR'S DIALOGUE, SHEWING
the manner of casting up of sundry fashions of Land, with the Scale and Compass, with Tables of computation for ease in accompting.

THE FOURTH BOOK.

Bailiff I see you are busied, and I perceive you are casting up the quantity of this square piece of land.

Surveyor So I am.

Bailiff This, I take it, is plain and easy to be measured.

Fig. 1   A 'square piece of land'; from *The Surveiors Dialogue* (1618), p. 147.

Surveyor I pray let me see your skill. What containeth it?

Bailiff I think if it were upon the ground, I could tell you; but upon the plot I cannot, because, I remember, you do it by your scale; I would gladly see the use of it, and how you apply your scale to the perches; and, if I saw it once, I think I could then guess at it. Where is your scale?

Surveyor This that you see like a ruler divided.

Fig. 2   Scale of inches and perches; from *The Surveiors Dialogue* (1618), p. 148.

Bailiff If you will give me leave, and if I trouble you not, I will try how near I can come to it. I apply the compass to the one side of the figure of the close, and then letting the compass stand, I lay the compass to the scale, and I find it is just one inch, which is 1/3 of the whole scale; and, as I remember, you made your scale twenty perches to an inch.[1]

Surveyor You say right, and your apprehension is good.

Bailiff Then is the one side 20 perches. And having laid my compass to the rest of the sides, I find them twenty of each side. What now is to be done?

Surveyor Multiply the one side by the other.

Bailiff Then I must say twenty times twenty; that makes four hundred perches. But now am I at a stand again: How shall I know how many Acres is in this figure?

Surveyor You must know, that there go 160 perches to one acre; 80 perches to half an acre; 40 perches to one rood, which is 1/4 of an acre; ten day's work to a rood; four perches to a day's work; 16 foot and a half to a perch.[2]

Bailiff Then I perceive, that as many times as I find 160 perches in 400 perches, so many Acres the piece is; and if the overplus come to 80 perches, it makes half and acre more; if to forty, one rood; if to four perches, a day's work; and so according to the odd perches, it maketh parts of an acre.

Surveyor You take it rightly.

Bailiff Then I divide 400 by 160, and I find 160 twice in 400 and 80 over: so it amounts to two Acres and a half.

Surveyor It is well done, but I would have you to observe a form in setting down your quantities; for as the parts are four, so set them down in four columns: as, for

---

[1]   In Fig. 2, the numbers refer to perches: 20 perches mark 1 inch, with the entire scale representing 60 perches (or 3 inches).

[2]   'The parts of an Acre'. See n. 40, p. 25.

example, 2-2-0-0. The first is Acres, the second is roods, the third is day works, and the fourth perches.

Bailiff   I thank you, Sir; I pray let us see some other form.

Surveyor   This form following is also a square; let me see how you will cast it up.

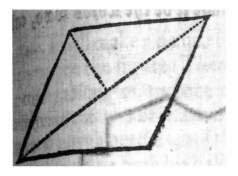

Fig. 3   Casting up a piece of land; from *The Surveiors Dialogue* (1618), p. 149.

Bailiff   I have laid the compass to the sides, as before; and by the scale, all the sides are 20 perches apiece, as were the first, and so I find no difference in the quantity.

Surveyor   But you shall find you are in an error; for it is not the length of the sides that justifies the quantity,[3] but the angles must be considered; for you see there is great difference between the angles of the first figure, and the angles of this; for the angles of the first are all right angles, but this hath two sharp or acute angles, and two blunt or obtuse angles, which maketh difference in the quantity, though the sides be equal in every way to the former.

Bailiff   I pray you shew me the reason.

Surveyor   Your eye may discern there is inequality in the bigness of these two, but you shall prove it thus: The first is a just square of twenty perches every way, which maketh the area and content as big as possible like sides may make; but this last, by bending two sides, makes the two angles unequal to the other, and must be measured by drawing a line from the two sharp angles, and then raising a perpendicular from that base to one of the obtuse equal angles:[4] multiply the base, which is 34, by half the perpendicular, and that maketh in the whole 2-0-0-3, the base serving to both the perpendiculars being equal.

---

[3]   'Pieces of equal sides may make unequal quantities'.
[4]   'How to cast up a Triangle'.

Bailiff This is almost two parts of an Acre less than the former. And by this reason there may be a piece of land 20 perches every side that shall not contain above two parts of an acre.

Surveyor It is true.

Bailiff I see in your plot a crooked piece of land to be measured, as I take it, and I think it be the Lord's wood, called *Frith-wood.*[5]

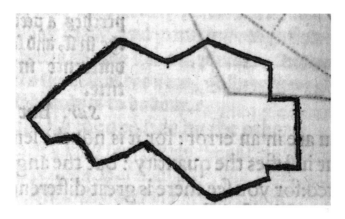

Fig. 4   Plot of Frith-wood, a 'crooked piece of land'; from *The Surveiors Dialogue* (1618), p. 150.

Surveyor This is that you see, and it is troublesome to measure indeed; and without a Geometrical instrument, it can very hardly be measured, because there are woods about it, and the wood itself thick of trees and bushes.

Bailiff You have indeed laid it out in his true form; but it hath so many angles and curvings that I dare not adventure to measure it upon your plot. I pray, what course take you in casting up such a piece of land?

Surveyor The truest course, for that it is so irregular, is to put it into as many triangles as you conveniently may, making no more than necessity requireth; and if you can do this, you may do any other form.

---

[5] *Frith-wood* This piece of land, surveyed by foot in the last book (p. 121), is here converted into an abstract, mathematically-defined 'plot'. For discussion of the epistemological and artistic permutations of 'plotting', see especially Henry S. Turner, 'Plotting Early Modernity', in Turner (ed.), *The Culture of Capital: Property, Cities, and Knowledge in Early Modern England* (New York, 2002), pp. 85–127, as well as Martin Bruckner and Kristen Poole, 'The Plot Thickens: Surveying Manuals, Drama, and the Materiality of Narrative Form in Early Modern England', *ELH* 69 (2002): 617–48.

Bailiff   I pray you, shew me the manner.

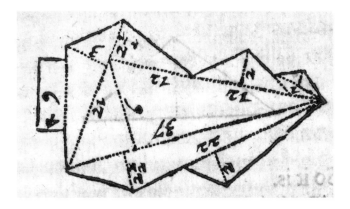

Fig. 5   Converting Frith-wood into triangles; from *The Surveiors Dialogue* (1618), p. 151.

Surveyor   I will make a demonstration unto you, and mark it. You see the figure: There are contained within this figure seven triangles, and one long square; the base of the first triangle is 22 perches, the half perpendicular thereof is two perches, and that containeth 0–1–0–0. The second triangle hath his base 37 perches, the half perpendicular, two and a half, which maketh 0–2–3–1. The third hath the base 37, the half perpendicular six, which maketh 1–1–5–2. The fourth hath the base 21, the perpendicular three, maketh 0–1–5–3. The fifth is in the base 12, perp. two and a half, and maketh 0–0–7–2. The sixth base 12, perp. two, maketh 0–0–6–0. The long square, six in length, and four in breadth, 0–0–6–0. The two last are equal triangles, base eight, perp. one and a half, 0–0–3–0. All which several sums being added together, do amount unto 3–0–8–0.[6]

Bailiff   But which do you call the base, and which perpendicular lines?

Surveyor   The longest line in any triangle is the base, and the perpendicular is a line imagined to rise from the base to the obtuse, or blunt angle:[7] as in the example following.

Bailiff   That which is done with pricks, you call the perpendicular, and the lower line you call the base, as in this figure?[8]

---

[6]   As a reminder, an acre is equal to four roods, 40 day works, and 160 perches; in other words, a day's work is four times the size of a perch, while a rood is 40 times its size, and an acre is 160 times its size.

[7]   'Base and perpendicular, quid'.

[8]   'Base and perpendicular, questions'.

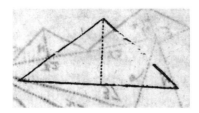

Fig. 6   A triangle; from *The Surveiors Dialogue* (1618), p. 152.

Surveyor   So it is.

Bailiff   But how do you cast up the quantity, by a triangle thus? You cannot, as I take it, by multiplying the base by the perpendicular, find the content; for it is by that computation, more than indeed the triangle containeth.

Surveyor   You say true, if you multiply the whole base by the whole perpendicular;[9] but you must multiply the one by the half of the other.

Bailiff   Do you imagine that the truest measure is by triangles?

Surveyor   Yea, where you find many angles in one field;[10] there are other kinds, and manners of measuring, but this is speedy and certain.

Bailiff   How if a piece of land is directly round? I think you measure it round, and then cast it into a square, as if the circle be 40 perches round, it maketh 10 square.

Surveyor   Indeed, many vulgar measurers do use to measure many sorts of land round, and cast the whole into a square, which is for the most part false. But for a round and circular piece of land, you must indeed measure it round, and take the half of the number of perches for the length;[11] then take the semidiameter, namely, as many perches, as are from the center to the extreme, and multiply the half of the circle by the semidiameter. And for a half circle, multiply half the half circuit by the semidiameter, and divide as I shewed you.

Bailiff   I thank you, Sir; I keep you from your business; yet I pray you, let me ask you one question more for my learning: How are hills and valleys measured?

Surveyor   There is indeed some difficulty in them, without great industry;[12] for commonly, hills and valleys lie very irregularly, sides, heights, and depths very

---

9   'The base multiplied by the perpendicular'.
10   'Triangles surest measuring'.
11   'A circular form'.
12   'Measuring hills and valleys'.

unequal. And therefore to demonstrate any certain rule for these kind of contents, many have endeavored to do, to whom as unto uncertainties I refer you; but for such kind of grounds, there must special diligence be had, in bringing them into certain parts, distinguishing the parts by marks, and so by degrees to bring these parts into a certain content general, and that upon the ground; otherwise, I see not, how by measuring a whole irregular circuit together, as irregular heights or depths, and applying the numbers to a general computation, according to the rules of arithmetic, a certainty may be procured;[13] although the rules be true, yet in regard of the inequality of forms, the working may fail, upon a plain plot, which cannot possibly truly demonstrate the true forms, nor consequently the quantities of unequal hills and dales.

Bailiff　Sir, loath I am to be troublesome unto you, for that I know you have much business, and the casting up of particulars of this whole Manor, will be very laborious; for to cast up every particular angle of a ground by arithmetic, will be very tedious.

Surveyor　But I have certain tables of ease, which yield more speedier dispatch, than to cast up every content with the pen.

Bailiff　I pray you, let me be bold to crave the sight of those tables.

Surveyor　I have set them down in a little book, and here follows.

Bailiff　Were these of your own invention?

Surveyor　Many have endeavored several manners and methods of computation: as one *Benese*, a Canon of *Martin Abbey*, near *Mecham in Surrey*,[14] who did it by sundry square Tables, increasing by ten, as from one to ten times ten, from one [times] twenty to ten times twenty, and so increasing by ten, until he come to an hundred times 120, that is, from one perch to 75 Acres.

Bailiff　Truly, these are very necessary tables: Is yours in another form?

Surveyor　It is in that kind, but it worketh by the increase from one to twenty times twenty, from one to forty times forty, from one to sixty times sixty, eighty times eighty, &c.

Bailiff　This differs not much from the former, yet I take it to be more ready.

13　'Irregular forms must be measured by regular parts'.

14　'Many rules of casting up contents, [by] Benese a Canon'. Richard Benese was the author of *This Boke Sheweth the Measurynge of all Maner of Land* (London, 1537), a popular text that went through four more editions by 1565.

Surveyor   So it is.

Bailiff   Who, I pray you, found out this way first?

Surveyor   Surely I had certain papers of that method, of M. *Randolph Agas*,[15] but they were so [imperfect as I have been enforced] to calculate them since, to make them [more large and more exact]. But surely his diligence deserves commendation.

Bailiff   Did *M. Agas* first contrive them so?

Surveyor   [M. *Valentine Leigh*][16] and M. *Digges*[17] had in manner the like, increasing by the multiplication of greater sums; but of all other, I take this to be the most readiest that you see here[, as I have digested them].

Bailiff   Is this the Book, and are these the Tables?

Surveyor   [These are they.][18]

Bailiff   Surely this is a necessary book for him that is employed in matters of great quantity. For if it should be all cast up with the pen, it would ask much labor, and waste much paper; and yet I know simple Country fellows will cast it up very speedily, even by their memories, by money:[19] as one penny to a Perch, four perches to a Day work, 10 day works to one Rood, four roods one Acre; three shillings four pence, is forty pence, and forty perches, one Rood; one hundred and threescore pence, make thirteen shillings and four pence, or a Mark of money; and one hundred and threescore perches one Acre. So that twenty pound makes three Acres; forty pound, threescore Acres; a hundred pound, one hundred and fifty Acres, and so forth.[20] But this kind of casting is troublesome, when it riseth

---

[15]   'Randolph Agas'. Ralph (or Randolph) Agas was the author of *A Preparative to Platting of Lands and tenements for Surveigh* (London, 1596).

[16]   'Valentine Leigh'. Norden refers to the author of *The moste profitable and commendable science of surueying of lands* (London, 1577, with four more editions by 1596).

[17]   'M. Digges'. Leonard Digges, author of *Tectonicon* (London, 1556) and *Pantometria* (London, 1571); along with his son Tomas, Digges introduced Euclidian geometry and advanced surveying instruments to an English reading public. Richeson discusses Digges' technical innovations in *English Land Measuring*, pp. 52–67.

[18]   As the Surveyor explains, the four figures within each square refer to the numbers of acres (upper-left), roods (upper-right), day works (lower-left), and perches (lower-right). Norden derives this system from Benese's 1537 text (see n. 14, p. 133). Norden's text contains 20 of these tables, the first and last of which have been reproduced as Figs 8 and 9.

[19]   'Country land measurers will cast by memory'.

[20]   'Casting by the parts of money'. A *shilling* had the value of 12 pence, or one-twentieth of a pound. A *mark*— a unit of measure, not a minted coin—was equal in value to two-thirds of a pound. (Also see n. 4, p. 194.) In using monetary denominations to determine

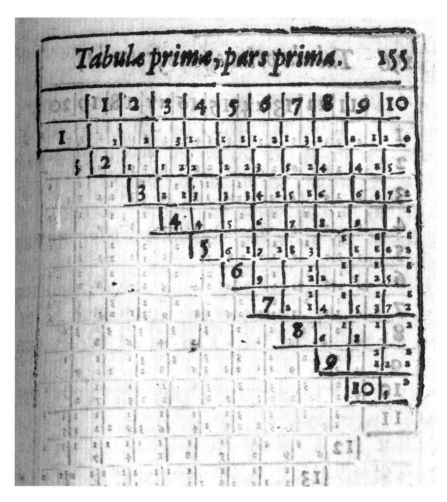

Fig. 7   Table for calculating the size of a plot of land; from *The Surveiors Dialogue* (1618), p. 155.

land size, the mark was made equivalent to an acre and served as a common denominator for calculations. In another text that features a surveyor engaging in a dialogue, Edward Worsop is forced to resort to this simpler accounting system in order to explain how to calculate the size of a plot of land: see *A discoverie of sundrie errors and faults daily committed by Landemeaters, ignorant of Arithmetike and Geometrie* (London, 1582), sig. C3v.

174 Tabulæ quartæ, pars octaua.

	71	72	73	74	75	76	77	78	79	80
61	27	27	27	28	28	28	29	29	30	30
62	27	27	28	28	29	29	29	30	31	31
63	27	28	28	29	29	29	30	30	31	31
64	28	28	29	29	30	30	30	31	31	32
65	28	29	29	30	30	30	31	31	32	32
66	29	29	30	30	20	31	31	32	32	33
67	29	30	30	30	31	31	32	32	33	33
68	30	30	31	30	31	32	32	33	33	34
69	30	31	30	31	32	32	33	33	34	34
70	31	31	31	32	32	33	33	34	34	35
71	31	31	32	32	33	33	34	34	35	31
72		32	32	33	33	34	34	35	35	36
73			33	33	34	34	35	35	36	35
74				34	34	36	35	36	36	37
75					35	35	36	36	37	37
76						36	36	37	37	38
77							37	37	38	39
78								38	38	39
79									39	39
80										40

Bayly.

Fig. 8   Table for calculating the size of a plot of land; from *The Surveiors Dialogue* (1618), p. 174.

to great portions and many parcels. And therefore, for my part, I could willingly embrace these tables for my ease, and leave this accompt by money unto such as have not the use of learning to aid their memories.

Surveyor   I have observed, that many unlearned men have better and more retentive memories than have some Scholars.

Bailiff   So have I noted, and I know some, that will by memory do very much, and no doubt, the reason is, because Scholars do commit their memories to the pen;[21] where such as have not the use of the pen, must use the memory only, which being fed with continual pondering the things they delight in, becomes as a Calendar of their accounts.[22] King *Cyrus* could name all his soldiers by memory. And *Pliny* reporteth of *Mithridates*, that having under his government 22 kingdoms, or nations, he could speak all their languages, and understand any tongue without an interpreter.[23] And *Scipio* could remember the names of the soldiers of all the Roman army.

Surveyor   Use memory, and have the use of memory, either Scholars or unlearned: if they use not their memories, they can make little use of their memories. On the other side, he that imprinteth too many things in his memory, shall, and some have often times wished, they could not remember so well,[24] and that they had the art of forgetting, to clear the memory of that they would not retain in memory; for many times a fresh and free memory heapeth up so many things in his thought, that it breedeth such confusion, that what it should indeed retain is often confounded with that which it would forget.

Bailiff   I wish therefore that my memory could retain according to occasion, to forget things whereof I have no necessary use, and to remember things expedient; yet surely, although the thought can apprehend but one object at one instant, the memory may well apprehend and retain many things. But, Sir, omitting this, I entreat you to shew me the use of these Tables which you have shewed me.

Surveyor   The use is very plain and easy: propound you a number of perches, the length and breadth of a ground.[25]

Bailiff   If a piece of ground be in length 52 perches, and in breadth 26, where and how shall I find the content in the Tables?

---

21   'All Scholars have not best memories'.
22   'Admirable memories of some great persons'.
23   Mithridates VI, King of Pontus (132–63 BC). Norden derives these three anecdotes from Pliny the Elder's *Historia Naturalis* [Natural History], vol. 7, Book XXIV (H. Rackham [trans.], Loeb Classical Library [Cambridge, MA, 1956], p. 88).
24   'Some would forget, and cannot'.
25   'The use of the former Tables'.

Surveyor   Look the third Table, the fourth part of the Table, in the upper rank whereof in the third Column, you shall find 52. Then look in the first Column for [25]. Then refer your finger and eye towards the right hand, till you come right under 52, and that square answers the content to be thus:[26]

Bailiff   What mean you by making the figures in the angles of the square?

Surveyor   Because the four angles do demonstrate the Acres and parts of an acre. The upper angle on the left hand shews the Acres; the upper angle on the right hand, the roods; the lower angle on the left hand, the day works; and the lower angle on the right hand, the odd perches.

Bailiff   This is very easy. But I see there are no figures in the two angles on the right hand, neither above nor below.

Surveyor   When it falleth so out, that there are none of the denominations found in the number, then his place is left blank.

Bailiff   Then this above said quantity is 8 acre and 5 day's works, which is twenty perches, and twenty perches is half a Rood.

Surveyor   You are right.

Bailiff   Then if the number of perches be less, I must seek them in the lesser Tables; if greater, in the greater.

Surveyor   You must do so.

Bailiff   Yet there resteth one scruple in my mind, which, if it should happen before I be resolved, would breed a great doubt, and therefore I am bold to ask it. That is, if the length of a ground be more perches than is expressed in any of the Tables, how shall I find it, when no Table reacheth so far?

Surveyor   You do well to cast all doubts. If the length be more than the tables will yield, whereof indeed the most is four score perches,[27] take first 80 perches out of the whole sum, and then seeking the breadth in the Table as before is shewed, you shall find the content of that part. Then if the breadth be more than the remnant of

---

[26]   Norden is referring to the table on page 164 of the 1618 edition, which has not been reproduced in this edition.

[27]   'How to find the quantity, when the number of perches exceed any table in the book'.

the length, let the breadth be the length, and the remnant of the length the breadth. And seek them likewise in the Tables, and what ariseth of both the numbers, add together: as, for example, a ground is 119 perches in length, and 67 in breadth; the whole length is not in the Tables to be found; then I find 80, and that is the length, and 67 the breadth, which the Table sheweth to be 33–2–0–0. There remaineth of the whole length 39, which is a lesser number than the breadth; therefore I make 39 the breadth, and 67 the length, which the Table sheweth to be 16–1–3–1; which added to the first number 33–2–0–0, maketh in the whole 49–3–3–1.

Bailiff   I see this Table will serve for the finding of the quantity of any sum, and I do understand it well. But I pray you, what Table is that you have here?

Surveyor   A necessary Table for some purposes. It sheweth how to lay out a just acre of land, the length or breadth being given.

Bailiff   Indeed, it is a necessary Table, for every man cannot upon the sudden; for, I take it, it is very hard without Arithmetic to lay out a just Acre to every length or breadth.

Surveyor   This can indeed hardly be done by guess; it requireth Art.

Bailiff   This is the Table; I pray you shew me the use of it.

Surveyor   The use of this Table is only to be required when a man is suddenly to set forth an Acre of land limited in length or breadth, how far it shall extend. As, for example, there is a piece of land containing many Acres, and there are to be set out of this 1, 2, 3, 4, or more Acres. First, the length must be considered. If the length be 77 perches: find that in the first Column of the Table, and right against it, you shall find the breadth to be two perches, one foot, four inches, which maketh an Acre.

Bailiff   But where you say I shall find the length in the first Column of the Table, it is in the head of the Column noted for the breadth.

Surveyor   It is so indeed, for that Column may be reputed to contain both the length and breadth.

Bailiff   How can that be?

Surveyor   Until the breadth do exceed the length, it may be said the Column of breadth. But when the breadth surmounteth the length, the length may be said the breadth.

Bailiff   I understand you: reason will observe that, without serious instruction. But this Table, I see, extendeth but to the length and breadth of one Acre: if a man be occasioned to lay out more, he is as far to seek, as if he had no Table at all.

Bredth. Perches broad.	Length of an Acre. Perches long, & their parts.	Feete, & their parts.	Bredth. Perches broad.	Length of an Acre. Perches long, & their parts.	Feete & their parts.
1	160	—	21	$7\frac{1}{2}$	$2\frac{2}{12}$
2	80		22	$7\frac{1}{4}$	$\frac{4}{12}$
3	$53\frac{1}{4}$	$1\frac{1}{2}$	23	$6\frac{3}{4}$	$3\frac{2}{12}$
4	40		24	$6\frac{1}{2}$	$2\frac{8}{12}$
5	32		25	$6\frac{1}{4}$	$2\frac{6}{12}$
6	$26\frac{1}{2}$	3	26	6	$2\frac{7}{12}$
7	$22\frac{3}{4}$	$1\frac{11}{12}$	27	$5\frac{3}{4}$	3
8	20		28	$5\frac{1}{2}$	3
9	$17\frac{3}{4}$	6	29	$5\frac{1}{2}$	$\frac{4}{12}$
10	16		30	$5\frac{1}{4}$	$\frac{4}{12}$
11	$14\frac{1}{2}$	9	31	5	$2\frac{7}{12}$
12	$13\frac{1}{4}$	$1\frac{1}{2}$	32	5	
13	$12\frac{1}{4}$	1	33	$4\frac{3}{4}$	$1\frac{8}{12}$
14	$11\frac{1}{4}$	3	34	$4\frac{1}{3}$	$3\frac{4}{12}$
15	$10\frac{1}{2}$	3	35	$4\frac{1}{2}$	$1\frac{2}{12}$
16	10		36	$4\frac{1}{4}$	$3\frac{2}{12}$
17	$9\frac{1}{4}$	$2\frac{7}{12}$	37	$4\frac{1}{4}$	$1\frac{3}{12}$
18	$8\frac{3}{4}$	1	38	4	$3\frac{5}{12}$
19	$8\frac{1}{4}$	3	39	4	$1\frac{8}{12}$
20	8		40	4	

N 3   Bredth.

Fig. 9   Table for converting length and breadth of acreage; from *The Surveiors Dialogue* (1618), p. 183.

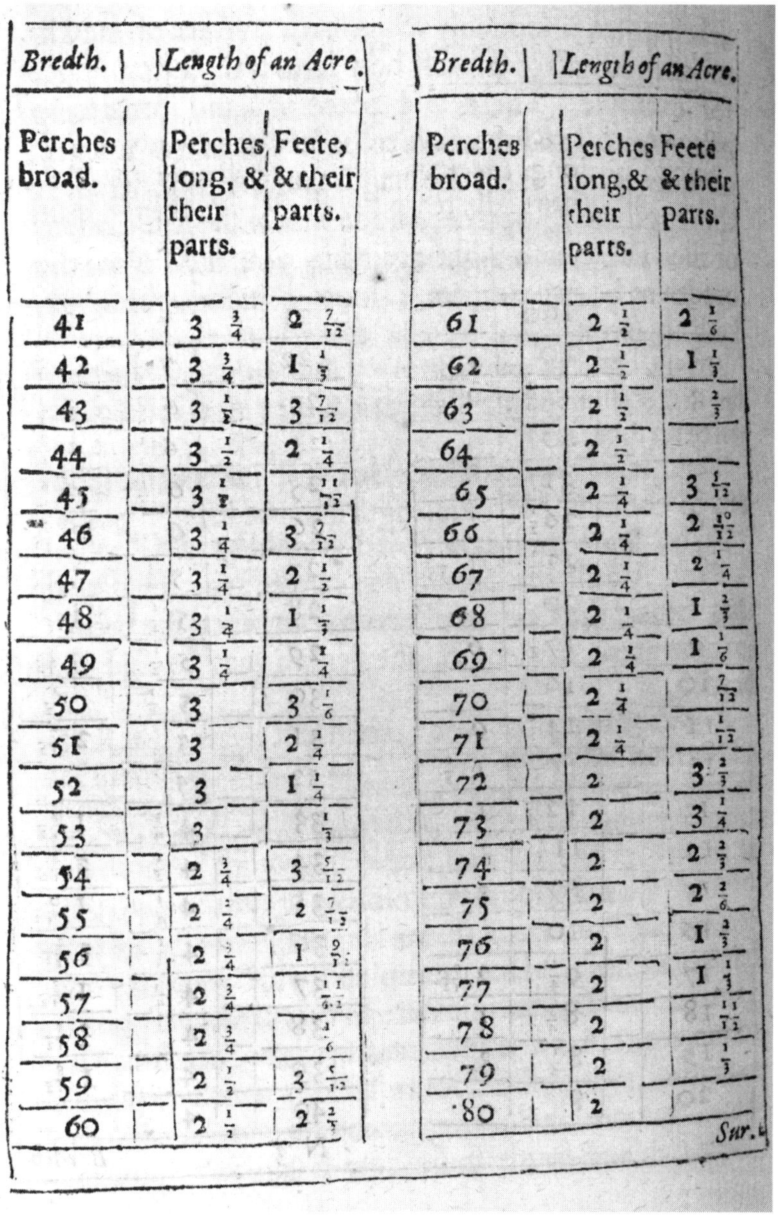

Breadth.	Length of an Acre.		Breadth.	Length of an Acre.	
Perches broad.	Perches long, & their parts.	Feete, & their parts.	Perches broad.	Perches long,& their parts.	Feete & their parts.
41	3 3/4	2 7/12	61	2 1/2	2 1/6
42	3 3/4	1 1/3	62	2 1/2	1 1/3
43	3 1/2	3 7/12	63	2 1/2	2/3
44	3 1/2	2 1/4	64	2 1/2	
45	3 1/2	11/12	65	2 1/4	3 5/12
46	3 1/4	3 2/13	66	2 1/4	2 10/12
47	3 1/4	2 1/2	67	2 1/4	2 1/4
48	3 1/2	1 1/3	68	2 1/4	1 2/3
49	3 1/4	1/4	69	2 1/4	1 1/6
50	3	3 1/6	70	2 1/4	2/12
51	3	2 1/4	71	2 1/4	1/12
52	3	1 1/4	72	2	3 2/3
53	3	1/3	73	2	3 1/4
54	2 3/4	3 5/12	74	2	2 2/3
55	2 1/4	2 7/12	75	2	2 2/6
56	2 3/4	1 2/3	76	2	1 2/3
57	2 3/4	1 1/12	77	2	1 1/3
58	2 3/4	1/6	78	2	11/12
59	2 1/2	3 5/12	79	2	1/3
60	2 1/2	2 2/3	80	2	

Sur.

Fig. 10   Table for converting length and breadth of acreage; from *The Surveiors Dialogue* (1618), p. 184.

Surveyor   Not so: for if you observe it, you are to double, treble, or quadreble the length or breadth, as you have occasion. As, for example,[28] if you would lay out 3 Acres, and admit your length be 48 perches, which to make one Acre is to have in breadth three perches and a quarter, 1 foot and 4 inches; which three perches, one-quarter and one foot, and one third being taken three times, make nine perches, one quarter and four foot:[29] and thus of length and breadth, how many Acres soever are to be set out.

Bailiff   I see, indeed, this Table may serve by due observation for the laying out of any quantity. But now, Sir, there is one thing which will breed some difficulty, for the difference of the quantities of Acres is great in divers Countries by the custom of the Countries:[30] for by the custom of some Countries, the measure is 24 foot to the Pole, in some 20, in some 18, and yet the statute alloweth only 16-1/2 foot.

Surveyor   You say truly. Yet when a *Surveyor* undertaketh to lay out the land in any of these, he is to measure it by the standard chain, that is, by the chain of 16-1/2 foot.

Bailiff   But the Country people, peradventure, will be obstinate, and will have the custom measure, because they will have the content of their land seem the less; and so shall they rent their ground more easily, having it by the greater measure.

Surveyor   That is but a conceit that they shall have it the cheaper: for admit that an Acre were as big as the *Cornish Acre*,[31] near 140 statute Acres. Will any man think a Lord or his officers so simple as to grant the same, because it hath but the name of an Acre, as he would let the statute Acre? It is nothing to the Lord what measure they take; for he must, and will apportion the price, according to the quantity and quality, be the Acre great or little.[32]

Bailiff   But Woods are always measured with the Pole of 18 foot.[33]

Surveyor   It is as the Buyer and Seller agree; for there is no such matter decreed by any statute, neither is any bound of necessity.

Bailiff   Why is it then in use?

---

[28]   'How to lay out many Acres by the former Table'.

[29]   Norden refers to 'Length of an Acre' as listed in Fig. 10 for a plot with a breadth of 48 perches.

[30]   'Perches divers in divers Countries'. By *Countries*, Norden refers to English counties.

[31]   'A Cornish Acre'.

[32]   'The great or small measure, all one to the Lords'.

[33]   'Wood measure'.

Surveyor   I take it, because in underwoods (for they are they that are thus measured for sale), have in many places sundry void places and gales,[34] wherein groweth little or no wood, or very thin. And to supply these defects, the buyer claimeth this supply by measure.

Bailiff   The difference is but a foot and a half in a pole, which is nothing.

Surveyor   Yes, it is something, for in every 5-1/2 Acre, it gaineth above an Acre.[35]

Bailiff   So might I have been deceived, for truly I did not think it had gotten so much. But, I pray, whence is the word *Acre* derived?

Surveyor   As I take it, from the Latin word *Actus*, a deed: a day's work of a plow, in tilling the ground.[36]

Bailiff   It may be so, for a plow will ayre[37] an Acre a day.

Surveyor   We read in 1 Samuel 14:14 that half an Acre of land was as much as two Oxen could plow; and that is it which the *Burgundians*, and others in *France*, do call *Journaux*, which, I take, is as much as *Ingerum* in Latin,[38] which containeth as much as two Oxen or Horse can till in a day: in length 240 foot, and in breadth 120, which seemeth near to agree with our Acre.

Bailiff   We have four or five Horses, or two or three yoke of Oxen, to till an Acre a day, where the former *Ingerum* hath but two. But the French have another kind of *Acre*, which they call an *Arpent*;[39] which amongst them differeth in quantity, as ours do differ in several kinds of Poles, and their *Arpent* is 100 Pole, howsoever the Poles do differ. One Pole they have, which containeth 22 foot, and that is called *The King's Arpent*, and used most in measuring of wood:[40] another of 20 foot, another of 19-1/2 foot, another of 18 foot. So that indeed their *Arpent* doth little differ in the several quantities from our Acre.

Surveyor   I observe one thing by the way, because you speak of *the King's Arpent* in *France*, and other measures there. I have seen in ancient Records, and books of *Survey* of great antiquity, which do shew, that the *Lord's demesnes* were measured

---

34   'Why Woods are measured with the 18 foot pole'; *gales*   bare spots.
35   'Great difference between the 18 and 16-1/2 pole'.
36   'Whence an Acre taketh name'.
37   *ayre*   plough.
38   *Ingerum*   a unit of land slightly larger than two Acres.
39   'An Arpent, or French Acre'. An arpent is 100 square perches, varying in size from less than an acre to an acre and one-quarter.
40   'The King's Arpent'.

with a Pole of 20 foot, which was called *major mensura*, and the customary by a Pole, called *mensura minor*,[41] which I take to be but 16-1/2 foot, though in some places the Tenants claim the 18 foot Pole.

Bailiff   Then, let me ask you another question: You shall shortly come into a Manor of my Landlord's, where the Copies do speak of an *Acre ware*, or *war*,[42] which I never could find or hear what it truly meant, nor what quantity it containeth. But the Tenants make good use, in their conceits, of the name: for under that title, they will carry away 2, 3, 6, 10 Acres; though they lie in 20 parcels, it is all but an *Acre war*; and yet I have seen some, under that title, not three Roods of ordinary measure. How comes it to pass, think you?

Surveyor   To speak truly, I cannot precisely tell you, for I have seen the like, especially in *Suffolk, Norfolk* and *Essex*. But, as I conjecture, it is a measured Acre, as an Acre by warrant. *Acra warr*, briefly written, an approved Acre, and the true sense being lost by time, they make it like a figure of wax, to draw it more or less as will best serve their purpose.

Bailiff   I have also seen Land, under the name of *Molland*,[43] and I have heard much disputation about the *etymon* of the word: some hold it to be *de Mollendo*, of custom grinding at the Lord's Mill; some otherwise, and leave it uncertain.

Surveyor   There is no difficulty in it: for *Molland* is upland, or high ground, and the contrary is *Fenland*, low ground,[44] a matter ordinary, where they use to distinguish between these two kinds. But we will leave these ambiguous words, and so take my leave, and betake me to my task.

Bailiff   Sir, I will not be troublesome unto you; only, when you have cast up your particulars, and finished your business of this Survey, I will be bold to trouble you again, to see what every man holdeth, and the value both of the customary leased lands, and the Lord's demesnes. May I be so bold?

Surveyor   It is a thing which I seldom consent unto; for I must tell you this, he is no true Surveyor for the Lord, that will make the same known to strangers.[45] I have undertaken the business for the Lord, not for strangers. And as he putteth me in trust, so will I be secret in these things; and therefore I pray you in this pardon me.

------

[41]   'Major and minor mensura'. A Lord's demesnes were measured with a pole of 20 feet (*major mensura*), while the customary lands of tenants were measured by a pole of 16-1/2 feet (*minor mensura*).

[42]   *Acre war*   an 'approved acre'.

[43]   'Molland'.

[44]   'Molland and Fenland contrary'.

[45]   'A Surveyor must be secret for his Lord'.

Bailiff   You shew me reason, and I was too rash. But, by your leave, how shall the Jury give their allowance to your doings (as you say, you will acquaint them with them) unless you deliver every particular plainly?

Surveyor   You must think there are some things which may be public, as the names of grounds, the owners, their estates, butts, bounds, and such like, and their answers to the Articles; and some things private, and to be concealed, as the quantities, and supposed yearly values. These are for the Lord.

Bailiff   I thought I should have seen the whole method of your collections and observations, to the end, that seeing I have waded thus far into the Art, I might be somewhat instructed how to have marshaled and engrossed my Book when such a work were done.

Surveyor   Every man in that case may use his own method; yet if you be desirous to see an exact course, in that kind, I must refer you to the most commendable work of [Master] *Valentine Leigh*,[46] whom in that if you imitate,[47] you shall tread the right way to the mark.

Bailiff   Then I shall only remain thankful unto you, for your patience and pains, and be studious evermore, to do you any service.

Surveyor   I thank you. I have a desire to have some communication with you, when I have passed over this little work in hand.

Bailiff   Willingly, Sir, I will give my diligent attendance. But I pray you, Sir, in what especially do you purpose to confer with me? To pose me, I fear, whether I have forgotten that you taught me.

Surveyor   Not so: but you being Bailiff of this Manor (about which I have, as you see, taken a serious perambulation) have not, as I persuade me, been so careful and provident for the Lord's profit, as you may; for there be divers grounds, which by good and industrious husbandry would be much bettered, as I will tell you further, at our next leisurable meeting. For this time, fare you well.

The end of the fourth Book.

---

[46]   *Valentine Leigh*   see n. 16, p. 134.

[47]   'M. Leigh's book of Surveying'.

THE SURVEYOR'S
DIALOGUE, SHEWING
the different natures of Grounds,
how they may be employed, how they
may be bettered, reformed,
and amended.

THE FIFTH BOOK.

Bailiff   I perceive, Sir, you are now at some leisure; you are walking abroad to take the air, after your long and tedious sitting, and I think indeed you are weary.

Surveyor   I am somewhat weary; but a man that undertaketh a business, must apply it, and not be weary, or at least, not seem to be so.

Bailiff   But methinks you apply it too hard; you might sometimes ease you, and give yourself to some game for recreation.

Surveyor   They that are idle, may take their pleasures in gaming; but such as are called to live by their labors, and have a delight therein, do (as all men ought) take pleasure, and think it a pleasing sport, to get means by their lawful labors to live.[1]

Bailiff   You say truth indeed: for the old Proverb is, *Dulcis labor cum lucro.*[2] But I pray you, [whither] walk you?

Surveyor   Into this next piece of ground.

Bailiff   Nay, it is an ill ground to walk in, for it is full of bogs, a very Moorish plot, overcome with weeds, and, indeed, is of no use.

Surveyor   I therefore go to see it, and worthily to [tax] you the Lord's Bailiff, of remissness and negligent looking unto the Lord's profit, suffering such a piece of ground as this, to lie idle and waste, and to foster nothing but Bogs, Sedges,[3]

---

[1]   'Labor that lawfully gets, is a game of delight'.
[2]   *Dulce ... lucro* ['reward sweetens labor'].
[3]   *Sedges*   coarse grass found in wetlands.

Flags,[4] Rushes, and such superfluous and noisome weeds, where, if it were duly drained, and carefully husbanded, it would make good meadow in short time.

Bailiff   I think that impossible; for there be many such plots you see in this level, and in many men's occupations, and some of them think themselves good husbands, I can tell you; and they see, that it is a matter of difficulty and charge, and therefore they think, and so do I, that it is to no purpose to begin to amend it.

Surveyor   I think they have more land than they or you have experience how to convert to best use: they their own, and you your Lord's.

Bailiff   If you be so skillful, I pray tell me for the Lord's profit how it may be amended.

Surveyor   If you be ignorant how to amend it, and simply desire to learn, it were a fault in me to conceal from you the means how to do it. But if you be careless or willful, it were good to leave you in your ignorance, and to inform the Lord of your unfitness, that a more skillful might take the place.

Bailiff   That is the worst that you can do. But I trust I may be a Bailiff good enough, and yet want one part of that which my place requireth to perform.

Surveyor   Even as well as a horse may be said to travail well enough, and yet lack one leg.

Bailiff   I would be sorry that comparison should hold; for then I could not but confess, that I were a lame Officer, as there be in other kinds, even of your own profession many. But I am not only not willful, but I am willing to learn; and I do not think any man so absolute in his place and calling, but he may learn some point of his function,[5] if at least he will confess his own imperfections.

Surveyor   Whether he verbally confess them or not, the execution will bewray them, and the world will observe them in him by the fruits. And therefore it behooveth all such as undertake and enter into any office or function, to examine the duties appertaining to such an office, and finding his fitness or unfitness, to perform it, so to leave or take (though few stagger at any). If his ability be weak, reason and duty may move him to seek expedient knowledge, lest he shame himself, and slander the place he is in, deceive his master, and wrong the people. And therefore I wish you to ask advice, not only in this case, but in all other belonging to your charge. For as it is commendable to know more and more, so is it no shame to ask often.

---

4   *Flags*   rocks
5   'All men may learn'.

Bailiff   I pray you then tell me, Sir, how must this piece of ground be handled, to be made meadow (as you say it will be made) or good pasture.

Surveyor   It must be drained.

Bailiff   If that be all, I think, I can say it is to little purpose, for I have made trenches to that end, as you may see where and how. But it became little or nothing the better, and therefore I think, cost will be but cast away upon it.

Surveyor   It is a true Proverb: *Ignorance is an enemy to Art and experience.*[6] What you did, it may be, you had good will to do the Lord service in it, but the course you took was not in the right kind. It is not enough to make such ditches, as appeareth you have done: they are too few and too wide. Neither did you rightly observe the fall of the water.

Bailiff   That were hard to be done in such a place as this, where the water hath no fall at all; neither is the water seen much, as you see, but it is the moistness of the earth that mars the land.

Surveyor   But the moisture comes by water, and the water is swallowed up in this spongy ground, and lies unseen; yet if you mark it well, you may observe which ways it rills:[7] for, as you see, though this plot of ground be very level in appearance, yet if it were tried by a just level, it would be found declining towards yonder forlorn brook, which you see is stopped up with weeds, that it permitteth not the water convenient pass. Therefore the first work is, to rid the Sewer or chief water-course, and then shall you see that the grounds near the cleansed brook will become more dry, by the moisture soaking into the Sewer; then make your other drains, using discretion therein, namely, in cutting them straight, from the most boggy places to the main brook, every of them as it were parallely; then cut you some other drains sloping, which may carry the water into these first drains, which again will convey it into the main.

Bailiff   You see the ditches that I made; they were broad enough and deep, fit to convey much water, yet they did no good: Can you prescribe a better form?

Surveyor   Your ditches, for the form, were too broad, and (as it seems) too deep, and that makes the water to stand in them, and, being broad above and narrow in the bottom, makes the loose earth to fall in and choke the ditch. But if you will make profitable drains, you must first observe how the water will run in them, for so will it appear presently, and to make them as narrow above as at the bottom, which at

---

6   'Ignorance enemy to Art'. Norden cites the Latin proverb, 'art has no enemy except experience'.

7   *rills*   flows in a small stream.

the most must not be above one foot and a half broad, and the crust of the earth will hold that the earth fall not in again. So will it in short time make it appear, that the moisture will decay, and the grounds become more dry; and as it becomes freed of that superfluous moisture, so will the weeds that are nourished by it begin to wither as they are deprived of their nouriture, which is too much water, which breedeth too much cold, and too much cold is the life of such weeds as increase in this ground;[8] and therefore the weeds should be often cut down in the spring time, and by that means they will consume, and better grass come in their stead; and the better, if cattle feed the ground, upon the draining, as bare as may be.

Bailiff   But the drains you speak of, may be dangerous for cattle, especially for sheep and lambs.

Surveyor   Not if they be kept always cleansed and open, that sheep and cattle may see them; for the bigger sort may step over them, and the lesser may have little bridges of the same crust, by undermining the earth some three or four foot, that the water may pass under.[9]

Bailiff   Indeed, if the crust of the earth will bear it, this course is necessary. But there is much land in England lost for want of draining, as the *Fens*[10] and low grounds in Lincolnshire, Cambridgeshire, Norfolk, and other places, which I did think impossible ever to be made dry, by the art and industry of man.[11] And yet, as I hear, much of it is made lately firm ground, by the skill of one *Captain Lovell*, and by M. *William Englebert* an excellent [*Engineer*], and others.[12] And truly it is much to their commendation, and to the common good of the inhabitants near[, and to the whole commonweal]. But these grounds are not drained by such means as you speak of.

Surveyor   Indeed, the drains are of unlike quantity, but like in quality: one and the same rule of reason doth work both the one and the other effect. But to say truly unto thee, the people of those Countries (especially the poorer sort) where this

---

[8]   'Cold ground breeds weeds'.

[9]   'Bridges over drains'.

[10]   'The Fens'.

[11]   The drainage of the Fens was one of the largest improvement projects of the early seventeenth century. But even though these works were authorized by statute in 1600, and surveyed in 1604, most ended in failure while others provoked popular resistance (H.C. Darby, *The Draining of the Fens* [Cambridge, 1956], esp. pp. 28–38; Clive Holmes, 'Drainers and Fenmen: The Problem of Popular Political Consciousness in the Seventeenth Century', in Anthony Fletcher and John Stevenson [eds], *Order and Disorder in Early Modern England* [Cambridge, 1985], pp. 166–95).

[12]   'Captain Lovell. M. Wiliam Englebert'. Captain Thomas Lovell's efforts to drain the Fenlands of Lincolnshire were countered by the active opposition of local residents, who rioted and destroyed dikes in 1602 (Thirsk, *Rural Economy*, p. 140).

kind of public benefit is thus gotten, had rather have want by their fathers' error, than to reap good and more plenty by other men's art and charge. And in their conceits they had rather catch a *Pike*, than feed an Ox.

Bailiff They are either very unwise, or very willful. But (no doubt) authority is above such country willfulness, and doth or may enjoin them, for the Common weale, to consent and yield all aid in the business. But if they will needs fish and fowl, and refuse rich relief, we will leave them to their wills, till reason in themselves, or compulsion, bring them to a more general desire of so great a blessing.

Surveyor Let it be so: What *Alders* are in the next ground?

Bailiff They are the Lord's too, Sir; but the ground is so rotten, that no cattle can feed in it.

Surveyor The *Alder* tree is enemy to all grounds where it grows;[13] for the root thereof is of that nature, that it draweth to it so much moisture to nourish itself, as the ground near it is good for no use.

Bailiff Do you think this ground would be good, if the trees were gone?

Surveyor Yes: for commonly the ground is good enough of itself, only it is impaired by this kind of wood; and therefore if the cause were taken away, the effect would die.

Bailiff Then will I cause them to be stocked up.

Surveyor Nay, first it behooveth you to consider, whether it be expedient or not; for although this tree be not friendly to pasture, meadow, or arable land, yet it yields her due commodity too,[14] without whose aid, in some places, where other wood is scant, men can hardly husband their lands without this. For of it they make many necessary implements of husbandry, as Ladders, Rails, Hop-poles, Plow-stuff, and handles for many tools, besides firing.

Bailiff If it be so commodious, it is not only good to stock them, but expedient to cherish them, and where none are, to plant.

Surveyor There is great difference between *necessity* and the *superabundance* of every necessary. For *Want* is a great commander,[15] and enforceth often times [to make proof of improbable experiments, by which they get experience], and in

---

[13] 'The Alder tree enemy to all grounds'.
[14] 'The Alder necessary for many purposes'.
[15] 'Necessity a commander'.

many places they desire and search for that which *Will* in the time of plenty merely neglecteth. And therefore where none of this kind of wood groweth (the place destitute of other means, and fit for this kind of commodity), *Will* may be forced to give place to *occasion*, as in other things.

Bailiff   I have heard that this kind of wood is also good to make the foundations of buildings, in rivers, fens, and standing waters, as also piles for many purposes in moorish and wet grounds.

Surveyor   It is true, this kind of wood is of greater continuance in watery places than any other timber;[16] for it is observed, that in these places it seldom or never rots.

Bailiff   It loved the water and moisture well in growing, and therefore it brooketh it the better, being laid in it. But I think the Fir-tree is much of the same nature; for I have seen infinite many of them, taken out of the earth in a moorish ground in Shropshire, between the Lordships of Oswestry[17] and [Ellesmere], which (as it is supposed) have [lain] in the moist earth ever since the Flood,[18] and being daily taken up, the people make walking staves and pikes of them, firm and strong, and use the chips instead of candles in poor houses; so fat is the wood to this day, and the smell also strong and sweet [the like is found in Lincolnshire in many places].

Surveyor   I know the [places] well, and I have seen *pales* made of an Oak taken out of the same ground, of the same continuance, firm and strong, black as *Ebony*, and might have fitly been employed to better uses; and I take it, that most wood will last long under the earth, where it never taketh the open air. But the wood now most in use for the purposes abovesaid is *Alder* and *Elm*.

Bailiff   May a man sow the seeds of the *Alder*?

Surveyor   It beareth a kind of seed, yet some have affirmed the contrary.[19] But the seeds will hardly grow by art, though the plant by nature may. The branches of the tree and the roots, are aptest to grow, if they be set so as the water and moisture may be above the plant, for it delighteth only in the moistest grounds. Is not this next close the Lord's, called *Broad-meadow*?

Bailiff   It is so: I perceive you had a good memory, being but once, and so long since, upon the ground.

---

[16]   'Alder good to make Piles'.

[17]   Norden had surveyed the liberties of Oswestry, Shropshire in 1602 (Kitchen, 'Cosmo-choro-polygrapher', p. 387).

[18]   'Fir-trees [lain] in the ground since the flood'.

[19]   'Alder hath no seed'.

Surveyor   It is most necessary for a Surveyor to remember what he hath observed, and to consider well the natures and qualities of all kinds of grounds, and to inform the Lord, of the means how to better his estate by lawful means, especially in bettering his own *demesnes*. So shall he the less to surcharge his Tenants by uncharitable exactions. And forasmuch as of all other grounds none are (of their own nature) so profitable, and less chargeable, as meadow grounds,[20] which are always ready to benefit the owner, summer and winter, they especially are to be regarded.

Bailiff   That is true indeed, and peradventure it takes the name of the readiness; for we call it in Latin *Pratum*, as if it were *semper paratum*,[21] either with the fleece for hay, or with the pasture to seed; and this meadow wherein now we are, is the best meadow that I know, and I think for sweetness and burthen there is not a better in England.

Surveyor   You do well to advance the credit of the Lord's land, and you speak, I think, as you conceive, because you are not acquainted with the meadows upon *Dove Bank*, in *Tan Dean*, upon *Severn side, [Allensmore], the Lord's meadow in Crediton*, and the meadows about the *Welsh-pool*,[22] and especially a meadow not far from Salisbury, near a Bourn under the plain, that bears grass yearly above 10 foot long; though many think it incredible, yet it is apparent that the grass is commonly 16 foot long. It is made shorter before cattle can feed on it, and when the cattle have [fed their fill], hogs are made fat with the remnant, namely, with the knots and sap of the grass.

Bailiff   This is the strangest thing that [ever] I heard of, but surely these meadows are made so good by Art; but naturally, I think, this may match the best of them.

Surveyor   Indeed, meadows very mean by nature, may be made excellent by charge, but they will decay, unless they be always relieved. But these that I speak of, require little or no help at the owner's hand, only the aid of these rivers and fat of the hills overflowing, do feed them fat, gives great burden, and very sweet.

Bailiff   These yearly overflowings of fat waters after floods, no doubt are very beneficial, as appeareth by the [annual] and yearly overflowing of the river *Nilus* in *Egypt*,[23] which maketh the adjacent grounds so fat and fruitful, as they be famous through the world for their fertility, and was allotted to Joseph's brethren in Egypt for their habitation.

---

[20]   'Meadows'.

[21]   'Pratum, quasi semper paratum' ['A meadow, just as if it were always prepared'].

[22]   'Best meadows in England'. The Surveyor names locales in Staffordshire (Dove Bank), Herefordshire (Allensmore), Devon (Crediton), and the Anglo-Welsh border (Tan Dean, Welsh-pool).

[23]   'Rivers overflowing good. Nilus in Egypt, Joshua 3:15'.

Surveyor   You speak of a matter wonderful in the conceits of some, that the river should so overflow in the summer, and yet it never rains in those parts at any time of the year.

Bailiff   So I have heard indeed; [and *Leo Africanus, Vadianus, Zieglerus*,[24] and other famous writers report it, as I have heard;] and that the floods grow in the heat of the year, about harvest, between July and September, with the snow melting, that falls in the wintertime, among the Mountains.

Surveyor   We have in England matter more strange, as the river near Chichester in Sussex called the *Lavant*,[25] which in the winter is dry, and in the driest summer full to her banks; so is the *Leam*, a River in Berkshire, near *Lambourn*.

Bailiff   That is strange indeed: one studious in natural Philosophy could tell the cause of this.

Surveyor   I take it to be, because they are only fed with springs, which run only when they are at the highest, namely, in the summer, when the Sun is highest. And that also is the reason, why many *Bourns* break out of the earth in sundry places,[26] as we may read it hath done sometimes near *Mergate*[27] in Hertfordshire, corruptly called *Market*, and near *Croydon* in Surrey, near *Hangleton* and *Patcham* in *Sussex*, and in many other places in this Realm, which break forth suddenly out of the driest [hills], in summer, and run for a time in such abundance, as it would drive many Mills. Not yearly, but in 6, 8, or 10 years.

Bailiff   Because you speak of *Hangleton*, I can assure you there is a Well, that sometimes yieldeth water, which when you wash your hands with, it smelleth like violets.[28] Some would (no doubt) give much for such excellent water.

Surveyor   Though the smell be sweet, I hold not the water so wholesome; for it is in itself *levis putredo*,[29] a kind of putrefaction, which, passing lightly by the sense of smelling, deceiveth the sense, which if it took a more serious note of it, would find it a kind of stink,[30] as your purest Musk and Civit: the more nearer the sense

---

[24]   Leo Africanus (1488–1554), writer of *A Geographical Historie of Africa* (trans. 1600); Joachim Vadianus (1484–1551), author of *Epitome trium terrae partium* (Zurich, 1534); Jacobus Zieglerus (or Ziegler) (1470–1549), Vienna-based cartographer.

[25]   'The Lavant and the Leam'.

[26]   'Bourns'. The term refers to streams or brooks that break out of chalky ground.

[27]   *Mergate*   Norden also mentions this locale in *Speculi Britaniae Pars. A Description of Hartfordshire* [*sic*] (1598), W.B. Gerish (ed.) (London, 1903), p. 21.

[28]   'Water smelling like Violets'.

[29]   'Levis putredo' ['Slightly rotten'].

[30]   'Sense deceived'.

it cometh, and the more the sense chargeth itself with the whole scent, the more loathsome it will prove. But these are things coming into our talk by the way: let us return to our matter of meadows, the cause of whose goodness is the soil, and overflowing with the most muddy water.

Bailiff   No doubt, it is an admirable help unto them.[31] Nay, I by small experience that have found, can tell you a pretty Paradox: How say you to this? Boggy and spongy ground, whereof we discoursed before, though in [its] own nature it be too moist, yet if it be overflowed with water often, it will settle and become firm; which, howsoever in my poor understanding, it would seem opposite to reason, that water should help watery ground, yet experience findeth it so.

Surveyor   All overflowing waters do bring a slimy and fat substance with them, and leave it behind them, which together with the working of the water, through the spongy ground you speak of, worketh that effect in all grounds where it comes.

Bailiff   But waters cannot be brought into all kinds of boggy grounds, nor into all kinds of Meadows.

Surveyor   No, for there are two sorts of Meadows:[32] low and moist, and upland and dry meadows; of these kinds the low is commonly the best, because they are aptest to receive these falling and swelling waters, which for the most part brings fatness with it; and besides it moisteneth the ground, and makes the grass to grow cheerfully; yet howsoever fat and fruitful they be, continual mowing yearly without intermission, may weaken them, and impair their goodness, and will require some help, unless they be such meadows as I recommended unto you erewhile, that are so fed with fat overflowing waters, as do still maintain them in strength.

Bailiff   Then must the upland meadow, by often and continual sheering,[33] needs decay.

Surveyor   The upland meadows have but the name of meadows;[34] for, indeed, they are but the best pasture grounds laid for hay. And to distinguish between that kind of meadow and pasture ground, or between pasture and arable, is frivolous; for that kind of meadow is most properly pasture, and all pasture grounds may be tilled.[35] For when we say arable, it is as much, as if we said, it is subject to the plough, or land which may be plowed: and why then may not a man say, that which

---

[31]   'Boggy grounds helped by overflowing'.
[32]   'Two sorts of Meadows'.
[33]   *sheering*   clearing.
[34]   'Upland Meadows have but the name'.
[35]   'Hard to distinguish grounds'.

is now pasture, is arable, that is, convenient to be tilled? And, on the contrary, that which is now tilled, may be pasturable, namely, apt to graze and to feed cattle.

Bailiff   You prove that it is superfluous in manner, to distinguish the qualities of grounds.

Surveyor   I confess, a Surveyor may note the quality of every kind, as he findeth it in the time of his perambulation and view. But peradventure, the next year, he that comes to distinguish them, may enter them clean contrary to the former. And therefore it is not amiss, in all such entries, to add the word 'now': as to say, now tilled or now pasture, now used for meadow, unless it be low meadow always mown. But he that shall enter a piece of upland ground (though it be sometimes mown), under the name of meadow, erreth in his entry. But for that, let all men follow their own fancies. But because we speak of upland meadows, we will accept all mowable grounds in that sense. And of such I will first speak. They are either of a clay soil, and so naturally fat or stiff, or a sandy earth, enriched and made fat by industry;[36] and both of these by mowing yearly without intermission, and supply of help, may be so impaired, as it will yield little benefit to the owner. The nature therefore of every ground must be considered: for the upland and high ground may be also watery, and consequently cold and moist, which kind of grounds are generally clay; for a sandy and gravelly ground lying high and depending, is seldom or never found moist by nature but dry and consequently hot. So that all upland grounds are commonly either too cold and moist, or too hot and dry: either of which must have his several help. For as the constitution of a man's body is found by the effects of *fatness, leanness, heat*, and *cold*, so do the earths discover their natures by their fruit, which nature causeth them to bring forth in infinite kinds. The cold and watery grounds yield long but sour and unprofitable grass, rushes, and rank moss, which kind of ground must be cured, if need require, with drains; but commonly these grounds are of clay, and clay will never give way or evacuation to the water, because the ground is hard and stiff, contrary to the open and spongy ground which is thin and open. And therefore the hottest chalk or lime is best to kill the sour grass and unprofitable moss. So is coal-dust ashes, and fine dry sand, and chimney soot, if sufficient quantity can be gotten; and after these things thus laid, it is expedient to give it a tilth[37] or two, and then to let it lie again, if it be to be used for Meadow or Pasture. And for the other grounds which are hot and dry by nature, the contrary is to be used, by using means to cool the heat and to moisten the dryness, and that is, by bestowing some fat and slimy *Marl*[38] upon them, which will much cherish and revive the parched grass, and kill the hungry moss that groweth by the dryness of the earth, as a *scurf* or *tetter*[39] on the body, by

---

[36]   'Meadows of different natures'.

[37]   *tilth*   tilling, plowing.

[38]   *Marl*   clay with deposits of calcium.

[39]   *scurf* and *tetter* are eczema-like inflammations of the skin.

the heat that proceedeth of a salt humor. The natures of these two kinds of grounds are also found out, whether they be cold and moist or hot and dry, by the quantity and quality of their fruits, as the seasons of the year be dry or moist; for that ground that groweth best in a moist year, is hot and dry. The clay ground in a moist year (if it be not too moist) may be also comforted, because in too dry a year, the clay becometh so strongly bound, that the tender grass can hardly make way through the obdurate earth,[40] whereas moderate moisture mollifieth the same, cherisheth the root, and gives way for the grass; and if it have too much moisture, it becometh so slimy, and the roots so drenched, as it turneth the grass into a spiry kind, and that but short, and by the cold that cometh of the too much moisture, it increaseth rushes abundantly, and thick moss. So that it appeareth, that the seasons of the year do either help or hinder the increase of all kinds of grounds, which the art or industry of man cannot prevent. For many times the helps that man useth to assist and help nature do hinder it:[41] as where compost and stable soil is laid upon a dry ground, reserved for grass, if a dry year follow, the heat of the soil and dryness of the year do so impoverish the grass that it yieldeth the owner less increase than if he had bestowed no soil at all; yet men ought not to be remiss in soiling their lands, for if it prevail not in one year, they shall find it at another time very profitable; and for all seasons, I persuade men to make means, where it may be done, to induce out of streets, lands, ways, and ditches, all the water, that by some extraordinary rain passeth through them, into their grounds, by making some little dam or bar to draw them into their grounds;[42] for the matter which this water bringeth with it, is commonly so rich and fat, as it yieldeth a marvelous refection to all the grounds, high or low, into which it may be brought; which kind of husbandry is much used in [Somerset], Devon, and Cornwall, to their admirable advantage, and in some other places here, and there, but not so generally, as in providence men might, for a richer experiment is not neglected.

Bailiff This is a good course, no doubt, in places where it may be put in execution; but as you say, all men are not so provident, and painful, which indeed is a great fault, and wherein I myself I confess, I have been culpable; but I will be more careful as well in that, as in other things, whereof you have put me in mind. And truly I think, there is much profit willfully lost in many places by negligence, want of skill, and sparing of some small charge. You have hitherunto spoken only of upland meadow grounds, but you divided meadows into two sorts: what say you to the second, namely, low meadows? For I have seen and observed as great defects in them, by reason of their too often mowing without rest, as may require some consideration how to repair them; for some of these grounds are as much annoyed by too much moisture, as the upland with the want of it.

---

[40] 'Clay ground'.

[41] 'Helps intended sometimes hinder'.

[42] 'Bringing of street water into grounds profitable'.

Surveyor   For the too much moisture, if it be but in the winter season, and continue but until the middle or end of April, it doth not only no harm, but good;[43] for if you mark and observe it well, you seldom or never see bogs, where the water overflows and stands in the winter time. But if it be more permanent, and of a longer stay, there must be means used for evacuation; for in many places you may perceive certain low places in meadow grounds, where if the water once take a standing, it will cause the ground to sink more and more, and therefore that kind of water must be vented betimes, for otherwise it killeth the grass, and makes the place bare in a dry summer, when the water is gone, or else it will cause such a coldness to the earth, as it will bring forth more rushes than grass.[44] And therefore it must be a principal care, to have all rivers, Sewers, and water drains, well cleansed and scoured, that upon occasion, when time requireth, when you will convey the water from the Meadows, it may have a due current, and likewise upon occasion to stop the rivers, to the end the water may overflow at times convenient.

Bailiff   But estoppels[45] of water-courses do in some places grow by such means, as one private man or two cannot by force or discretion make remedy. As when Sewers be common sometime between Lordship and Lordship, parish and parish, or between a multitude, among whom it is always seen, some will be perverse and willful, and hinder the best public action that is, though the doing of it be never so profitable to themselves, and the omitting hindrance. Besides this, you see upon divers streams *Water-mills*, which by reason of their high pitch, bar back the water that should have clear pass,[46] so that sundry men's grounds are drowned, even until, and at the time of haying. And for the most part, these Mills do appertain to great persons, who rather than they will lose a penny of their profit, will hazard the loss of a pound to poor men. What remedy is there for any of these mischiefs?

Surveyor   For every of them the law hath provided remedy. And the greatest hindrance is either neglect or fear of complaint; and upon complaint in places, and to persons appointed to reform, neglect of justice to be executed; *Leets or Law-days, general Sessions, Commissioners of Sewers, and actions at the common law* are provided to right these wrongs; therefore speak no more of this, as matter of impeachment of the grounds, which of themselves are naturally good or evil. But rather seek the means to better and help the ground, which, as you object, is weakened by often cutting. When a man observeth such decay in his Meadow, let it lie some few years to pasture, and be eaten very low; it will procure some heart again.[47] If not, take the fattest earth that may be gotten, and let it lie a year if you can, to dissolve, and when it is dry and will crumble small, mingle it with good

---

43   'How waters doth good to meadows'.
44   'Water, how it may be hurtful to grounds'.
45   *estoppels*   dams.
46   'Mills of too high a pitch pen the water'.
47   'How to amend weakened meadow'.

and well-fatted dung, and lay them awhile in a heap, until they be sufficiently incorporated, which will be in one winter; then carry it into your meadow about the beginning of March, or before, and then cast it abroad upon the meadows, not too thick, nor the clods too great; it will revive the weakened mold, and make the grass spring again very freshly.

Bailiff   I think this be good also for barren pasture.

Surveyor   It is very excellent for pasture, for he that will bestow the cost, shall find his recompense in short time. It is worthy the observance, though the care, cost, and pain be great.

Bailiff   I see in some meadows gally[48] places, where little or no grass at all groweth,[49] by reason (as I take it) of the too long standing of the water; for such places are commonly low where the water standeth, not having vent to pass away, and therefore means must be first made for the evacuation of the water, for the continual standing of the water consumeth the grass, and makes the place bare, and sinketh it.

Surveyor   In such a place, therefore, sow in the spring time some hay seed, especially the seed of the Clover-grass,[50] or the grass honeysuckle, and other seeds that fall out of the finest and purest hay; and, in the sowing of it, mingle with it some good earth. But sow not the honeysuckle grass in too moist a ground, for it liketh it not; therefore you must drain the place before you sow it.

Bailiff   Is it not good sometimes to till and sow the meadow grounds?[51]

Surveyor   Yes, upon good occasion, as you find by the slender crop of hay it beareth in a seasonable summer [and by the moss] that the ground begins to faint, as it were under the burden of continual bearing; fallow it, and let it lie a whole summer, and in the fall of the leaf plot it again, and at the season sow it with peas or fetches,[52] next with wheat, and lastly with fetches and hay dust, laying it as plain and level as you can. Then feed it the next summer, and after that, hain[53] it and mow it, and within a year or two, the grass will be fat, sweet and good.

---

48   *gally*   bare.
49   'Gally places in meadows'.
50   'Clover-grass'.
51   'To till meadow grounds'.
52   *fetches*   vetches, a bean-like plant.
53   *hain*   left to grow.

Bailiff   I have seen meadows, as well as other arable lands, namely, the crust of the earth cut in turfs[54] and burned, and so sown as aforesaid.[55]

Surveyor   This kind of husbandry is neither usual nor expedient in all places, especially in meadow grounds, unless the meadows be too much overgrown with moss, through too much moisture and cold; yet indeed I have seen it in some part of *Shropshire*. But I have thought it rather done for the [corn's] sake, than for restoration of the meadow.

Bailiff   But I like not this husbandry in any sort, in good meadow grounds, for I think it weakens the earth.

Surveyor   You need not fear it, for experience hath found that it hurteth no kind of ground, if it be not overmuch and too often burned. But I leave every man to his own fancy.

Bailiff   Surely, I think there needs no help to good meadow grounds, for it requireth small [travail], and less charge, and of all grounds (as was said in the beginning of our speech) it is most beneficial.[56]

Surveyor   Every thing hath his time and course, a growing, a perfection and decay. And the best ground may be overcharged, the plow and the scythe will weaken, if there be no help by Art or Nature, even the best earth; for though nature wake and work when we sleep and are idle, yet [when nature faileth, wit] and industry must work and supply what Nature [wanteth]. And therefore he that hath best meadow grounds, if he be a good husband, will observe how they stand in force or [feebleness], and accordingly endeavor to help the defects; he must neither sleep for the too much heat in summer nor keep house in winter for too much cold, but both winter and summer give such attendance and aid unto his land as in discretion he shall find most behooveful: for land is like the body;[57] if it be not fed with nutriture, and comforted and adorned with the most expedient commodities, it will pine away and become forlorn, as the mind that hath no rest or recreation waxeth lumpish and heavy. So that ground that wanteth due disposing and right manurance waxeth out of kind; even the best meadows will become ragged, and full of unprofitable weeds, if it be not cut and eaten: some will become too moist, and so grow to bogs; some too dry, and so to a hungry moss. And therefore according to the natural inclination, men are to endeavor to prepare preservations or reformations, namely, to keep the good in good case and to bring the evil to a

---

54   *turfs*   layer of sod.
55   'Meadow ground burned'.
56   'Meadow most beneficial'.
57   'Land like the body'.

better state. If it be too moist, you must seek to dry it; if it be too dry, you must use means to moisten it.

Bailiff   What if there be such places in a meadow, as neither Art nor charge can conveniently make dry, or fit for grass, as I know many, and (no doubt) so do you, which will be unprofitable whatsoever course be taken, unless more charge be laid upon it, than it can requite?

Surveyor   In such places the best course is to plant willows red or white, namely, in every void plot of low ground that is too moist, and of little [use], as also near unto, and in hedge-rows.[58] For those kinds of willows are very profitable and little hurtful, and delight most in watery places, where profitable and sweet grass likes not; they grow speedily, and bear much, and serve for many uses in husbandry.

Bailiff   In this indeed I can approve your Judgment by mine own Art and experience; for about seven or eight years since, I set a certain number of these kinds of Willow poles,[59] shaped and cut for the purpose, and indeed I cut them and set them in a dry time, for I can tell you, although they love the water well in their growing, wet is an enemy unto them being cut from the tree, and in the time of their replanting: some I set in the end of *January*, some in the beginning of *February*, when the extremity of the cold in near gone. I set some in a meadow by a river's side, some in a bottom, where the water falls most in the time of rain, and I set every one of them 6 foot asunder, and for three years' space I kept them pruned very carefully: and at this present time they have heads and branches of very great burden, every three trees near a load of wood. And I do not think, but every five or six years will afford as much and more; for as the body of the tree doth increase, the branches will augment in greatness, and this without loss of much ground, or hindrance to the grass. Nay, I find that under these trees, the grass is most rank and fruitful, not only by reason of the dropping of the boughs but by the fall of the leaf in *autumn*, as also by the cattle sheltering and shadowing under them. And, moreover, I have planted an *Osier-hope*[60] (for so they call it in *Essex*, and in some places an *Osier-bed*) in a surrounded ground, fit before for no other use, for the too much moisture and overflowing of it. And, to tell you truly, I think it yieldeth me now a greater benefit yearly, Acre for Acre, than an Acre of best wheat, and that without any great [travail] or charge, and the ordinary increase seldom failing. Only I find, that this kind of tree brooketh not the shadow of any other tree,[61] but delighteth in the open air, and in the Sun beams: so imperial or sullen is this little plant. And, truly, I conceive that men that have such grounds, as befit this kind of commodity, come short of good husbands, if they plant them not.

---

58   'To plant Willows'.
59   'Setting of Willows'.
60   'Osier-hope'.
61   'Osier brooketh no shadow'.

Surveyor   You say in this very truly, and it is a great shame for many capable wits, and able bodies, that they having livings and leisure, employ neither of them to their uttermost profitable ends: for land is given to man, to the end he should till it, manure it, and dress it; namely, he should set, sow, and plant upon it, and in due discretion to convert every place to his fittest fruit. For I am of opinion, that there is no kind of soil, be it never so wild, boggy, clay, or sandy, but will yield one kind of beneficial fruit or other.[62]

Bailiff   Nay, by your leave, I think the pebbles of beach stones upon the sea coast, about [*Orford*] *Ness*[63] in [*Suffolk*,] the *Camber* in *Sussex*, and such like, are good for no use, especially for any profitable fruit; for, I think, there is no firm soil within a spear's length of some part of the highest of them.

Surveyor   You speak not now of soil, you speak of stones, and yet have I eaten of good and nourishing fruit, growing even there, as *peas*, pleasant, wholesome, and good, growing of their own accord, never set or sown:[64] but they differ in the manner of branching only; the blossoms differ not much, but the cods hang in clusters, eight, 10, or 12 in a bunch, and taste as other peas.

Bailiff   That is strange, that they should grow where no firm earth is near, and without setting or sowing; methinks, if they be of any abundance, poor people might make use of them, if they be wholesome and not forbidden.

Surveyor   So do they in the times of dearth and scarcity.

Bailiff   I have seen upon these grounds, store of *Peewits*,[65] *Olives*, and *Cobs* breed, fowls of great request at most honorable tables.[66]

Surveyor   So have I; but to allure them, it is good to strew rushes and grass upon the *beach*, whereon to lay their eggs about March, unless there be store of sea-weeds to serve for that purpose. But for your other sorts of grounds, as boggy, and hot and sandy grounds, commonly barren, I see not how they may be employed to any great profit. For the first, namely, your low and spongy grounds, trenched, is good for hops,[67] as *Essex*, and *Surrey*, and other places do find to their

---

[62]   'All [grounds] good for some use'.

[63]   *Orford Ness*   Norden was familiar with this region after having surveyed Orford and neighboring areas in 1600–1601. These surveys have been published as *Orford Ness: A Selection of Maps mainly by John Norden*, James Alfred Steers (ed.) (Cambridge, 1966).

[64]   'Peas upon the beach grow naturally'.

[65]   *Peewits*   lapwings; *olives*   birds also known as oystercatchers; *cob*   a male swan.

[66]   'Peewits and Olives, &c'.

[67]   'Hops'.

profit. The hot and sandy (omitting grain), is good for *Carrot roots*,[68] a beneficial fruit, as at *Orford, Ipswich*, and many sea towns in *Suffolk*, as also Inland towns, [*Bury*],[69] [*Framlingham*], and others in some measure, in the same shire, *Norwich*, and many places in *Norfolk, Colchester* in *Essex, Fulham*, and other places near *London*. And it begins to increase in all places of this Realm, where discretion and industry sway the minds of the inhabitants; and I do not a little marvel, that husbandmen and Farmers do not imitate this, for their own families at least, and to sell to their poor neighbors, as in some places they begin, to their great profit. I have also observed in many places, where I have had occasion to travel, that many crofts, tofts, pingles, pitles, and other small quillets of Land,[70] about farm houses and tenements, are suffered to lie altogether idle: some overgrown with nettles, mallows, thistles, wild teasels, and divers other unprofitable weeds, which are fat and fertile;[71] where, if the Farmer would use the means, would grow sundry commodities, as *hemp* and *mustard-seed*,[72] both which are so strong enemies to all other superfluous and unprofitable weeds, as they will not suffer any of them to grow where they are sown. The hemp is of great use in a Farmer's house, as is found in [*Lincolnshire*,] *Suffolk, Norfolk, Sussex, Dorset*, and in many places in *Somerset*, especially about [*Bridport*] and *Lyme*, where the people do find by it great advantage, not only for cordage for shipping, but also for linen and other necessaries about the house. So is also the *flax*,[73] which is also sown in many places, where good huswives endeavor their wits, wills, and hands to that commodious and profitable course, and the *flax* will like well enough in a more light and gentle and leaner soil than the hemp. And indeed there is not a place so rude and unlikely, but diligence and discretion may convert it to some profitable end; and among many other commodities, I marvel men are no more forward in planting of *Apple-trees*,[74] *Pear-trees*, Crab-stocks, and such like in their hedges, between their fields, as well as in Orchards: a matter praiseworthy, and profitable to the planter, and to the commonwealth very beneficial.

Bailiff   Indeed, I have thought upon this kind of husbandry, but I have been prevented of mine own desires by a prejudicate conceit, that these fruits would redound little to my benefit, for that I think they will be stolen, the hedges trodden down, and the trees broken for the fruit's sake.

Surveyor   Negligence may easily find excuse, but this objection is frivolous; for I know in *Kent, Worcestershire, Shropshire, Gloucestershire, Somerset*, and *Devon*,

---

[68] 'Carrot roots'.

[69] *Bury*   Bury St Edmunds.

[70] *tofts, pingles, pitles*, and *quillets* are small enclosed plots of land.

[71] 'Many waste grounds might yield profit'.

[72] 'Hemp. Mustard-Seed'.

[73] 'Flax'.

[74] 'Apple-trees'.

and many parts in *Wales*, full of this commodity, even in their remote hedge-rows. And although some few be lost, sith the rest come so easily, so fully, and so freely, a good mind will not grudge at a wayfaring passenger, taking for his refection, and to qualify the heat of his [travail], an apple or a pear, for the remnant will content the well conditioned owner. For I have known, that (all the stolen allowed) the fruit thus dispersedly planted, have made in some little Farms, or (as they call them in those parts) *Bargains*,[75] a tun, two, three, four of *Cider* and *Perry*,[76] which kind of drink resembling white-wine, hath, without any further supply of Ale or Beer, sufficed a good householder and his family the whole year following, and sometimes hath made of the overplus 20 nobles, or 10 pounds, more or less; [yea, there is a Parish in Devonshire called *Stofordton*,[77] wherein is commonly yearly made as much *Cider* as the tithe thereof amounteth yearly at two pence the hogshead, unto above 40 marks, and yet not above 70 Tenants in the whole Parish].

Bailiff   This surely cannot be but confessed to be very beneficial, both for the private and [public weal].[78] And I myself have noted that [*Middlesex*], in former times, hath had regard to this kind of commodity; for many Apple-trees, Pear-trees, Service-trees,[79] and such like, hath been planted in the fields, and hedge-rows, especially in the North and East part of the shire, as also in the South part of Hertfordshire, which are at this day very beneficial to the inhabitants, both for their own use and relief, as also to vent divers ways at London by the good huswife. But the trees are now for the most part very ancient, and I do not see such a continual inclination in the time present to continue or increase this benefit for the use of posterity; neither did I ever know much Cider or Perry made in these parts, neither do I think they have sufficient skill or means.

Surveyor   I think indeed little *Cider* is made there; some *Perry* there is here and there, but more in the West Country, and in *Kent*,[80] a place very fructiferous of that kind of fruit.

Bailiff   Yet is there not so much *Cider* made, for all the great abundance of fruit, as there might be, but in the Inland.

Surveyor   The reason is, because that near *London*, and the *Thames* side, the fruit is vented in kind, not only to the Fruiterers in gross, but by the country wives,

---

[75]   *Bargains*   small farms.

[76]   'Cider. Perry'. The latter is a cider made from pear juice.

[77]   *Stofordton*   Stoford, Devon.

[78]   *public weal*   a term associated with more radical strains of the sixteenth-century complaint tradition. On the implications of Norden's use of this term, see the Introduction (p. xxxix).

[79]   *Service-trees*   trees bearing small pear-like fruit.

[80]   'Kent'.

in the nearest part of *Kent, Middlesex, Essex* and *Surrey*, who utter them in the markets, as they do all other vendible things else.

Bailiff   But above all others, I think, the *Kentishmen* be most apt and industrious, in planting Orchards with *Pippins* and *Cherries*, especially near the *Thames* about *Faversham* and *Sittingbourne*. And the order of the planting is such, as the form delighteth the eye, the fruit the taste, and the walks infinite recreate the body. Besides, the grass and herbage, notwithstanding the trees, yieldeth as much benefit, in manner, as if there were no trees planted at all, especially for hay.

Surveyor   It is true; and, in mine opinion, many men having tenements, and time in them, make not half the profit, which by due and discreet industry they might.

Bailiff   Truly, I now so conceive it: for you have in many things made me see mine own indiscretion and negligence,[81] but in many of them *fear* hath more prevailed with me than *willful refusal*. And so I think it doth in other men, who also with myself, are ignorant of many points of providence and good husbandry, because they are not generally travellers to see other places, neither hath their breeding been judicious, but plain, according to a slubbered[82] pattern of ancient *ignorance*,[83] by which they only shape all their courses, as their Fathers did, never putting in practice any new device, by the rule of more reason. And therefore indeed, we that live in this age of ignorance and idleness may betake us to a better course without any disparagement, if we conform us to new and probable precedents, as time and trial will yield experience. But surely I hold your opinion good for the planting of *fruit trees*, not only in Orchards, but in the hedge-rows and fields, for I think we have of no tree more necessary use.

Surveyor   It is true in respect of fruit. But in other respects, the *Oak, Elm* and *Ash* are more precious.[84]

Bailiff   These indeed are building trees, and of the three, the *Oak* is of most request, a timber most firm and durable. I have been no great traveller, and therefore I can speak little of the increase or decrease of them, other than in the places where I am most resident, and where my ordinary affairs do lie. And for those parts, I can say, that they increase not, though they seem not to be wanted: for you see this Country inclinable to Wood and Timber much, yet within these 20 years they have been diminished two parts of three, and if it go on by like proportion, our children will surely want. How it is in other Countries I know not.

---

[81]   'Men untaught know little'.
[82]   *slubbered*   careless.
[83]   'Many follow old husbandry'.
[84]   'Oak, Ash, and Elm'.

Surveyor   I have seen many places of note for this kind of commodity (for so it is, howsoever it hath been little preserved), and I find, that it hath universally received a mortal blow within the time of my memory: notwithstanding there is a Statute for the preservation and maintenance of the same,[85] and the same continued to this day, but not with wished effect, as we have thereof spoken before.

Bailiff   I will tell you, Sir, careless Gentlemen, that have Manors and Parks well wooded, left them by their careful ancestors, that would not strip a tree for gold, are of the mind (as it seemeth) that the shadow of the high trees do dazzle their eyes; they cannot see to play the good husbands, nor look about them to sell the land, till the trees be taken out of their sight.

Surveyor   Can you break a jest so boldly upon men of worth?

Bailiff   You see as well as I, some do it in earnest; and I think indeed, it is partly your fault that are *Surveyors*: for when Gentlemen have sunk themselves by rowing in *Vanity's* boat, you blow them the bladders of lavishing helps, to make them swim again awhile, counseling first to clear the land of the wood (in the sale whereof is great abuse), persuading them they shall sell the land little the cheaper.[86] And indeed I hold it providence, where necessity commands, to choose of two, the lesser evil: namely, to sell part of a superfluous quantity of wood, where the remnant will serve the party in use, rather than the land. But withal, it is the part of a good Surveyor, to counsel frugality, and a sparing spending,[87] according to the proportion of the means of him he [travails] for. And if that great Emperor *Necessity* will needs have havoc, sell the wood, or prize it so, as he that buys the land have not the wood for nought, as is often seen, when the wood and timber sometimes is worth the price of wood and land.

Surveyor   It seems, when you come to be a Surveyor, as you labor to be, you will be very careful in your counsel;[88] but it may be, when you seem to have best skill, and earnest desire to draw the line straight for a man inclinable to his own will, he will rather give into the hands of some one that feeds his conceits with flattery,[89] and he shall manage the building, when you have laid the foundation; and what he doth, be it right or crooked, is level with the mark. And therefore, leaving every man to him he likes, I say only this, that sith timber, and timber-trees, and wood by due observation, are found to decay so fast, methinks in common discretion it

---

[85]   'Oak much decayeth. 33 Henry VIII'. Norden refers to the proclamation 'Enlarging Hatfield Chase', 3 November 1541 (Paul L. Hughes and James F. Larkin [eds], *Tudor Royal Proclamations*, vol. 1 [New Haven, CT, 1964], pp. 303–5).

[86]   'Gentlemen sell their woods too fast'.

[87]   'A Surveyor must counsel frugality'.

[88]   'Affection'.

[89]   'Simple men do manage men's business through flattery'.

should behoove every good husband (for all would be so accounted), both upon his own land as also upon such as he holds of other [men],[90] not only to maintain and to the uttermost to preserve the timber-trees and saplings likely to become timber-trees, Oak, Elm, and Ash, but voluntarily to plant young; and because there is not only an universal inclination to hurl down, it were expedient that sith *Will* will not, *Authority* should constrain some mean of restoration, namely, to enjoin men, as well Lords as Tenants, to plant for every sum of Acres a number of trees, or to sow or set a quantity of ground with Acorns, Ash-keys,[91] Hawberries, Nuts, &c.

Bailiff   I remember there is a Statute made, 35 *Henry* the 8 and the 1 *Elizabeth*,[92] for the preservation of timber-trees, *Oak, Ash, Elm, Asp*, and *Beech*, and that 12 storers and standels[93] should be left standing at every fall upon an acre; but methinks, this Statute is deluded, and the meaning abused, for I have seen in many places at the [fall], where indeed they leave the number of standels and more, but instead they cut down them that were preserved before, and, at the next fall, them that were left to answer the Statute,[94] and young left again in their steads; so that there can be no increase of timber-trees, notwithstanding the words of the Statute, by this kind of reservation, unless such as were thus left were continued to become timber-trees indeed. And, therefore, it were not amiss that some provision were made to maintain the meaning of the Statute in more force; but I leave that to such as see more abuse than I see, and have power to reform it.[95]

Surveyor   It is a thing indeed to be regarded, for the abuses of woods are infinite and intolerable.

---

[90]   'All men ought to preserve Timber'.

[91]   *Ash-keys*   seeds of the Ash-tree; *Hawberries*   fruit of the Hawthorn.

[92]   '35 Henry VIII, 1 Elizabeth'. Norden refers to the proclamations 'Suspending Statute on Fuel', 11 February 1544, and 'Prohibiting Sale of Ships to Foreigners', 23 August 1559 (Hughes and Larkin [eds], *Tudor Royal Proclamations*, vol. 1, pp. 325–6 and vol. 3, p. 135).

[93]   *standels*   like storers, a term for a stock of spare trees.

[94]   'The Statute abused'.

[95]   For discussion of Norden's comments on deforestation, see the Introduction (p. xxxix). Norden is appropriately cautious in broaching this subject, for the loss of England's forests was a site of ongoing debate in the early Jacobean period. Arthur Standish's text *The Commons Complaint* (London, 1611) viewed the Midland Rising as a response to the unprecedented loss of England's forests in the previous 30 years. The official acceptance of this view is reflected in the fact that Standish's sequel, *New Directions of Experience to the Commons Complaint* (London, 1613), contained a prefatory letter from King James approving of the text. Another text on the subject, John Manwood's *A Treatise and Discovrse of the Lawes of the Forrest* (London, 1598), which, in its original form, treated forests primarily as a site of aristocratic privilege and retreat, was republished in 1615, with five additional chapters concerned with the legal rights of tenants in forests. The need to restock England's forests was also the main topic of another dialogue involving a figure of a Surveyor, Rooke Churche's *An olde thrift newly revived* (London, 1612).

Bailiff   Surely it is, especially in places where little timber grows, for there is no Country, how barren of timber so ever, but hath use of timber;[96] and therefore, if neither men's own wills, seeing the eminent[97] want, nor force of justice will move and work a reformation, we may say as the Proverb is, *Let them live longest, fetch their wood farthest.*[98]

Surveyor   But some Countries are yet well stored, and for the abundance of timber and wood, were excepted in the Statute, as the welds of *Kent, Sussex* and *Surrey* which were all anciently comprehended under the name of *Holmes dale.*[99] There are divers places also in *Derbyshire, Cheshire,* and *Shropshire* well [wooded]. And yet he that well observes it, and hath known the Welds of *Sussex, Surrey* and *Kent,* the grand nursery of those kinds of trees, especially Oak and Beech, shall find an alteration within less than 30 years, as may well strike a fear, lest few years more, as pestilent as the former, will leave few good trees standing in those Welds.[100] Such a heat issueth out of the many forges and furnaces, for the making of Iron, and out of the Glass-kilns,[101] as hath devoured many famous woods within the [Welds]: as about *Burningfold, Loxwood Green,* the *Menns, Kirdford, Petworth Parks, Ebernowe, Wassals, Rusper, Balcombe, Dallington,* the *Dyker,* and some forests and other places infinite.[102] *Tantum aevi longinqua valet mutare vetustas.*[103] The force of time, and men's inclination, make great changes in mighty things; but the crop of this commodious fruit of the earth, which nature itself doth sow, being thus reaped and cut down by the sickle of time, hath been in some plentiful places, in regard of the superfluous abundance, rather held a hurtful weed, than a profitable fruit, and therefore the wasting of it held providence, to the end that corn, a more profitable increase, might be brought in instead of it, which hath made Inhabitants so fast to hasten the confusion of the one to have the other.[104] But it is to be feared, that posterities will find want, where now they think is too much.

---

[96]   'Want of wood and timber feared'.

[97]   *eminent*   'conspicuously displayed' (*OED*, II.4).

[98]   *Let ... farthest*   Norden cites the proverb 'they that live longest must fetch his Wood farthest' (Morris Palmer Tilley, *A Dictionary of Proverbs in England in the Sixteenth and Seventeenth Centuries* [1950; Ann Arbor, MI, 1966], p. 750).

[99]   'Holmes dale'. Like Kent, this region was associated with resistance to foreign invasion: as William Camden wrote, 'The vale of Holmesdall [*sic*] / Never wonne, ne never shall' (*Britain* [1610 edition], p. 296).

[100]   'Thirty years have consumed much wood and timber'.

[101]   'Glass houses'.

[102]   'Great Woods wasted'. These erstwhile woods, located in Surrey and Sussex, became the site of extensive ironworks in the early modern period.

[103]   *Tantum ... vetustas* ['such vast change can length of time effect']; from Virgil, *The Aeneid,* Book 3, l.415 (*Virgil, I: Eclogues, Georgics, Aeneid I–VI,* H. Rushton Fairclough [trans.], Loeb Classical Library [Cambridge, MA, 1999]).

[104]   'Woods destroyed for corn's sake'.

Virtutem incolumem odimus, sublatam sero saepe quarimus invidi.[105] Things that we have too common are not regarded, but being deprived of them they are often times sought for in vain.

Bailiff   It is no marvel, if *Sussex* and other places you speak of, be deprived of this benefit; for I have heard, there are, or lately were in *Sussex*, near 140 hammers and furnaces for Iron,[106] and in it and *Surrey* adjoining, three or four glass-houses: the hammers and furnaces spend, each of them in every 24 hours, two, three, or four loads of Charcoal, which in a year amounteth to an infinite quantity, as you can better account by your Arithmetic than I.

Surveyor   That which you say is true; but they work not all, all the year, for many of them lack water in the summer to blow their bellows. And to say truth, the consuming of much of these in the Weld, is no such great prejudice to the [weal public],[107] as is the overthrow of wood and timber, in places where there is no great quantity; for I have observed, that the cleansing of many of these weld grounds, hath redounded rather to the benefit than to the hurt of the Country; for where woods did grow in superfluous abundance, there was lack of pasture for Kine,[108] and of arable land for corn, without the which, a Country or country farm cannot stand, or be relieved, but by neighbor helps, as the *Downs*[109] have their wood from the Weld. Beside, people bred amongst woods, are naturally more stubborn, and uncivil, than in the *Champion*[110] Countries.

Bailiff   What, are men's manners commonly guided by the disposition and quality of the places where they are bred?[111]

Surveyor   There is no necessity in it, I take it, but by observation it hath been much collected, that *Montani sunt asperi atque inculti: Molliores corpore atque moribus Pratenses: Campestres mansueti et Civiles: Rudes et refractarii Silvicola:*

---

[105]   *Virtutem ... invidi*   a slight variation from Horace, *Liber III, Ode* XXIV ('The Curse of Mammon'): 'virtutem incolumem odimus, sublatam ex oculis quaerimus, indivi' ['with envy filled, (we) hate Virtue while it lives and mourn it only when snatched from sight'] (*Horace, the Odes and Epodes*, C.E. Bennett [trans.], Loeb Classical Library [Cambridge, MA, 1927], pp. 254–5).

[106]   '140 Ironworks in Sussex'.

[107]   'Wasting of woods in Sussex, good for the commonwealth'.

[108]   *Kine*   cattle.

[109]   *Downs*   the South Downs, located north of the Hampshire and Surrey coasts and running from Southampton to Eastbourne.

[110]   *Champion*   or 'champaign', open and unenclosed land.

[111]   'Men's manners of their place of breed'. Among recent discussions of the influence of classical models of climate theory on early modern definitions of cultural difference, see John Gillies, *Shakespeare and the Geography of Difference* (Cambridge, 1994) and Mary Floyd-Wilson, *English Ethnicity and Race in Early Modern Drama* (Cambridge, 2003).

Paludicolae inconstantes et hebeti ingenio: Littorales duri, horrendi, immanes, latrociniis dediti, omniumque deniq; pessimi, & c.[112] So that if this observation hold, men vary in wit, manners and disposition of body and mind, much after the nature of the place where they are brought up. But let us not think that follows always, but that education and divine grace doth shape new minds, [manners] and dispositions in men, as they are trained up in the knowledge and fear of God.[113] But woods are commonly most desert, so are Sea coasts subject to violent winds and vapors, and therefore these above other places are most condemned, and the inhabitants more need to seek the means of reformation.

Bailiff   Truly, I think all the places you name, the *Mountains, Meadows, Woods, Marshes,* and the *Sea-coast,* breed by nature all *rudes, refractarios et immanes,*[114] without the grace of God directing them. And therefore we will leave to censure conditions of men, in one continent, and, as it were, under one climate, by the places of their breed. That in my conceit, were to give sentence against God's secret Counsel and providence, as also to say: such a complexion were always an argument of ill condition, and such of good, which never holdeth generally true.[115] Let us, I pray you, return to our former communication, for time passeth, and I know, you would not be letted long.

Surveyor   Then I say, where in former times, a farm stood in those parts, wholly upon these unprofitable bushy and woody grounds, having only some small and ragged pastures for some kind of cattle, now I see as I [travel], and where I have had business, that these unprofitable grounds are converted to beneficial tillage in so much as the people lack not, but can to their great benefit, yearly afford to others, both Butter, Cheese, and Corn, even where was little or none at all;[116] yet I hold a moderation necessary, lest that the too much overthrowing of timber trees, and stocking up of Woods, bring such a scarcity of that necessary commodity, as men build not for lack of timber, but use *Peats, Turf, Heath, Furze, Broom,* and

---

[112] *Montani ... pessimi:* 'Mountain people are savage and uncouth. Meadow folk are gentle in aspect and character. Those of the plains are subdued and courteous. Woodlanders are ignorant and stubborn. Marsh folk are fickle and by nature obtuse. Coast dwellers are hard, terrible and monstrous: devoted pirates, the worst of all' (trans. Brian Philips, from 'John Norden's Judgements on the Weald Re-Examined', *Sussex History* 2, 9 [1985]: 26–32, qtd in Kitchen, 'Cosmo-Choro-Polygrapher', n. 24, pp. 257–8).

[113] 'Divine grace shapes new minds'.

[114] *rudes ... immanes* ['uncultivated, stubborn, and savage'].

[115] 'Complexion never a true argument of good or evil men'. For discussions of the historical construction of race, see especially Kim F. Hall, *Things of Darkness: Economies of Race and Gender in Early Modern England* (Ithaca, NY, 1995) and Sujata Iyengar, *Shades of Difference: Mythologies of Skin Color in Early Modern England* (Philadelphia, 2005).

[116] 'The benefit that Sussex findeth by decay of Woods'.

such like fuel for firing,[117] where they may be gotten, yea, and Neat's dung, as in some places of *Wiltshire,* [*Lincolnshire,* the Isle of *Portland,*] and elsewhere men are enforced to use; which cannot but ensue, if there be neither prevention for the subversion of the present, nor provision to plant or spare for the time to come: who seeth not that the general extirpation and stocking up of copy grounds in *Middlesex*[118] *will breed want to them that shall succeed*?

Bailiff But that may be the more tolerated, because it bringeth a great profit in tillage and pasture, the ground being good, bringeth forth Wheat and Oats, and other commodious grain, instead of stubs and shrubs.

Surveyor Stubs and shrubs are also necessary; but as we desire food, so we must preserve the means to prepare it for food: for as corn availeth not without Mills to grind, so many other necessaries, without firing, are of little use.[119] If all were arable, which is the life of corn, then meadow and pasture, the life of cattle, were dead: to covet one peculiar for all necessary things is a true resemblance of *Midas'* wish. Therefore it is good to foresee, and to avoid a mischief to come, by desiring or using present commodities moderately and providently. For when there is a true concurrence between the use, and preservation, and increase of necessary commodities without willful consuming, there seldom followeth too much want; but if, for the overgreedy use of things present, there be no regard of future occasion, it cannot be, but if the *earth*, the mother of man and other creatures, could verbally complain, she might well say, *she were even robbed of her fruits by her own children*:[120] and namely, when for one commodity's sake, another is abandoned by some private men, more expedient for the [public weal].[121] [It was ordained by the *Romans* that the *Consuls* should have charge of the Woods, to the end there should be no timber wanting, for building of houses and Ships, as also other timber-works. The state of *Venice* at this day observeth the same order, appointing private officers to oversee their Woods, and some to have the charge to see young Woods yearly planted. Woods were, in *Virgil's* time, in high esteem. *Eclogue* 4: *Si [canimus] silvas, silvae [sint] consule dignae.*[122] And much it is to be lamented, that so common and general devastation of this special commodity,

---

[117] 'Fuel of constraint'.

[118] 'Middlesex stocking'.

[119] 'The use of firing necessary'.

[120] *she ... own children* Norden draws on Psalm 127: 3: 'children are the inheritance of the Lord, and the frute of the womb.'

[121] 'A commodity present should not deprive future times of a better'.

[122] From Virgil's *Eclogue 4*, line 3 ['If our song is of the woodland, let the woods be worthy of a consul'] (*Virgil, I*, Loeb Classical Library, p. 49).

is no way sought to be prevented, which threateneth a grievous weakening of this commonwealth.][123]

Bailiff [Devastation, that is,] when farms or townships are by private men dispeopled, and the houses pulled down, and the land converted to some more private use: as only to sheep pastures, or grazing for cattle only, you mean, the *Corn* the more commodious is abandoned for these less profitable.[124]

Surveyor Both these are necessary in their places; no man can deny it. But when the *Ox* and *Sheep* shall feed where good houses stood, where honest men and good subjects dwelled, where hospitality was kept, the poor relieved, the King better served, and the commonwealth more steaded: who will not say it is the bane of a commonwealth, an apparent badge of *Atheism*, and an argument of apish ambition, or wolvish emulation? But because there is a statute carefully providing reformation,[125] I will be sparing to accuse, though a man might point at the places and persons, depopulators of houses, and spoilers of woods: Is not this next, *Fern-hill*, a close of the Lord's demesnes?

Bailiff You remember well; it is so.

Surveyor If my memory fail not, there is a deep bottom in this field, and a little rill of water rising out of the hill runs through it.

Bailiff If you look but over this hill, you shall see it.

Surveyor I see it, and I marvel that there hath been no respect had of this place; for it is a desert bottom, full of bushes and shrubs, yielding now little or no benefit.

Bailiff What can you advise to be done with it, to make it more profitable?

Surveyor I could wish some cost to be bestowed here, in making a *fish-pond*;[126] nay, it would make at the least two or three, one below the other.

Bailiff Alas, that were to little purpose, as I take it, considering the charge of making the ponds, the clearing of the water-course, the cleansing of the bodies,

---

[123] This section, beginning with the reference to Roman policy, is new to the 1618 edition. See the Textual Notes (p. 210).

[124] '[Depopulation] dangerous'.

[125] The Tudor state had enacted a series of statutes that attempted to forestall depopulation and enclosure: for discussion, see Joan Thirsk, 'Tudor Enclosures', in *The Rural Economy of England*, pp. 72–4.

[126] 'Fish-ponds'.

the making of the dams or heads of the ponds, will be more chargeable, than the fish will be profitable.

Surveyor   As you conceive it[. The *Romans*, especially the Nobility, were wont to make fair fish ponds about their houses, which yielded them both pleasure and profit, and therefore spared they not for costs: *Hortensius, Hiricius, Lucullus,* and others, are famous for this kind of husbandry, as testifieth *Marcus Varro*.[127] And therefore], where reason or experience teach not, there the will follows to be untoward in all actions; and seldom men practice doubtful things, howsoever probable, for [experience's] sake. But in this there is no doubt at all, the benefit is certain by approved experience, and it payeth the charge to the founder in short time, and afterward the benefit comes without much labor or cost[, besides the pleasure]. He that hath travelled, and is acquainted with *Sussex* and *Surrey*,[128] and hath observed this commodity, may find that Gentlemen, and others able in those parts, will not suffer such a convenient place as this for the purpose to lie unprepared for this use; and the sweetness of the gain they yearly make of it, hath bred such an increase of ponds for fish, as I think these two shires have more of them than any 20 other shires in England.

Bailiff   That were very much, but, I take it, the making of them is very chargeable; for the cleansing and digging, the ridding of the stuff, the making the head, I think will consume a greater charge than many years will pay, or redeem again[, as I said before.

Surveyor   That which commonly cometh out of these kind of places, is good soil for other lands, and will of itself quit the costs of cleansing and carrying. As for the head wherein the greatest charge consisteth, may be done, for a mark or a pound a pole at the most; but where there is good fast earth, as is here, I think less will do it. This pond may be 20 pole at the head, few so much, and after two or three years being well stored, it will yield requital, not only for domestical use, but to be vented very beneficially; for the Fish-mongers of London do use to buy the Fish by the score or hundred, of a competent scantling, when the ponds in the country

---

[127] *Varro*   Marcus Terentius Varro's *Rerum rusticarum libri tres* [*On Agriculture*] (first century BCE) mentions the stocking of fish ponds by Roman aristocrats, including the three figures named by Norden (William Davis Hooper and Harrison Boyd Ash [trans.], Loeb Classical Library [Cambridge, MA, 1960], pp. 525–9). Joan Thirsk has argued that a reading of classical writers such as Varro inspired aristocratic landowners to begin farming their own demesnes ('Making a Fresh Start: Sixteenth-Century Agriculture and the Classical Inspiration', in Michael Leslie and Timothy Raylor [eds], *Culture and Cultivation in Early Modern England: Writing and the Land* [Leicester, 1992], pp. 15–34). Norden distances his own text from this classical tradition, however, referring to Varro only twice (also see n. 192, p. 184) and never citing other classical agricultural manuals, such as those by Xenophon, Cato, Columella, or Palladius.

[128]   'Fish-ponds many in Sussex and Surrey'.

be sewed,[129] and bring them to London in cask 20, 30, 40, 50 miles, and vent them by retail;[130] and if the ponds be so remote from the main Mart London, as the Fish cannot be conveniently transferred, other confining Cities, Towns, and Inhabitants, besides the owners' private families, will find good use of them: and many times also, these kinds of ponds may have sufficient fall of water for corn Mills, fulling, or wake Mills,[131] [sith] Mills, and Mills of other kinds,[132] as the country where such convenient places are, may require; and it is found, by such as duly observe the courses of Countries, and inclinations of men, that want of providence and fear of charge, withholdeth men's minds from many benefits, private and public, and that many times where they are voluntarily moved to consume far more in matter of mere vanity, and things which right reason holdeth very frivolous.

Bailiff Truly, I have observed this that you say to be true in many, especially in such as ambition moveth without necessity to build more fair and stately piles[133] than their estate or abilities will well bear, and covet nothing more than to raise their fame by their folly, not respecting commodities so much as pleasures, as if the name of a fair house were made meat, drink and credit unto them; where if they were forced by necessity to raise an habitacle,[134] it might be so marshaled in discretion, that it should not exceed the quality of the person, neither stand without such supply of all convenient appendances, as might both argue the party provident, and add means unto all necessaries for alike the family's relief.[135]

Surveyor Men will have their humors; but he is wise, that can learn by others' harms to avoid, and by others' good example to follow the like.

Bailiff Sir, you see this piece of ground; it hath not the name for nought: it is called *Ferny close*, and, as you see, it is full, and so overgrown with these brakes, that all the Art we can devise and labor we can use cannot rid them.

Surveyor *Neglectis urenda filix innascitur agris*, saith *Horace*.[136] But in many places they serve to good use;[137] and, therefore, where they grow, it must be considered,

---

[129] *sewed* drained.

[130] 'Fish-mongers buy pond fish far off'.

[131] *wake Mills* also known as 'walk' or 'wauk' mills, these mills—like fulling mills—were used to process woolen cloth.

[132] 'Ponds necessary for Mills'.

[133] 'Ambitious building ridiculous'.

[134] *habitacle* home.

[135] 'A house with necessaries commendable'.

[136] 'Horace'. From Horace, *Satire I.III*, l. 37 ['for in neglected fields there springs up bracken, which you must burn'] (*Satires, Epistles and Ars Poetica*, H. Rushton Fairclough [trans.], Loeb Classical Library [Cambridge, MA, 1939], p. 35).

[137] 'Fern'.

whether it be better to destroy them or to foster them, for they seldom or never grow in a fat soil, nor cold, but in a sandy and hot ground: and, as *Theophrastus* saith, in his eight book, it cometh not up in manured places, but withereth away.[138]

Bailiff   How? Meaneth he by manured places, plowed grounds?

Surveyor   Plowed grounds may be said to be manured; but it is not so meant by *Theophrastus*, for he meaneth grounds well soiled, with good fat marl and dung:[139] for plowing without this kind of manurance, will hardly kill it, for the ground being naturally barren, it will not quit cost to plow it, till they grow no more. And if there be no other soil to manure it, take the brakes themselves, to kill the brakes.

Bailiff   I think that were the way to raise more, for it is like the adding more fuel to put out fire.

Surveyor   But you see that though the oil feed the lamp, oil will extinguish it.[140]

Bailiff   That is, if you drown the match with oil.

Surveyor   So if you cut the brakes often, while they are young, and a little before Midsummer, when they are grown, and cast them upon the same land, and set the fold upon it, and use it thus two or three years, feeding it often with cattle or sheep, you shall find a great decay of them. In the Welds of *Sussex* and *Surrey*, places inclinable to brakes, you may learn how the inhabitants by their endeavors do make good use of this kind of husbandry,[141] both for corn and to increase their pasture, by cutting them in August, and after, when they are withered, laying them upon their grounds with the fold, as I told you, which causeth the grass to spring very fast and freshly; and they are so far from coveting to kill them, that they fetch them for this use far off, but the continuance of this course will impair them much. Moreover, they bring the brakes into their yards, where their cattle lodge in the winter, and there they rot; and when they be well dissolved among their other soil, they carry it about September and October into their arable fields to their good advantage. And in some places they lay it in the common highways (as in *Hertfordshire* and other places) and about March carry it into their grounds. It is of so lively, slimy and vegetable a nature, as it seldom becomes utterly consumed, but by fat marl, and soil, and continual plowing, as I told you before. But I see,

---

[138] 'Theophrastus, lib. 8'. Book VIII of Theophrastus's *Historia Plantarum* [Enquiry into Plants] discusses summer crops (*Theophrastus, II, Enquiry into Plants, Books VI–IX*, Arthur F. Hort [trans.], Loeb Classical Library [Cambridge, MA, 1961]).

[139] 'Manuring, what is meant by it'.

[140] 'Fern destroyed by fern'.

[141] 'The use of Fern, in divers places'.

here is a ground next unto this, of another nature, full of bushes and briars: he is no good husband that oweth it.

Bailiff Neither he that owes it, nor a better husband can prevent this inconvenience;[142] for besides the bushes, the moss is so full and rank, as the ground is good for nothing, but for that small pasture, that is in it here and there.

Surveyor The ground of itself, I see is good enough, and not so prone to moss as you take it, but the cause of the moss is the bushes;[143] for after every shower of rain, the bushes hang full of drops, which often falling on the ground, makes the upper part of the earth so cold, that it increaseth this kind of moss; but without the aid and industry of a skillful husband, fairest grounds will become ugly, and best land evil, and will bring forth unprofitable weeds, bushes, brakes, briars, thorns, and all kind of hurtful things, according to the curse inflicted upon it for man's fault, at the beginning.

Bailiff Admit, no man did manure the earth, yet surely there be many grounds, in my conceit, would never become worse than they be.[144]

Surveyor You are in a great error; for the freest grounds that you see, the fairest pastures and greenest meadows, would become in short time, overgrown with bushes, woods, weeds, and things unprofitable, as they were before they were rid and cleansed of the same by the industry of man, who was enjoined that care and travail to manure the earth, which for his disobedience should bring forth these things.

Bailiff How then was the state of this Island of great *Britain* at the beginning when it was first peopled?

Surveyor A very Desert and wilderness, full of woods, fells, moors, bogs, heaths, and all kind of forlorn places;[145] and howsoever we find the state of this Island now], Records do witness unto us, that it was for the most part an universal wilderness, until people finding it a place desolate and forlorn, began to set footing here, and by degrees grew into multitudes, though for the time brutish and rude. Time taught them, and Nature drew them to find the means how to stock up trees, bushes, briars, and thorns, and instead thereof, to plow the land, to sow, set, and plant, to build Cities for defense, as well against the force of Wild beasts, then plentiful in these grounds which now we manure, as against enemies, as the ruins of *Silchester*

---

[142] 'Bushy ground'.

[143] 'The cause of Moss'.

[144] 'The earth not manured, what it becomes'.

[145] 'Great Britain sometimes a desert'.

in *Hampshire*, among the woods, and of *Verulamium* in *Hertfordshire*,[146] and other Roman Monuments of antiquity, do lay before our eyes at this day. After Cities (as the land became more and more peopled), they built lesser Towns, Villages, and Dorps,[147] and after more security, Country Farms and Granges; and, as these increased, wild beasts, as Bears, Boars, Wolves, and such like decreased,[148] for when their shelters, great woods, were cut down, and the Country made more and more champion, then the people more and more increased, and more and more decreasing the inconveniences that offended them.

Bailiff   I observe in this your discourse some doubts, as whether all this Island, now *Great Britain*, were a Wilderness and Desert, and whether there were ever such wild beasts in it, as you speak of.

Surveyor   If you will be satisfied by records, you may find that most of the Shires in *England* were *Forestae*; and, as for the wild beasts, Authors very authentic report of the *Caledonian* Bear, Boar, Bull, and Kine,[149] which were in this Island, with infinite many Wolves, as by reason of the great woods and vastness there are yet in *Ireland*.[150]

Bailiff   This our discourse is somewhat from our matter, yet not altogether impertinent; for if this lie hidden, and men be ignorant of the state of former times, our present swelling and ambitious conceits may seem to assume more commendation for present Art and industry, in reforming the earth, than Ages of old: wherein I perceive, and by your discourse collect, that our forefathers did more in 10 years than we in 40.[151]

Surveyor   It is true, because we saw not the earth's former deformities, we dream it was then, as now it is, from the beginning, whereas indeed our forefathers, by their diligence and travail, left unto our forefathers, and they by increasing experience and endeavor, left unto us that fair and fruitful, free from briars, bushes, and thorns, whereof they found it full.[152] And this field wherein now we are, may be an instance; for you see by the ancient ridges or lands, though now overgrown with bushes, it hath been arable land, and now become fit for no use, unless it be

---

[146]   'Silchester, Verulamium'. A Roman fort and the British town of Calleva Atrebatum were located nearby what is now Silchester, Hampshire; Verulamium, near modern St Albans, was the third-largest city in Roman Britain.

[147]   *Dorps*   villages.

[148]   'Wild beasts in Britain'.

[149]   'Caledonian Bear and Boar'.

[150]   The comparison of early modern Ireland to ancient Britain was a commonplace in English colonial literature: for discussion, see Andrew Hadfield, *Shakespeare, Spenser and the Matter of Britain* (New York and Basingstoke, 2004), p. 100.

[151]   'Former ages had more art and industry than ours'.

[152]   'The earth not in the beginning as now it is'.

reformed.[153] And the bushes that are in this field, you see, are such shrubs and dwarfy bushes, and fruitless briars, as are never like to prove good underwood, nor good haying or hedging stuff. If it were fit for either, and the Country scant of such provision, it might be preserved. But sith they have been so cropped and bruised with cattle, and sith this country is full and most inclinable by nature to this kind of stuff, more than sufficient for fencing and fuel, and corn ground and good pasture nothing plentiful, if the Tenant were a good husband he would stock it up and plow it.

Bailiff   I think it is so full of Moss, it will bear little corn.

Surveyor   The Moss[154] being turned in by the plow, will rot, and these hillocks, mole-hills, and ant-hills will enrich the ground, and cherish the seed sown.

Bailiff   What grain is best to be sown first after the stocking?

Surveyor   It seemeth to be a good stiff cold clay ground, and therefore Oats are best to heat and prepare the earth, to make it fit for wheat the next season;[155] and, after it, as the ground may be by the skillful husbandman thought fit, for wheat again or peas. But if the soil were lean and light, barley would agree better in it,[156] and a light red rush wheat, where, in the more stronger ground, the white Wheat and gray Ball (as they call it in the West parts) is best. And in some more hot and sandy grounds, Rye, as men shall by experience find the land to like the grain, and the grain the ground. For there is a natural affinity and enmity between grains and grounds, as between stomachs and meats.[157] And therefore the husbandman's experience will best guide him. But I do not a little wonder at men in this age, whom, whether I may rather accuse of idleness or ignorance, I cannot tell; for where I have travelled in sundry parts of *England*, I have in many of them found many old dry pits, anciently digged in fields, Commons, Moors, and other grounds, many of them bearing still the names of *Marl pits*,[158] and by search have been found to yield very excellent Marl, first found and digged by the providence and industry of our forefathers, and left and lost by the negligence of latter times.

Bailiff   But by your favor, fat Marl, methinks, is not good for this kind of ground, because it is a strong clay; it is better, I take it, for a hot and sandy soil, and a hot chalk better for this.

---

[153] 'Lands formerly arable, now wood'.

[154] 'Moss'.

[155] 'Oats in clay'.

[156] 'Barley in sand'.

[157] 'A mutual agreement between grains and grounds'.

[158] 'Marl pits'.

Surveyor   It is very true that observation should not have been forgotten, but is well remembered of you.

Bailiff   We have, indeed, a kind of plodding and common course of husbandry hereabouts, and a kind of peevish imitation of the most, who (as wise men note) are the worst husbands, who only try what the earth will do of itself, and seek not to help it with such means as nature hath provided; whereas if men were careful and industrious, they should find that the earth would yield in recompense for a good husband's [travail] and charge, [*Centuplum*],[159] without corrupt usury[, an hundred for one].[160]

Surveyor   I am glad you can now approve it so in reason, for I think experience doth not yet so fully teach you. I have known where land hath been very base and barren, and so continued many generations, as ground in manner forsaken and forlorn, abandoned of the plow, which after hath come into the hands of a discreet and industrious husband, that knew how, and would take the pains, and bestow the cost to manure it in kind, hath much enriched himself by it, and where before it would not bear a crop of requiteful increase, by marling and good usage hath born crop after crop, 12, 16, or 20 years, without intermission.[161] The benefit of marling, *Lancashire, Cheshire, Shropshire, Somerset, Middlesex, Sussex, Surrey*, among many other places, yea, all the shires of England can witness, though not all by one kind of soiling and marling. For neither is all kind of Marl in one place, neither any one kind in all places. But few places are so defective, but it yieldeth of itself, or is near unto some place of help. And men that will have profit must use the means; they must not sit and give aim, and wish and repine at others' increase. There must be observation, to mark how others thrive, inclination and imitation, to do the like by endeavor and charge. And if one experiment fail, try a second, a third, and many: look into places and persons, not the qualities of the land of other men, and confer it with thine own; and where there is a resemblance, mark what the best husband doth upon his land like unto thine; if it prosper, practice it, and follow the example of him that is commonly reported a thrifty husband. And, by this means, will experience grow, and of one principle of reason, many conclusions will proceed. If a man look into *Cornwall* [and some part of *Devonshire*], there shall he find, that in divers [places], that the inhabitant Farmers do soil their Lands with sea sand;[162] which, because the Country affordeth not in all places pass for cart carriage, men fetch this kind of sand 3, 4, 5 miles in sacks on horseback. And poor men live by fetching and selling it to the more wealthy. In *Devon* and *Somerset*, and in some places of *Cornwall, Sussex*, and in the South part of *Surrey*, besides their other commendable courses of husbandry, they burn their land, and call it in

---

[159] *Centuplum*   hundred-fold.

[160] 'Grounds well manured, greatest interest'.

[161] 'Ill ground made good'.

[162] 'Sea sand a good soil in Cornwall'.

the West parts, *Burning of [Beat]*, and in the South-East parts, *Devonshiring*,[163] and by that means in barren earth have excellent Rye, and in abundance. In *Shropshire, Denbeighshire, Flintshire,* and now lately in some part of *Sussex,* the industrious people are at a more extraordinary charge and toil. For the poor husbandmen and Farmers do buy, dig, and fetch limestones,[164] 2, 3, 4 miles off, and in their fields build lime-kilns, burn it, and cast it on their fields, to their great advantage: which kind of lime is of the nature of hot chalk, great helps to cold and moist grounds.

Bailiff   But this kind of stone is not to be had in all places.

Surveyor   That kind or some other is to be found in or near most places, and there is no kind of stone, for the most part, but being burned will work the like effect. So will also and especially the beach or pebble stones burned that frequent the sea shore in many places,[165] as upon the *Camber* shore near *Rye,* and at *Eastbourne* in *Sussex,* near [*Pevensey*], about *Folkestone,* and upon the coast of *Kent,* upon *Orford Ness,* and about [*Aldeburgh*], [*Hollesley*], and upon that coast in *Suffolk,* and sundry other places upon the Seashore: in some places in so great abundance, as if there were wood in competent measure, would make good and great store of lime for building, though some hold opinion they will not burn.

Bailiff   This may be far to fetch, but I do not think but every load fetched 5 miles is worth 5 shillings the carriage: this is very chargeable.

Surveyor   Yet it quiteth the cost well enough, he that is able doth find it profitable. But you are in the mind of some that I have heard, when they have been moved to entertain a help for their land, either it is too dear, or too far to fetch, or too deep in the earth, or some difficulty they pretend in it,[166] that few undertake the right way to good husbandry, like unto them that *Solomon* speaketh of,[167] that in winter will hold his lazy hands in [lousy] [ambry],[168] and for sloth will not look about his land in the cold, and sleep out the time in summer. Many difficulties and impediments prevent them that will never be good husbands nor thrifty. But such as mean to live like men, will shake off the cold with [travail], and put by sleep by their labor, and think no cost too great, no labor too painful, no way too far to preserve or better their estates. Such they be that search the earth for her fatness, and fetch it for fruit's sake. [About *Hitchin* in *Hertfordshire,* is a kind of chalk which they call *Hurlock*,[169]

---

[163] 'Devonshiring'.

[164] 'Lime-stones'.

[165] 'Pebble and Beach, good to make lime'.

[166] 'Difficulties pretended, where is no will'.

[167] *Solomon speaketh of*   Norden alludes to Proverbs 26:14: 'As the dore turneth vpon his henges, so doeth the slouthful man vpon his bed'.

[168] *lousy ambry*   dirty hovel ('ambry' refers to a closet or cupboard).

[169] *Hurlock*   also known as 'hard chalk'.

a stony marl, more fit to make lime than of itself to soil land, yet being mixed with a more fragile and gentle marl, which also aboundeth thereabout, they find it very helpful to their common fields.] Many fetch Moor-earth or Murgeon,[170] from the river between *Colebrook*[171] and *Uxbridge*, and carry it to their barren grounds in *Buckinghamshire, Hertfordshire*, and *Middlesex*, 8 or 10 miles off. And the grounds whereupon this kind of soil is employed, will endure tilth[172] above a dozen years after, without further supply, if it be thoroughly bestowed. [In *Devonshire*, about *Ashburton, Buckfastleigh*, and those parts, are certain main rocks of a most hard black flint, which the country husbandmen beat out with extreme toil, and with intolerable difficulty beat it as small as a man's fist, and cast it on their land, which doth yearly cast a kind of scale, which fats the earth so as it needs no other help in a dozen years.] In part of *Hampshire*, they have another kind of earth for their dry and sandy grounds, especially between *Fordingbridge* and *Ringwood*, and that is, the [stub] of the River of *Avon*, which they call *Mawme*,[173] which they dig in the shallow parts of the river; and the pits where they dig it, will in few years fill again: and this *Mawme* is very beneficial for their hot and sandy grounds, arable and pasture. And about *Christchurch* [*Twynham*], and up the river of [*Stour*], they cut and dig their low and best meadows to help their upland hot and heathy grounds.[174] And now of late the Farmers near *London* have found a benefit by bringing the Scavengers'[175] street-soil, which, being mixed as it is with the stone coal-dust, is very helpful to their clay [ground; for the coal-dust], being hot and dry by nature, qualifieth the stiffness and cold of the soil thereabouts. The soil of the stables of *London*, especially near the *Thames* side, is carried Westward by water, to *Chelsea, Fulham, Battersea, Putney*, and those parts, for their sandy grounds.[176]

Bailiff   Whether do you account the better, the stall or stable dung?[177]

Surveyor   The stable dung is best for cold ground, and the stall dung for hot grounds, if they be both rightly applied.[178] And of all other things, the Ashes that proceed of the great roots of stocked ground, is fittest and most helpful to a cold clay. So is the cinders that come from the Iron, where hammers or forges are, being made small and laid thin upon the cold moist land.

---

[170] 'Moor earth, or Murgeon'.

[171] *Colebrook*   most likely Coleshill, Buckinghamshire, located northwest of Uxbridge.

[172] *tilth*   tilling.

[173] 'Mawme'. Also known as 'malm', a white loamy soil produced by the mud of the river Avon.

[174] 'Meadows cut and carried into dry grounds'.

[175] 'Scavengers'.

[176] 'London soil'.

[177] *stall dung*   the mixture of waste and bedding from livestock kept indoors; *stable dung* refers to the same mixture produced from outdoor barnyards.

[178] 'Difference of stable and stall dung'.

Bailiff   I was once in *Somersetshire*, about a place near *Taunton*, called *Tandeane*;[179] I did like their land and their husbandry well.

Surveyor   You speak [not of the land of *Cabul*, the barren and dirty cities which *Solomon* gave to *Hiram, 1 Kings 9:13*,[180] but] of the *Paradise of England*;[181] and indeed their husbandry is good if it be not decayed since my being in those parts, as indeed (to be lamented) men in all places give themselves to too much ease and pleasure, to vain expense, and idle exercises, and leave the true delight, which indeed should be in the true and due prosecution of their callings: as the artificer to his trade; the husbandman to the plow; the Gentleman, not to what he list, but to what befits a Gentleman, that is, if he be called to place in the common weal, to respect his execution of Justice; if he be an inferior, he may be his own Bailiff, and see the managing and manuring of his own revenues, and not to leave it to the discretion and diligence of lither[182] swains, that covet only to get and eat. The eye of the [provident Master] may be worth two working servants. But where the Master standeth upon terms of his quality and condition, and will refuse to put (though not his hand) his eye toward the plow, he may (if it be not the greater, for I speak of the meaner) gentlelize it awhile, but he shall find it far better, and more sweet in the end, to give his fellow workmen a congee[183] early in the morning, and affably to call them, and kindly to incite them to their business, though he soil not his fingers in the labor. Thus have I seen men of good quality behave them towards their people, and in surveying of their hirelings. But indeed it is become now contemptible and reproachful, for a mean Master to look to his laborers, and that is the reason that many well left leave it again before the time, through prodigality and improvidence, and mean men industrious step in; and where the former disdained to look to his charge, this doth both look and labor, and he it is that becomes able to buy that which the idle and wanton are forced to sell. Now I say, if this sweet country of *Tandeane* and the Western part of *Somersetshire* be not degenerated, surely, as their land is fruitful by nature, so do they their best by art and industry.[184] And that makes poor men to live as well by a matter of 20 pounds *per annum*, as he that hath an hundred pounds by year in some other parts.

Bailiff   I pray you, Sir, what do they more than other men upon their grounds?

---

[179]   *Tandeane*   The Vale of Taunton Deane, northwest of the city of Taunton.

[180]   *Cabul*   Also spelled *Kavul*, a desolate area of west Galilee, given to Hiram for his aid in constructing Solomon's temple.

[181]   'Tandeane, the Paradise of England'.

[182]   *lither*   slothful, careless.

[183]   *congee*   farewell.

[184]   'Good husbandry in the West'.

Surveyor   They take extraordinary pains, in soiling, plowing, and dressing their lands.[185] After the plow, there goeth some three or four with mattocks to break the clods, and draw up the earth out of the furrows, that the lands may lie round, that the water annoy not the seed; and to that end they most carefully cut out gutters and trenches in all places, where the water is likeliest to annoy. And for the better enriching of their plowing grounds, they cut up, cast, and carry in the unplowed headlands and places of no use. Their hearts, hands, eyes, and all their powers concur in one, to force the earth to yield her utmost fruit, and the earth again in recompense of their love to her, vouchsafeth them an incredible increase.

Bailiff   What, I pray you, in quantity upon an acre, more than the ordinary rate of wheat, which is the principal grain in other Countries?

Surveyor   They have sometimes, and in some places, 4, 5, 6, 8, yea, 10 quarters in an ordinary Acre.[186]

Bailiff   I would think it impossible.

Surveyor   The earth, I say, is good unto them, and their cost and pain great to it, and there followeth a blessing, though these great proportions always hold not. The land about *Ilchester, Long Sutton, Somerton, Andrey, Middlezoy, Weston,* [*Milton Faulconbridge*],[187] and many other parts, are also rich, and there are many good husbands.

Bailiff   Do they not help their Land much by the fold?

Surveyor   Not much in those parts, but in *Dorset, Wiltshire, Hampshire, Berkshire,* and other places champion, the Farmers do much enrich their Land indeed with the sheep-fold.[188] A most easy, and a most profitable course, and who so neglecteth it, having means, may be condemned for an ill husband: nay, I know it is good husbandry, to drive a stock of sheep over a field of wheat, rye, or barley, newly sown, especially if the ground be light and dry; for the trampling of the sheep, and their treading, doth settle the earth about the corn, keeping it the more moist and warm, and causeth it to stand the faster, that the wind shake it not so easily, as it will do when the root lieth too hollow under the earth.[189]

---

[185]   'The manner of husbandry in the West'.

[186]   'Great yielding of Wheat'.

[187]   *Ilchester … Faulconbridge*   these towns and manors are located in the southeastern portion of Somerset, Norden's home county.

[188]   'The [sheepfold.]'.

[189]   'Sheep's treading good for corn'.

Bailiff   I cannot reprove you. But I know grounds of a strange nature in mine opinion; for if they be once plowed, they will hardly graze again in six or seven years,[190] yet have I seen as rich wheat and barley on it as may well approve the ground to be very fruitful. And if a stranger that knoweth not the ground look upon it after a crop, he will say it is very barren.

Surveyor   Such ground I know in many places, as in the Northwest part of *Essex*, in some places in *Cambridgeshire, Hertfordshire, Buckinghamshire,* [and] *Wiltshire*. But commonly, where you find this kind of earth, it is a red or brown soil, mixed with a kind of white, and is a mould between hot and cold, so brittle in the upper part, and so fickle, as it hath no firm setting for the grass to take rooting so soon, and in such sort as in other firmer grounds;[191] and for this kind of ground, good and well rotted stable dung is fittest. [*Varro de signis idoniae terrae ad collendum*, saith, *Si sit terra alba, quae cum fodiatur, facile [frietur], bona:*[192] white earth which when it is digged up, or plowed, if it may be easily made small, it is good for tillage; and of this very nature is the earth which you speak of, that is good for corn, not for grass.] Let us, I pray thee, walk into the next field, the Lord's demesnes, called as I take it, *Highfield*.

Bailiff   It is indeed: a large ground you see it is, and good pasture, but so overgone with *Thistles*, as we can by no means destroy them.

Surveyor   This kind of Thistle approveth the goodness of the ground; they seldom or never grow in a barren soil.

Bailiff   Yes, I have seen Thistles in mean ground.

Surveyor   It may be so, a kind of small hungry dwarfy thistle, but this kind which you see, large, high, and fatty, you shall never see in abundance in a weak soil.

Bailiff   But I wish they were fewer in number; though they may be a note of good ground, I find them nothing profitable, unless it [be] to shroud the under grass in the parching summer from the heat of the scorching Sun, for they are good for no other use that I can find.

Surveyor   That is some benefit; but the best way to kill them, is to take them up often by the roots, ever as they begin to spring, and either presently to take them

---

[190]   'Grounds long in grazing'.

[191]   'The cause why grounds will not graze in long time'.

[192]   *Varro ... bona*   from Varro's *Of Agriculture*, Book I ['you can judge whether land is fit for cultivation or not, either from the soil itself or the vegetation growing on it: from the soil according as it is ... light and crumbling easily when it is dug, of a consistency not ashy and not excessively heavy'] (Loeb Classical Library, pp. 205–6).

up, and carry them out of the fields, or else to beat them in small pieces;[193] for their nature is to revive again like an Adder, that is not thoroughly battered in the head and cut in pieces. Such is the nature of this kind of Thistle,[194] that though it be plucked up by the root, if it lie still upon the ground, as soon as it receiveth the evaporation of the earth, his slimy nature gathers a kind of new life, and begins to fasten and cleave itself to the earth again, and to shoot forth small strings, which, entering into the earth again, will bring forth many for one.

Bailiff   That is, if they be cut when they are seeded, the seeds fall and increase.

Surveyor   Nay, if you cut them in their infancy; for if they be not cut often, and that as soon as they shew themselves a foot high or less, the root will recover, and bud again: the root is as the liver in the body, from whence proceedeth all the blood that feedeth the veins, and quickeneth the body, which by obstruction and stopping of the passages putrifieth.[195] So the roots of these vegetables, when the branches are again and again cut off as they spring, the root is left so overcharged with moisture, that it will in the end yield, and give over bearing, and die: as will also Rushes, Flags, and such like,[196] which though they be strong by nature, yet by this means they will be destroyed soonest.

Bailiff   But what say you to this heathy ground? I think of all other grounds that it is the most unprofitable.

Surveyor   Indeed, naturally all heathy grounds are barren, and that comes by the saltness of the soil.

Bailiff   Doth all barrenness proceed of saltness?

Surveyor   As leanness in a man's body is principally procured by saltness of the humor,[197] so is barrenness in grounds; for salt is hot, and heat drieth, and too much drought breeds barrenness and leanness. And according to the measure and proportion of the degree of hot and cold, moisture and dryness, are all grounds fruitful and barren, as the body by these causes is fat or lean, hot or cold. Therefore, though heathy grounds be commonly in the highest degree of barrenness, yet are some more in the mean than some. Some are more tractable and more easily reduced to some use than others, and therefore hath sundry names. Heath is the general common name, whereof there is one kind, called Heather, the other Ling.[198]

---

[193] 'Thistles, how to kill them'.

[194] 'Thistles, the nature'.

[195] 'The roots of vegetable things, like the Liver in the body'.

[196] 'Rushes. Flags. Heath'.

[197] 'Saltness, hot and dry'.

[198] 'Heather. Ling'. *Ling* refers to the plant *Culluna vulgaris*, a variety of heather.

And of the particulars, there are also sundry kinds, distinguished by their several growth, leaves, stalks, and flowers:[199] as not far from *Gravesend*, there is a kind of Heather that beareth a white flower, and is not so common as the rest, and the ground is not so exceeding barren as some other, but by manurance would be brought to profitable tillage. Some, and the most, doth bear a purple or reddish flower, as in the *Forest of Windsor*, and in *Suffolk*, and sundry other places; and this kind is most common, and groweth commonly in the worst ground. In the North parts, upon the Mountains and fells, there is a kind of Ling, that bears a berry; every of these hath his peculiar earth wherein it delighteth: some in sandy and hot grounds, as between *Wilford Bridge* and *Snape Bridge* in *Suffolk*, and that is bettered especially, and the Heath killed best and soonest, by good fat marl; some in gravelly and cold earth, and that is hard to be cured, but with good stable dung. But there is a kind of Heathy ground, that seemeth altogether unprofitable for tillage,[200] because that the gravel and clay together retaineth a kind of black water, which so drencheth the earth, and causeth so much cold, as no husbandry can relieve it; yet if there be chalk-hills near this kind of earth, there may be some good done upon it, for that only [chalk] or lime will comfort the earth, dry up the superfluous water, and kill the Heath. But the sandy Heathy ground is contrarily amended, as I told you, with fat marl, and that is commonly found near the Heathy grounds, if men were provident and forward to seek for it. Every of the heathy grounds are best known of what nature they be of, whether hot or cold, by the growing of it: as if it grow low and stubbed, it argues the ground to be gravelly, cold, and most barren; where it groweth rank and high, and the stalk great, the ground is more warm and more apt for tilth,[201] yet it requireth some kind of compost, else will it not bear past a crop or two, contenting the owner; but if men will not endeavor to search for the hidden blessings of God, which he hath laid up in store in the bowels of the earth, for their use that will be painful,[202] they may make a kind of idle and vain shew of good husbandry, when indeed they only plow, and sow, and charge the earth, to bring forth fruit of [its] own accord, when we know it was cursed for our sakes, and commanded to deny us increase, without labor, sweat, and charge, which also are little available, if we serve not him in fear and reverence, who is the Author of true labors, and of the blessings promised thereunto.

Bailiff   I think there is no disease in the body of man but nature hath given virtue to some other creatures, as to herbs, plants, and other things, to be medicines for the same: so is there no kind of ground so mean, barren, and defective, but God hath provided some mean to better it,[203] if man, to whom he hath given all, will

---

[199]   'Heath, divers kinds'.

[200]   'Heathy ground unprofitable'.

[201]   'How to find the nature of the heathy grounds'.

[202]   'The earth commanded to deny us fruit without labor'.

[203]   'All kind of grounds have their help'.

search for it, and use the same to that end it was provided for. And yet this piece of ground adjoining, hath had much labor and great cost bestowed on it, and the ground little or nothing the more reformed, this Furzy close.[204]

Surveyor   Indeed, it is a strong weed, called in the North Country, *Whins*.[205] It seldom gives place where it once footeth. I will go see the form of some of the furzes. These furzes are not worth the fostering: they be dwarfy furzes, and will never grow great, nor high, and of little use.[206]

Bailiff   I speak not to learn how to preserve them, but how to destroy them.

Surveyor   But there is a kind of Furze worth the preservation, if it grow in a Country barren of wood. And of that kind there grows much in the West part of *Devonshire*, and in some parts of *Cornwall*, where they call them *French Furze*:[207] they grow very high, and the stalk great, whereof the people make faggots, and vent them in neighbor Towns, especially in *Exeter*, and make great profit of them. And this kind of Furze groweth also upon the Sea coast of *Suffolk*, but that the people make not that use of them, as in *Devonshire* and *Cornwall*; for they suffer their Sheep and Cattle to browse and crop them when they be young, and so they grow [to] scrubbed and low tufts, seldom to that perfection that they might; yet in that part of *Suffolk* they make another use of them: they plant them in hedges, and the quick-set[208] of them make a strong Fence [in dry and hot grounds where other quick-set will not grow].

Bailiff   Very silly[209] quick-set hedges, I would think, can be made of simple furzes.

Surveyor   Such as after two or three years, being cut close to the earth, they will then branch and become so thick, as no Hedge, if the Ditch be well made and quick well set, can be more defensible, being set in two or three ranks.

Bailiff   I marvel they learn it not in *Cornwall*, where for want of quick-set, and haying or hedging stuff, especially in the West parts, they are forced to make their Fences with turfs and stones.[210]

---

[204]   'Furze'.

[205]   'Whins'. Another name for furze and other thorny shrubs.

[206]   'Dwarfy Furzes'.

[207]   'French Furze'.

[208]   'Quick-set hedges of Furze'. *Quick-set* refers to cuttings gathered together and planted as a hedge.

[209]   *silly*   simple.

[210]   'Fences of Turfs and Stones'.

Surveyor   They do so indeed upon the Moors there, but sheep will easily scale their walls. But the Furze hedges which I have seen in that part of *Suffolk*, no cattle can pierce them.

Bailiff   Then are these furzes good for nothing?

Surveyor   To brew withal and to bake, and to stop a little gap in a hedge.

Bailiff   Then may we hereabouts afford the standing of them, for we have no great plenty of these necessaries in these parts.

Surveyor   I see no store of Haybote,[211] unless it be in the Lord's wood, where I think it be not lawful for men at their pleasure to take.

Bailiff   What mean you by *Haybote*? I have read it often in Leases, and I promise you, I did never take it to be that which men commonly use in hay time, as to make their forks and tools, and lay in some kind of lofts or hay talets,[212] as they call them in the West, that are not boarded: And is not that the meaning?

Surveyor   I take it not: it is for hedging stuff, namely, to make a dead hedge or rail, to keep cattle from corn or grass to be mown.

Bailiff   What difference then is there between *Haybote* and *Hedgebote*?

Surveyor   Some there is: for a hedge implieth quick-set and trees, but a hay a dead fence, that may be made one year and pulled down another, as it is common upon the downs in many countries where men sow their corn, in undefensed grounds; there they make a dead hay next some common way to keep the cattle from the corn.[213]

Bailiff   If that be the difference, we have some use of it also in this Country, but we want it much, as you see, by the lying of our hedges.

Surveyor   I see the hedges lie very unhusbandly, a true note of few good husbands; for he that will suffer his hedges to lie open, and his houses uncovered, never put a good husband's hand to his head. Quick-set hedges are most commendable, for they increase and yield profit and supply, to repair decayed places; but dead hedges or hays devour and spend, and yet are seldom secure.[214]

---

[211]   *Haybote*   wood or thorns used for patching hedges; such material was generally taken from commons.

[212]   *talets*   haylofts in buildings used to shelter livestock.

[213]   'Haybote, what it is. Hedgebote and haybote, the difference'.

[214]   'Dead hedges devour'.

Bailiff   I pray, what is the best stuff to make quick-set of?

Surveyor   The plants of white thorn, mixed here and there with Oak and Ash.

Bailiff   But the plants are not easily gotten in all places.

Surveyor   Then the berries of the white or hawthorn, Acorns, Ash-keys,[215] mixed together, and these wrought or wound up in a rope of straw will serve, but that they will be somewhat longer in growing.[216]

Bailiff   How must the rope thus stuffed with the former berries be laid?

Surveyor   Make a Trench at the top or in the edge of the Ditch, and lay into it some fat soil; and then lay the rope all along the Ditch, and cover it with good soil also; then cover it with the earth, and ever as any weeds or grass begins to grow, pull it off, and keep it as clean as may be from all hindrances; and when the seeds begin to come, keep cattle from bruising them, and after some two or three years, cut the young spring by the earth, and so will they branch and grow thick; and if occasion serve, cut them so again, always preserving the Oak and Ash to become [trees].

Bailiff   What is the best time to lay the Berries in this manner?

Surveyor   In September or October, if the Berries be fully ripe.[217]

Bailiff   What if a man were desirous to make a little grovet,[218] where now no kind of such plants do grow?

Surveyor   Till the place with the plough, in manner of following,[219] and cross plough it, and beat the clods small as may be; then sow or set Acorns, Ash-keys, Haws, Hedgeberries, Nuts, and what else you desire, in a seasonable time, and then harrow it; and for some two or three years, it were good to keep it as free from grass or weeds as could be, until the seeds were above the grass, and when they be somewhat stronger, the superfluous weeds will be the more easily culled out: I know a Wood sown of Acorns about 32 years since, the Oaks whereof are now as high as an ordinary steeple. The ground in this case must be considered, for some grounds are more naturally inclined to foster such things and some are not.[220] Some kind of Wood also loveth one kind of soil more than another, as the

---

215   *Ash-keys*   seeds of the Ash tree.
216   'How to make a quick-set hedge'.
217   'Time of quick-setting'.
218   *grovet*   a small grove.
219   'How to make a Grovet'.
220   'Several trees and the grounds [they] like'.

Juniper delighteth in a chalky soil, as appeareth in *Kent* and *Surrey*; so doth also the Yew tree, which brooketh a light and barren soil; the Walnut tree likewise in mean ground being hot, and the Elm a sandy earth; the Asp, the [Poplar], the Alder, the Abele[221] trees moist ground; the Oak most kinds of ground.

Bailiff I have a piece of land, overcome with a kind of weed that is full of prickles, and groweth a foot or two foot high, whereof no cattle will feed, and I know no way to destroy it.

Surveyor By your description it should be Gorse,[222] or prickle-Broom, a weed that groweth commonly upon grounds overtilled, and worn out of heart, and it commonly groweth not but in cold clay ground, and is hardly killed but with Lime or Chalk, and so ploughed, and then sow it two or three crops together. And if you then let it lie, it will bear you the next year a crop of [coarse] Hay, and will then yearly increase in goodness for pasture or Hay, and so much the sweeter and thicker, if you keep it low eaten[, for this weed groweth in a clay ground].

Bailiff I think you mistake the weed; you mean, I take it, *Furze* or *Whins*, which some call also *Gorse*.

Surveyor I think I mistake it not, but such as call Furze, Gorse, are as much mistaken, as they that call Brakes, Broom.[223]

Bailiff Because you speak of *Broom*, I know a Lordship of my Landlord's, which no doubt you shall survey too; it is much pestered with *Broom*, and there hath been much charge and pains, and Art too, bestowed in destroying of them, but all in vain: they have been cut, stocked up by the roots, as was thought, burnt, ploughed, and yet they grow again.

Surveyor It is the nature of Furze, Broom, and Brakes, to keep their standing, and hardly will yield the possession once gotten in a field;[224] for commonly they like the soil well, and the soil them, and where there is a mutual congruity, there is seldom a voluntary separation. And therefore, as long as there is not a disturbance of their possession with a contrary earth, they will keep where they are: for as the Fish loveth and liveth in the water, the Chameleon by the air, the Salamander in the fire, and either of them being taken from his Element, will die; so these kinds of weeds (for so they may be called) as long as they possess the soil they affect, do

---

[221] *Able*   White Poplar.

[222] 'Gorse'. Also know as prickly shrub, and usually not distinguished from furze or whin.

[223] 'Broom'. A *brake* is a cluster of brushwood, whereas *broom* refers to a specific kind of shrub, the *Sarothamnus*.

[224] 'Furze, Broom, Brakes, their nature'.

what you can, they will live. And therefore as the soil is commonly barren, hot and dry wherein they live, make this ground fat and fruitful, and they will die.[225] And therefore the greatest enemy that may be set to encounter them, is good and rich Marl, and thereupon, the plough some few years together, and you shall see, they will shrink away, and hide their heads.

Bailiff   But commonly this kind of fat *Marl* is not to be gotten in all places: nay, seldom where these barren grounds are.

Surveyor   It is true, they commonly come not, and say to the lazy husbandman: 'Here I am'. It is the nature of all things to covet rest, and where dumb and dead things lurk, is not easily found without diligent search. Gold, Silver, Brass, Tin, Lead, Coal, Slate, and great Millstones, shew not themselves voluntarily, but are found by scrutation[226] and discretion.[227] And I think many treasurable blessings lie hid from slothful men, for want of search, and worthily. So doth this notable commodity of Marl, from the eyes of the Husbandman, until he dive into the bowels of the earth to seek: and admit he miss it here, he may find it there; if he fail today, he may get it tomorrow. But Thrift hath no greater enemies than Ignorance and Idleness:[228] the one persuades it cannot be, the other it will not be. And between these sluggards, these Weeds, Briars, Thorns, Thistles, Fuze, Broom, Gorse, and a thousand marks of the first curse annoy us, which by the blessing of God, industry and charge might easily and shortly be removed out of our sights. And yet if the view of them daily could make us, or move us to call our first disobedience to consideration and repentance, I would wish Thorns to grow where Corn stands. But sith no spectacle of former threats, no use of present blessings, will move the hard hearted, either to seek by labor or charge to reform these evils, easy to be reformed, let us leave to discourse, and he that hath understanding and will, let him use them here in this toilsome life, and be not idle;[229] for, if we do what we can, these Cankers will follow us, these inconveniences will annoy us, and will procure every day new labor, and new cost, and new diligence, and new Art, to make us know that *Omnia proposuit Labori Deus*: Man of necessity must labor. And when he hath sweat and toiled, and bestowed all his skill and utmost charge, if God add not a blessing, all is lost. *Paul* may plant, *Apollo* may water, but if God give not the increase, the labor is vain. *God maketh a fruitful land barren, for the wickedness of the people that dwell therein*:[230] there is a curse. Again, *A handful of Corn sown upon the tops of high Mountains, shall so prosper, as the*

---

[225] 'How to kill Furze, Broom, and Brakes'.

[226] *scrutation*   a Norden neologism, referring to a detailed search or examination (*OED*).

[227] 'All hidden benefits must be sought for'.

[228] 'Ignorance and Idleness enemies to thrift'.

[229] 'None should be idle'.

[230] 'Psalm 107:34'.

fruits and ears thereof shall shake like the high Cedars in Lebanon:[231] here is a blessing. It is a gracious thing therefore to fear and reverence him, whose blessing and cursing so much prevail, and to pray to him for success in our endeavors, and to glorify him for his blessings.

Bailiff You have divinely concluded: and I wish not only the words of your mouth, but the substance of your meaning were fully engraven, and truly seated in the hearts of all that labor. So, no doubt, but the Lord would be always ready to bless their endeavors: Although indeed *Job* saith, *The earth is given unto the hands of the wicked, and they wax old and wealthy.*[232] And *David* in divers and sundry places declareth that the wicked prosper most in the world. And I tell you, it is a daunting[233] unto weak men, that think they serve God truly, and many times it goeth worse with them, than with such as seem seldom or never to call upon his name.

Surveyor   But when *David* considered the end of these men, he could say, that *the Lord had set them in slippery places.* And that *they that are blessed of God, shall inherit the earth.* And *whatsoever they do, it shall prosper.*[234] Therefore, I say, that he that commendeth his labor unto the Lord, and the success of all his endeavors unto his divine providence, who doth and can always bring all things to pass for our best good, whether it be the full fruits of the earth for our relief and comfort, or scarcity and want, for our trial, he is sure to stand fast, and *shall be as a tree planted by the river's side, whose leaf shall never wither,* and *in the time of dearth, he shall have enough to sustain his necessity.*[235]

Bailiff   It is a good and holy resolution, on which all men ought to rest themselves with a faithful and patient expectation. And therefore he that hath *fat and fruitful ground,* let him be laborious and thankful, and he that hath lean and barren, let him be painful and patient.

Surveyor   You say well, and so I leave you: And for other matters, and better satisfaction in these things thus superficially discoursed, I refer you to the advice of the better able to resolve you. I will return to my former task.

Bailiff   I thank you for your patience and pains, and I commend you to your labors. And as your occasions shall challenge my further poor service, I shall be ready.

The end of the fifth Book.

---

[231] 'Psalm 72:26'. (Psalm 72:16).

[232] 'Job 9:24, 8, 21:7'. Norden combines three passages from the Book of Job: 9:24, Chapter 8, and 21:7.

[233] *daunting* discouragement.

[234] 'Psalm 37:22'.

[235] 'Psalm 1:3'.

THE SURVEYOR'S DIALOGUE, CONTAI-
ning a brief conference between a
PURCHASER of Land and a SURVEYOR:
Wherein are some points necessary to be
considered, of such as are able and willing to Purchase Land in Fee-
simple, or by Lease.

THE SIXTH BOOK.

Purchaser   Sir, as I take it, you did Survey a Manor wherein I dwell, called the Manor of Beauland.

Surveyor   I did Survey a Manor of that name indeed.

Purchaser   It may be you have forgotten me, yet I was one of your Jury of Survey there, and I did accompany you in your perambulation of the Manor. And I remember the Bailiff, among many other questions, demanded you one, wherein I would have been glad to have had your opinion, but that you had no fit opportunity at that time to give such satisfaction as I did wish.

Surveyor   What, I pray you, was the question?

Purchaser   Whether it were better for a man that had money in his purse, a thousand Marks or a thousand pounds, and would lay it out upon land, to purchase a Fee simple or to buy a Lease.[1]

Surveyor   I can hardly admit leisure to answer you by reason of other occasions. But in regard of former acquaintance to do you a pleasure, I will borrow so much time, as may [afford consideration to answer] this question. So you can be satisfied with some brief reasons, although I know that such are the different opinions of men

---

[1]   'A question touching Freehold and Lease to Purchase, when a man hath little money'.

in this point, as that which will fully satisfy one, will draw some others the further into doubt, as we see in divers other like cases: *Multa capita, multae sententiae.*[2]

Purchaser   I confess my Judgment is mean in this point, because I have not had hitherto any practice in the purchase of land. And I must also confess that I am not provided for that business, as some great Masters who can undergo matters of many thousands; yet I think it in my discretion, as fit to be well advised in the smallest, as in matters of greatest moment:[3] for a little well employed, may prove so far more beneficial than a greater portion, by how much the same is laid out with more discretion and better Judgment. And though, to tell you truly, my stock will not exceed a thousand Marks,[4] yet would I gladly bestow it upon such a thing as I might live thereby, and my children after me.

Surveyor   Then I perceive you would deal with some matter of perpetuity.

Purchaser   I mean some Fee simple.[5] For, you know, it is a good matter to be a Freeholder. It is a quietness to a man's mind, to dwell upon his own, and to know his Heir certain.[6] And, indeed, I see that men are best reputed of, that are seized of matter of inheritance: Leases are but of base account. For they have often times their livings taken over their heads. So hath the Freeholder of inheritance never. And many other fair preferments, are laid upon a man that holdeth to him and his Heirs, that never are bestowed upon men of inferior tenures and terms.

Surveyor   Are you a Scholar?

Purchaser   No, truly.

Surveyor   Then nature hath taught you the Art of Ambition.[7] And I fear you have set too fair a color upon so mean a proportion, as is between your portion of money you have to bestow, and the exceeding contentments which you expect to grow by the land you purpose to purchase with the same.

---

[2]   *Multa ... sententiae* ['So many minds, so many opinions'], a variation on Terence's proverb 'Quot hominess, tot sententia' ['there are as many opinions as there are people'] (*Phormio*, in *Terence*, vol. 2, John Barnsby [trans.], Loeb Classical Library [Cambridge, MA, 2001], l. 454).

[3]   'Good to be advised as well in small as great Purchases'.

[4]   *thousand Marks*   a Mark was a unit of value equal to 13 shillings and 4 pence, or approximately two-thirds of one pound. The Purchaser's estate is thus worth around 660 pounds, a sizeable amount by early modern standards.

[5]   *Fee simple*   the approximation of absolute property in the early modern period; right to pass on ownership to stipulated heirs (also see p. 45 and n. 29).

[6]   'Some men's vain opinions of Freeholds'.

[7]   'Nature teacheth Ambition'.

Purchaser   Is every man that desires to Purchase, ambitious?

Surveyor   Not as he is a Purchaser. But the humor of his aspiring, being discovered, discovereth his ambition to be the motive to the Purchase. Will, and Ableness to Purchase, are in themselves so far from Ambition, as it is a blessed benefit given of God to man:[8] and a great cause of rejoicing, is it to the heart of the most religious man, when from a low estate and small portion, God doth give means to raise himself, by lawful Purchase. But if all his aim therein be a vainglorious thirst, I cannot give it any other fitter title than Ambition, which is a vice. And, methinks, I smell it in yourself by all your former arguments of the happiness of a Freeholder.[9] It is a good thing you say, (and so do I), to be a Freeholder. But you must think he is not so free but he is subject to many services, whereunto some inferior tenures are not. As when you are a Freeholder experience will teach you. Also it is (as you say) a good thing to dwell upon a man's own. Freeholders only dwell not on their own; he that hath a Lease but for a year, dwells upon his own for a time. As for your Heir certain, and apparent; no doubt it is a comfort, so it be a comfort: for comforts prove in those casual and changeable inclinations sometimes crosses.[10] Tender Heirs are like young twigs: they will bend and be wreathed at the will of the parent; but, grown strong, they prove often strong distractions to best minded and wealthiest parents, especially when they have learned to say, *My Father cannot put away his Land from me*. Then he begins to feel his father's health to be his sickness, his father's long life, his lingering death.[11] I need not tell you what succeeds; if you see it not, the mist of partial observation dazzles your eyes: yet would I have you to know this, that I hold it great happiness for a man of that estate to have an heir, but greater, and the greatest, to have a virtuous, a frugal and thrifty Heir. Touching the *Reputation* which you pretend to gain by the title of a *Freeholder of inheritance*, that is seen to be won and lost, as is or shall be the report of your good or ill conversation among your neighbors, which often poor men get and rich men lose. The clearing of the fear of having your living to be taken over your head, is some [reason] indeed: but many times, the Heir to avoid the danger, sells it himself, sometimes before it come to his hand. For the preferments, commonly laid, or expected to be laid upon a man of that estate, howsoever ambitious men may think it glorious, men wise enough, of a temperate and moderate spirit, rather embrace their own freedom, and think it far more precious than the fairest imposed or assured preferments to office, commonly accompanied with care and controlment.[12]

---

8   'A blessing to be able to Purchase'.

9   'Ambition, what?'

10   'Seeming comforts may prove certain crosses'.

11   'Fathers' long life, some Sons' lingering death'.

12   'True freedom better than office'.

Purchaser   I perceive you favor not *estates of inheritance*, the best and most absolutely reputed tenure that any man can be endowed with.

Surveyor   You much mistake me, and the matter: for I ground not my objections upon any unworthiness of that most worthy tenure, but upon your ambitious assuming reputation, security, office, and vainglorious preferments, by reason of so small a mite of means as your stock (being but 1,000 Marks) is able to Purchase.

Purchaser   It will Purchase (as I take it) about forty pounds a year[, with my thousand Marks].

Surveyor   Thereabouts, at 16 years' Purchase. A weak revenue to support so weighty contentments, as you have propounded to yourself.

Purchaser   I must cut my coat according to my cloth: spend no more than will arise of the Farm.

Surveyor   But your thousand Marks being gone, where is then the mean to stock your Farm? For a Farm without stock, is like a Piece without Powder, or a Steeple without Bells.[13]

Purchaser   Truly, I confess it; but if I should reserve any of that portion for the stock, it would Purchase far less. And therefore I conceive it better to strain myself some other way to stock it, though I should give interest for awhile, or let it out for some few years, to enable me to stock it myself afterwards.

Surveyor   So shall you soon indeed make trial of your adventure, either to arrive safe with little advantage, or to suffer utter shipwreck[, to lose both yourself and your Ship]. For the first, *Interest*, the mother of misery,[14] the longer she goeth with her birth, the greater monster she breeds, that immediately devours him that begat it, worse than the Viper that kills the mother. Of two evils, the least is, to let it. If then thou be accompanied with a charge, thou and thy charge must be maintained. If that eat up thine income, or the better part of it, little will be laid up for the future stock, and so shalt thou rest *in statu quo prius*,[15] as able in the end, as at the beginning of the term.

Purchaser   I know of no other course to dispose of my money, in way of Purchase; for lives are casual, and years run out so swiftly, as I cannot think of a better employment of my money, than to lay it out upon land of inheritance, for that is perpetual.

---

[13]   'A Farm without stock, what like?'

[14]   'Interest the mother of miseries'.

[15]   *in statu quo prius* ['in the same state as before'].

Surveyor   There are many of your mind who, by the greatness of their spirits, undermine their own estates, and so hurl voluntary repentance upon their own heads, which they cannot avoid.

Purchaser   If a man have a competent bargain, there needs no repentance.

Surveyor   A convenient bargain requires more than a competent *quid* for a competent *quo*: that is a bargain barely worth a man's money.[16] As he that hath a thousand pounds in his purse, and bestows it upon a Jewel worth a thousand pounds, unless he purpose, and can dispose this Jewel for more than it cost, he may say he hath a Jewel worth a thousand pounds, and had a thousand pounds in money; but his money being gone, instead of using it to his gain, he looks on his Jewel with grief, especially when commanding necessity, requires needful supplies: then lies his Jewel dead, and cannot, but had he his money, it would have supplied his wants.

Purchaser   This in mine opinion is little to the matter in question, for I lay not out my money so, but that I have a yearly profit, answerable to the value of my money, and lies not dead, as doth his Jewel.

Surveyor   Little odds between nothing coming in, and something coming in and profit nothing: as doth your Farm, which either wanting stock, can yield little, or having stock of interest, eats the gain. But the question propounded was, whether a man of small means, were better for his profit to Purchase Fee simple, or to buy a Lease.[17]

Purchaser   That indeed is the question, and I think a more profitable course, to purchase land in Fee simple, than to buy a lease.

Surveyor   I say more expedient it cannot be, for a man that hath 10 or 20 or more thousand pounds in his purse; for thereby he may confirm his hope of hereditary succession, and consequently of Honor and Office.[18] But to speak in answer to your stock, at the most (as you say) 1,000 Marks, were it two or three thousand pounds, I affirm these kinds of Purchases are not most profitable.

Purchaser   What then in your opinion is the best course to lay so small portions of money in, as you speak of.

Surveyor   Leases.

---

[16] 'A competent bargain, what?'

[17] 'The question'.

[18] 'With whom the Purchase of Fee simple best agreeth'.

Purchaser Alas, a Lease is gone in the third part of a man's age, unless it be for fifty, sixty, or an hundred years: upon such a man might be content to lay out his money.

Surveyor I hold rather a Lease of one and twenty years more beneficial.[19]

Purchaser That were strange: How can you prove that?

Surveyor Admit you have 1,000 pound in your purse, and you will Purchase a Lease for 100 years. It will cost you thirteen years' Purchase at the least. So your 1,000 pound will buy about 80 pound *per annum*, which will not amount unto the interest of your money by twenty pounds a year. But if you buy a Lease of 21 years, you may have it for 7 years' Purchase. So will your 1,000 pound buy a Lease worth 140 pounds a year, exceeding the interest of your money 40 pounds a year. So there is threescore pounds more by a Lease of twenty one years, than by a Lease of a hundred years, which whether it be more profitable for a man to buy, that hath no great means, judge you.

Purchaser Truly for my part I do now conceive it so well, as I am utterly dissuaded from Purchasing land in *Fee simple*, or for more years than one and twenty, unless I had a greater portion, than indeed I have. And methinks I might compare myself (in the mind that I was) unto one that had four pence in his pocket, who would needs buy a purse to put it in, and so bought him a purse which cost him a groat:[20] and he had as much money left to put in his new purse, as I should have had to have stocked my new Farm, when I had bestowed my thousand Marks upon forty pounds a year.[21] But now buying a lease for one and twenty years, my thousand Marks will bring me near threescore pounds a year, and yet reserve money sufficient to stock the Farm: I do not think, but if other men of my poor means did well conceive of this, they would be of the same mind that now I am.

Surveyor I neither persuade nor dissuade any, to or from their own opinions; for I know, it is as hard a matter to draw some men to a truth, as to remove some from an error. And some I know are always most persuaded to embrace that which is most in use, and refuse the better, that few affect, and not many have proved:[22] And therefore to make a man's singular conceit (have it in experience and practice never so deserved allowance) the precedent of other men's imitation, will suspend it until it become as common as vice itself; and therefore to yourself I say, do not as I persuade, but persuade yourself, as your own conceit, in your seeming reason, shall tell you what is best or worse; though it be matter of fact, it is no matter of saving faith, therefore take right or left, as you list.

---

[19] 'A Lease of twenty one years most beneficial in some cases'.

[20] *groat* a coin equal in value to four pence.

[21] 'A fit comparison'.

[22] 'Some will embrace what is most in use'.

Purchaser   I am not so fickle in my fancy, as it should fly from one conceit to another, after such due satisfaction as you have given me; for whatsoever other men's judgments may yield in this behalf, I take it the truest course for best profit by smallest means, and I think no arguments can be so forcible to remove what I have conceived. Only one scruple remaineth, which I may rather term a frivolous doubt, because it may succeed otherwise than I fear, and that ariseth in my conceit by reason of the shortness of the term of one and twenty years:[23] for if a man leave his son a Farm for that term, either it may be taken over his head, or else he must be forced to buy it again within fifteen or sixteen years, which both are things very unpleasant and most distasteful to most men.

Surveyor   It is true, but the end of the term being truly known, it takes away some of the harshness, by a provident preparation against the time: for if a son to whom a man leaveth threescore pounds *per annum* (your own proportion) with a stock; if he, by his frugality, providence and careful husbandry, cannot lay up, in sixteen years so much, as will either procure the same again, or some other as valuable elsewhere, leave him to live as he may after the term ended; for it is not probable that he would be thrifty or become more wealthy if he had thrice as much, for it is not the quantity of the thing left, but the quality of him to whom it is left, that proveth this proposition true or false.

Purchaser   It is so; for I have known some meanly left with leases, have grown rich, and some rich of inheritance become poor.

Surveyor   As are men's dispositions good or ill, so commonly is the continuance of their estates prosperous or adverse.

[*Purchaser*]   Surely, it is true. It so appeareth by the carriage of young men in these days, who shew themselves most improvident and careless,[24] for the most part, only such as stand in possibility to be advanced by the ability of parents or friends, but such also (by a kind of impious imitation) as have no other means than either their own labors or sinister shifts. For as are the diseases of the body, of late become *yearly wonders* for their strangeness, so men's profane humors and vicious qualities grow yearly more strange, by taking new courses of chargeable wickedness: changeable fashions in apparel, gaming, the pot,[25] and their lascivious lives, rend patrimonies in pieces, and bring men to mere beggary, that before scorned the mere title of *Gentleman*. A due observer may well note, that where one, left by a careful father wealthy, and by the grace of God, is of discretion fit to manage what is left him, ten grow thereby the more insolent, secure, prodigal, vicious, and consume more in one year by their rank riot than their careful

---

[23]   'A doubt in a lease of 21 years'.

[24]   'The carriages of young men careless'.

[25]   *the pot*   alcohol.

fathers or regardful friends did get by their care and industry in ten.[26] Whereby groweth that strange vicissitude which we see in the world, the father to purchase, never continuing long in one line: many generations enjoy not one and the same inheritance. *Patrimonies* are like unto the feigned *wheel of Fortune*,[27] resembling also the waves of the Sea, driven now to the shore, and forthwith to the channel, as the tide and the winds; so are possessions posted from one to another, more in these latter days than ever before: minds become inconstant breed estates inconstant. In former ages an inheritance continued many generations, never altering either the line or the name of the owner; men had a kind of religious regard to preserve the inheritance of their ancestors. And, in these days, they think it a superstitious ceremony to keep [it:] the father buyeth in hope to better his son, and the son sells to dishonor himself: And therefore I think whether it be *Fee simple* or *Lease*, all is bait for a buyer, and a wasteful son is indifferent in both.

Surveyor   There is no cause so much to assure a son of future means by *Leases*, as by *Fee simples*:[28] for an eldest son is in part assured of his Patrimony, howsoever he carry himself; but leases may be given as a chattel, and therefore may make a son the more awful. But it is a hard thing, that neither the love of parents, in persuading, nor the law of Magistrates by punishing, can prevent these daily increasing mischiefs: I think it may be affirmed, that the fault is especially in parents, by given and suffering, as also in Magistrates in not correcting such willful transgressing the laws of love and obedience, and to shorten the line of that common liberty of young men whereby they live, do, and continue as they list. And so much the more, by how much they find their own strength, to rest in the ability and doting love of their abused parents, who (whilst they live) support these liberties by supplies of needless wants. And the hope of the whole, after their deaths, make young men dive into the deepest of the danger of causeless debts, which (the parents dead) forceth to be emboweled the best of his new fallen Patrimony: the relics whereof he must sacrifice, to appease the violence of that devouring *Hydra*, and piecemeal offers the rest to his own vice and vainglory.

Purchaser   Truly, these days affording such fruits, I wonder whether is more the cause, the folly of parents or the frenzy of children.

Surveyor   I think indeed many children (as it seemeth by their dissolute lives) are possessed with a kind of frenzy or madness; for they are as far from awe of government, as are such as are mad indeed. And yet I think of the two, the foolishness of doting parents is more the cause of their children's madness than is the mere natural inclination of the children:[29] for did parents keep a kind of power in their

---

[26]   'The cause of the confusion of Patrimony'.

[27]   'Patrimonies like Fortune's wheel'.

[28]   'A son cannot so much depend upon leases as upon Fee simple'.

[29]   'Fathers doting on their children, the cause often times of their children's hurt'.

own hands, and did not feed their children's humors too full, they could not but withdraw, though not their desires, yet their means from those wasteful courses.

Purchaser   It seemeth to me a matter almost impossible. My reason is, because it is now grown to so general a disease, if it were in the City only, and not in the Country, or were it in one shire, and not in another, or in one town or parish and not in another: nay, were it in one house and not in another, I would then think the Country might reclaim the City, one shire, one town, or one house might reform another: but being as it is, so universal, in Cities, country towns and houses, if any place or person be now free, it, or he, is in danger to be seduced; and therefore one father may endeavor by counsel, force, or fair words, to order his son in the way of hope to be happy, but what ten fathers by counsel can work in two children in much time, one impious, idle, vain, and vicious neighbor's son shall poison twenty in less. And therefore unless as the infection is general, there could be found a general preservative, it will grow, *ab hoc malo, ad illud pejus*, to be daily worse and worse.

Surveyor   So then let us leave them, and I leave you: fare you well.

Purchaser   Nay, I must needs entreat your opinion in one thing more; I will not be tedious. When a man doth purchase Land in *Fee simple* or Lease, are there not some special points of observation to be considered before a man either buy or sell?

Surveyor   I think none is so ignorant or simple, but if he buy a Horse, he will see what pace he hath, whether he be sound, and whether he that sells him have right to the Horse, and other circumstances fit to be considered in the buying of a Horse. And will any man be so mad as to buy or sell Land without due consideration, what he buys or sells?[30] And yet I must confess, that some do purchase, and some do sell, as they that cut wood over their heads: the chips fall into their eyes; they see not what they buy, or what they sell. Many have been and are daily deceived, for want of the true judgment of the things they buy or sell, not seeking to inform themselves by themselves; nor, for fear of charge, be informed by some of understanding to view the thing they buy or sell, a matter savoring either of little providence, or great security.

Purchaser   Wherein I pray you should a man seek especially to be informed in buying or selling Land?

Surveyor   Methinks it is a needless question, because these things are common to every man's conceit. But to satisfy your desire, I take it the *Title* is first to be duly considered, and then the drawing of the Evidence,[31] for in these days there go more

---

[30]   'None is so simple but will observe what he buys'.

[31]   'Things to be considered in a Purchase'.

words to a bargain of ten pound land a year, than in former times were used in the grant of an Earldom; and yet methinks many superfluous words might be omitted, and the assurance good, as they were in former times, with far fewer words, but that I leave to the learned, that know what is fit to be inserted or omitted, according to the quality of the thing purchased, only the true meaning should be the best assurance. Secondly, the *yearly and likely permanent value* is to be considered. The *quantity, quality*, and *nature of the soil*. The means to better it, as by cleansing and clearing of the grounds of bushes, and other inconveniences, draining of the low, boggy, and watery grounds; where and how to get *Marl, Chalk, Moor-earth, Sea-sand*, and such like means to improve and better mean grounds. The scarcity or plenty of *Wood* and *Timber*, which are either a help or hindrance to the sale. To observe the *Fences*, and the means to continue them. The *Water*, whether in Springs, River, or standing Pools, which last is most inconvenient. The *Housing*, how convenient and competent they are, and how they stand presently repaired, and the supposed charge to do it. The *situation of the place*, for air, sweet or contagious. The ways, good or cumbersome. *Commons of pasture, Commons of Estover*,[32] if any be. What *Commodities* it especially yieldeth: how and where they may be best vented; and where, and how far off *household necessaries* are to be had. Duties to the Church, and Commonwealth, with services due to the same. What issues out in Rent, or other charges; what is paid to it, and many other things may be considered in the view of a Manor, which at large are set down in the second and third Books.[33]

Purchaser   These are necessary notes of remembrance, which are fit to be considered, both by him that selleth, and him that buyeth any Land, the neglect whereof may prejudice either; and thereby no doubt many are deceived, and some abused. I am loath to trouble you further. I thank you for your patience; I will leave you to your occasions.

Prov. 17:2.

A discreet Servant shall have rule over an unthrifty Son.

FINIS.

---

[32]   *Commons of Estover*   the right to take wood from common lands for use as fuel; as E.P. Thompson notes, this customary usage was often a spark for conflict ('Custom', p. 104). For further discussion, see Peter Linebaugh, *The Magna Carta Manifesto: Liberties and Commons for All* (Berkeley, 2008).

[33]   The Surveyor breaks the diegetic frame of the dialogue by making a cross-reference to the earlier books of the text.

Textual Notes

Emendations to the copy-text (*1618*) are listed below, along with substantive variations among the previous editions of the text, and are keyed by page number and word to this edition.

Abbreviations of editions cited:

1607—John Norden, *The Surueyors Dialogue* (London: Hugh Astley, 1607) STC 18639

1610—John Norden, *The Surueiors Dialogue* (London: William Stansby and John Windet for John Busby, 1610) STC 18640

1618—John Norden, *The Surueiors Dialogue* (London: Thomas Snodham, 1618) STC 18641

1853—John Norden. The Surveyor's Dialogue. John W. Papworth (ed.) *Architectural Publication Society: Detached Essays and Illustrations issued during the years 1848 … 1852* (London: Thomas Richards, 1853)

Title Page

3   *Gentlemen*] *1618*; *all Gentlemen 1610*

3   *Farmers*] *or any other Farmar 1610*

3   and Husbandmen] *1618*; or Husbandman *1610*

3   hire,] *1618*; *not in 1610*

3   necessary] *1618*; excellent *1610*

3   The use] *1618*; The true and right use *1610*

3   fit as well *for* LORDS, *as for* TENANTS] *1618*; or Occupation thereof, as well in the Lords, as in the Tenants: being the true facultie of Surueying of all manner of Lands and Tenements, &c. *1610*

3   the third time] *1618*; newly *1610*

3   familiar] *1618*; familiar and pleasant *1610*

3   or by Lease] *1618*; or otherwise by Lease *1610*

3   Printed … 1618] *1618*; Printed by *I.W.* [*W.S.* in some editions] for *I. Busby*, and are to be sold at his shop in Saint Dunstanes Church yard in Fleetstreet, 1610 *1610*

Dedicatory Letter to Robert Cecil

6   27 Martii, *1610] 1610, 1618*; primo Ianuar. 1607 *1607*

Preface to Readers

7   its] *this edn*; it *1618*
8   caution] *1618*; prevention *1607, 1610*
8   travail] trauell 1618
8   revenues] *1610, 1618*; commands *1607*

The Author to His Book

11   alis] *this edn*; aliis *1618*

Contents

13   The sixth book ... or by Lease] *1610, 1618*; *not in 1607*

Book 1

16   condemned] *this edn*; contemned *1618*
18   reason] *this edn*; reasou *1618*
20   least] *this edn*; lest *1618*
25n   'Great ... freeholders'] *1618*; *not in 1610*
28   whereupon] *this edn*; whereupou *1618*
28n   Grounds] *this edn*; Gounds *1618*
29   its] *this edn*; it *1618*
30   Besides] *this edn*; Beside *1618*
32   attendance] *this edn*; attendants *1618*
33   politic] *this edn*; politique *1618*
35   whether] *this edn*; wherther *1618*
35   courses] *this edn*; couses *1618*
36   order's] *this edn*; order *1618*
36   outward] *this edn*; ontward *1618*
37n   Tenants] *1610*; Tenant *1618*

Book 2

42   practice] *this edn*; practicke *1618*
44   or *fermes* ... victual] *1618*; *not in 1610*

44	Furthermore … *Mainer,*] *1618*; It may also take the name of *Mainer 1610*
44n	Mesuage] *this edn*; M suage *1618*
47	than] *this edn*; the *1618*
47n	c. 3] *this edn*; 3.c. *1618*
50	, although … probable.] *1618*; *not in 1610*
50	for it] *1618*; for his rent behind *1610*
50–51	And if … the Land] *1618*; *not in 1610*
51	And it … apportioned] *1618*; *not in 1610*
51	, and … remedy] *1618*; *not in 1610*
53	manner] *this edn*; mannor *1618*
53	nearer] *this edn*; neere *1618*
54	forfeit,] *1618*; *not in 1610*
55	, or farelife] *1618*; *not in 1610*
55	belonged] *1610 (errata)*; belongeth *1618*
57	in some Manors two years,] *1618*; *not in 1610*
57	in Cornwall … five pence;] *1618*; *not in 1610*
58	half a yard land … Country] *1618*; *not in 1610*
58	But commonly] *1618*; So that every *1610*
58	hundred] *this edn*; hundreth *1618*
58	In *Shippon* … 10 Acres.] *1618*; *not in 1610*
58	So … I see] *1618*; *not in 1610*
58	The Earldom of Richmond,] *1618*; *not in 1610*
59n	2] *this edn*; 3 *1618*
60	as the statutes … exacted] *1618*; *not in 1610*
62	the use and waste thereof] *1618*; it *1610*
62n	are] *this edn*; ae *1618*
65	travail] *this edn*; travel *1618*
66	lineaments of body] *1618*; limes *1610*
66	parts] *1618*; lineaments *1610*
67n	34] *this edn*; 3.4 *1618*
68	others] *this edn*; other *1618*
68	the education and] *1618*; *not in 1610*
70	and so far] *1618*; and wherein *1610*
73	quasi servus] *this edn*; quasiseruus *1618*
73	mancipii] *1618*; *not in 1610*
73	many of them] *1618*; they *1610*
73	In Suffolk … meat] *1618*; *not in 1610*
73	, before their enfranchisement] *1618*; *not in 1610*
74	; as Solomon … 21] *1618*; *not in 1610*
75	But … forbid.] *1618*; *not in 1610*
77	smile] *1610 (errata)*; simple *1618*
77	as … hardly] *1618*; *not in 1610*

Book 3

80	For … lands.] *1618*; *not in 1610*
81	too] *1610*; to *1618*
82	The fire] *1618*; Nay truely, I will excuse that fault, the fire *1610*
82	of ambition] *1618*; in the ayre *1610*
82	of good hospitality from the poor,] *1618*; from earthly creatures *1610*
82	, as … bellies] *1618*; *not in 1610*
82	nos mutamur] *this edn*; nos fatuamur *1618*; omnia mutantur *1610*
82	especially] *1618*; Now too *1610*
82	body.] *1618*; body, I shall like it well. *1610*
83	A.B.] *1618*; *not in 1610*
83	, and every of them] *1618*; *not in 1610*
83	own letters] *1618*; letters *1610*
83n	'It … Lands.'] *1618*; *not in 1610*
84	, in words … discretion] *1618*; *not in 1610*
84	by how much] *1618*; as the *1610*
84	by] *1618*; of *1610*
85	travail] *this edn*; travel *1618*
85	of your own Evidences,] *1618*; *not in 1610*
85	being of inheritance] *1618*; *not in 1610*
85	or if you deny] *1618*; or denie *1610*
85	to himself or his posterity] *1618*; *not in 1610*
87	, as … Manors] *1618*; *not in 1610*
87	*Freeholders … And*] *1618*; *not in 1610*
87n	'Littleton … cap.5.'] *1618*; *not in 1610*
88	namely … holdeth,] *1618*; *not in 1610*
88	or daughter … husband] *1618*; *not in 1610*
90	But that Lords] *1618*; But that it should be generall, and that the Lords *1610*
90	But if … England] *1618*; *not in 1610*
91	*Commons … lies*] *1618*; *not in 1610*
93	her] *this edn*; here *1618*
93	courtesy, or … widower.] *1618*; courtesie? *1610*
93	*Gavelkind*] *1618*; *Gauelkind* at *Islington* neere *London 1610*
93	In *Ottery Saint Mary* … unmarried.] *1618*; *not in 1610*
93	inherit.] inherite, as *in Gauelkind.Kitch. 1610*
94	: the like … customs.] *1618*; *not in 1610*
94	Surveyor] *this edn*; *not in 1618*
95	, due for that acre] *1618*; *not in 1610*
95	many Tenants seem] *1618*; some close hearted Tenants will seeme *1610*
95	; wherein … again] *1618*; *not in 1610*
96	Wednesday] *1618*; munday *1610*

96–7	The title ... *St Michaelis*] *1618*; *not in 1610*
97	festum *St Michaelis*] *1853*; fectum *Sc Michis 1618*
97	, and what goods possess they] *1618*; *not in 1610*
97	*Solomon ... Proverbs 22:28.*] *1618*; *not in 1610*
97n	Neifes] Niefes *1618*
98	: a toft ... house] *1618*; *not in 1610*
98n	'New Cottages ... Land.'] *1618*; *not in 1610*
101	, nor ... articles] *1618*; *not in 1610*
102	, and whether ... answered] *1618*; *not in 1610*
102	, as also ... abused] *1618*; *not in 1610*
102	*Bushes*] *1618*; *not in 1610*
102	to the uttermost value] *1618*; *not in 1610*
102	fells] *1618*; fields *1610*
102	Lincolnshire, Cambridgeshire] *1618*; *not in 1610*
102	to the Lord, ... country] *1618*; *not in 1610*
103	For in many places ... as for] *1618*; You spake also of *1610*
103	with great profit] *1618*; *not in 1610*
104	, and consequently ... scallages] *1618*; *not in 1610*
104	Iam ... erat] *1610, 1618*; *not in 1607*
105	Surveyor] *this edn*; *not in 1618*
105	36. Whether ... courts] *1618*; *not in 1610*
105	37.] *1618*; 36. *1610*
105	muniments] *this edn*; mynuments *1618*; miniments *1607*; monuments *1610*
105	, and without records ... survey] *1618*; *not in 1610*
105	38.] *1618*; 37. *1610*
106	39. Whether ... Mortmain] *1618*; *not in 1610*
106	40.] *1618*; 38. *1610*
106	41.] *1618*; 39. *1610*
106	42.] *1618*; 40. *1610*
107	omniumque] *1853*; ominumq *1618*
108	praed] *1853*; pred *1618*
108	caeterae] *1853*; cater & *1618*
108	the former Tenants for] *1610* [errata]; *not in 1618*
108	the rent or fine,] *1618*; *not in 1610*
109	travail] *1607*; travell *1610, 1618*
110	Will you do it by instrument ... as many do?] *1618*; *not in 1610*
110	Will you do it by instrument ... whether they list (**185**)] *not in 1853*
110	man] *1618*; bird *1610*
110	more] *1618*; *not in 1610*
110	for ... skill] *1618*; *not in 1610*
111	manner] *this edn*; mannor *1618*
111	Plane] *this edn*; Plaine *1618*
112	Plane] *this edn*; plaine *1618*

113	Then I think ... I thank you; **(190)**] *not in 1853*
113	Plane] *this edn*; plaine *1618*
115	Gamut] *this edn*; Gammaoth *1618*
116	So, you that carry … Into the next field **(193)**] *not in 1853*
119	It is I confess … I pray you proceed **(198)**] *not in 1853*
121	of] *1618*; after *1610*
121	numbering them.] *1618*; numbring them: yet if you will follow my direction, wee will come neere the number.
Baylie	How, I pray you? Wee will all giue any ayd we can.
Sur.	Then goe you along by this hedge, and when I bid you stand, stand you still: and let another goe vp this path, and when he comes right against you, let him stand: likewise another must stand here at the end of the wood, and must not mooue, vntill I call him to remooue: and I and my man will account the number of trees, that are within the square, which you three and the corner of the wood doth make. Sirra, goe you along by the hedge, and let your eye be alwaies vpon the trees that are betweene vs, and as you see mee mooue, so mooue you: and I wil number the trees as I goe. So, now call away the man that stands at the end of the wood, and place them again in another square, and do as before: and so from place to place, til all the wood be viewed, and the trees numbred. *1610*
122	random] *this edn*; randon *1618*
123	Some … pass.] *1618*; It is true: *1610*
123	in deed] *this edn*; indeed *1618*
123	We] *1618*; It is true: we *1610*

Book 4

133	times] *this edn*; time *1618*
133n	by] *1618*; *not in 1610*
134	imperfect as I have been enforced] imperfect in the due progression: for they contayned the first, wanting the middle, & some of the end of the Tables: that I haue beene forced *1610*
134	more large and more exact] *1618*; perfect *1610*
134	M. Valentine Leigh] *1618*; So I take it, but M. *Valentine Lea 1610*
134	, as I have digested them] *1618*; *not in 1610*
134	These are they.] *1618*; These are they but that I haue set them into this forme, because they may the better fall into leaues of a Portable booke, being before in long and troublesome rols, and in another forme lesse convenient. *1610*
138	25] *this edn*; 26 *1618*
145	Master] *this edn*; Mastet *1618*

Book 5

147	whither] *this edn*; whether *1618*
147	tax] *1618*; attach *1610*
150	Engineer] *this edn*; Ingenor *1618*
150	, and to the whole commonweal] *1618*; *not in 1610*
151	to make proof … experience,] *1618*; *not in 1610*
152	Ellesmere] *this edn*; Elsemore *1618*
152	lain] *this edn*; lyen *1618*
152	the like … places] *1618*; *not in 1610*
152	places] *1618*; place *1610*
152n	lain] *this edn*; lien *1618*
153	Allensmore] *this edn*; Allermore *1618*
153	fed their fill] *1618*; fed *1610*
153	ever] *this edn*; every *1618*
153	annual] *this edn*; annale *1618*
154	and Leo Africanus … heard] *1618*; *not in 1610*
154	hills] *1610*; hill *1618*
155	its] *this edn*; it *1618*
157	Somerset] *1610*; Summersetshire *1618*
159	and by the moss] *1618*; *not in 1610*
160	corn's] *this edn*; corn *1618*
160	travail] *this edn*; travel *1618*
160	when nature faileth, wit] *1618*; it often faileth, when wit
160	wanteth] *1618*; leaueth *1610*
160	feebleness] *1618*; weakness *1610*
161	use] *1618*; use, but to plant them *1610*
161	travail] *this edn*; travel *1618*
162	Orford] *this edn*; Oxford *1618*
162	Suffolk,] *this edn*; Suff. *1618*
162n	grounds] *1618*; ground *1610*
163	Bury] *this edn*; Berrie *1618*
163	Framlingham] *this edn*; Framingham *1618*
163	Lincolnshire,] *1618*; *not in 1610*
163	Bridport] *this edn*; Burport *1618*
164	travail] *this edn*; travel *1618*
164	yea, there is … Parish] *1618*; *not in 1610*
164	public weal] *this edn*; publique weale *1618*
164	Middlesex] *this edn*; Mid. *1618*
166	travails] *this edn*; trauels *1618*
167	men] *this edn*; mens *1618*
167	fall] *this edn*; fals *1618*
168	wooded] *this edn*; wodded *1618*
168	Welds] *1610*; welds *1618*

169   weal public] *this edn*; weale publike *1618*
170   manners] *this edn*; mannors *1618*
170   travel] *this edn*; travell *1618*
171   *Lincolnshire*, the Isle of *Portland*,] *1618*; *not in 1610*
171   public weal] *this edn*; publike weale *1618*
171–2   It was ordained … this commonwealth.] *1618*; *not in 1610*
171   canimus] *this edn*; cavimus *1618*
171   sint] *this edn*; sunt *1618*
172   Devastation, that is] *1618*; I think your meaning is *1610*
172n   Depopulation] *this edn*; Depolution *1618*
173   The *Romans* … therefore] *1618*; for, *1610*
173   experience's] *this edn*; experience *1618*
173   , besides the pleasure] *1618*; *not in 1610*
173   [, as I said before. … howsoever we find the state of this Island now (**176**)]; this section, sigs P8v–Q3r, or six pages of text, is missing in the Folger/EEBO copy of *1618*
174   sith] *this edn*; syth *1618*
179   travail] *this edn*; trauell *1618*
179   Centuplum] *1618, 1610*; centum pro cento *1607*
179   , an hundred for one] *1618*; *not in 1610*
179   and some part of *Devonshire*] *1618*; *not in 1610*
179   places] *1618*; places, especially vpon the North coast, about *Padstow 1610*
180   Beat] *this edn*; Beach *1618*; beat *1610*
180   Pevensey] *this edn*; Pensey *1618*
180   Aldeburgh] *this edn*; Alborow *1618*
180   Hollesley] *this edn*; Hoseley *1618*
180   lousy] *this edn*; lowzie *1618*
180   ambry] *this edn*; aumery *1618*; amnerie *1607*; ambrie *1610*
180   travail] *this edn*; trauell *1618*
180–81   About *Hitchin* … common fields.] *1618*; *not in 1610*
181   In *Devonshire* … dozen years.] *1618*; *not in 1610*
181   stub] *1607, 1610*; shub *1618*
181   Twynham] *this edn*; twineam *1618*
181   Stour] *this edn*; Stowre *1618*
181   ground; for the coal-dust] *1607*; ground for he co e-dust *1618*
182   not of the land … but] *1618*; *not in 1610*
182   provident master] also with marginal note, 'A prouident Master.' *1610*; *not in 1618*
183   *Milton Faulconbridge*] *this edn*; Milton, Faulconbridge *1618*; *not in 1610*
183n   sheepfold] *this edn*; sheepfol. *1618*
184   and] *this edn*; *not in 1618*
184   Varro … not for grass] *1618*; *not in 1610*

184	frietur] *this edn*; fretur *1618*
184	be] *this edn*; b *1618*
186	chalk] *this edn*; *not in 1607, 1610, 1618*
186	its] *this edn*; it *1618*
187	to] *this edn*; too *1618*
187	in dry … grow] *1618*; *not in 1610*
189	trees] *this edn*; ttees *1618*
189n	they] *this edn*; the *1618*
190	Poplar] *this edn*; Popple *1618*
190	coarse] *this edn*; course *1607, 1610, 1618*
190	, for this weed … ground] *1618*; *not in 1610*

Book 6

193	afford consideration to answer] *1618*; suffice the answer of *1610*
195	reason] *1618*; assurance *1610*
196	, with my thousand Marks] *1618*; *not in 1610*
196	, to lose both yourself and your Ship] *1618*; *not in 1610*
199	Purchaser] *this edn*; Bayly *1618*
200	it:] *1618*; it. And therefore he that hath money, may now buy what his sonne may sell; *1610*

Works Cited

Manuscript Sources

Norden, John, commission for a survey of the King's woods in Surrey, Berkshire, and Devonshire (1608), British Library, Egerton MS 806 f. 42.
———, 'Perambulatio, &c. de Halimote' (1616), British Library, Landsdowne MS 905 ff. 95v–124v.
———, 'Reasons to prove that the inclosing of Wasts [*sic*] and Common Forest grounds and chases are Lawful, Profitable [and] Necessarie to the King and people' (1612), British Library, Additional MS 38445 ff. 5–9.
———, *Speculum Britanniae. The first parte of an historicall description of Middlesex* (London, 1593). Copy annotated by Lord Burghley. British Library, Harleian MS 570.

Primary Sources

Adames, Jonas, *The Order of keeping a Court Leete, and Court Baron* (London, 1593).
Africanus, Leo, *A Geographical Historie of Africa* (London, 1600).
Agas, Ralph, *A preparative to platting of Landes and Tenements for Surueigh* (London, 1596).
———, *To all persons whom these presents may concerne* (London, 1596).
Anon., *The Maner of Kepynge a courte baron and a lete* (London, 1538).
Bacon, Francis, *The Works of Francis Bacon*, James Spedding et al. (eds), 15 vols. (London: Longmans, 1857–1874).
Benese, Richard, *This Boke Sheweth the Measurynge of all Maner of Land* (London, 1537).
The Bible and Holy Scriptures [Geneva Bible] (Geneva, 1560).
Bracton, Henry de, *De Legibus et consuetidinibus Angliae* (London, 1569).
Breton, John le, *Britton cum priuilegio regali* (London, 1533).
Camden, William, *Britain, or a chorographicall description of the most flourishing kingdomes, England, Scotland and Ireland* (London, 1610).
Churche, Rooke, *An olde thrift newly revived* (London, 1612).
Cicero, *Cicero. De Senectute, De Amiticia, De Divinatione*, William Armistead Falconer (trans.), Loeb Classical Library (Cambridge, MA: Harvard University Press, 1923).
Cowell, John, *The Interpreter* (Cambridge, 1607).
Cuningham, William, *The Cosmographical Glasse* (London, 1559).
Digges, Leonard, *Pantometria* (London, 1571).
———, *Tectonicon* (London, 1556).

Fitzherbert, Sir Anthony, *The boke for a Iustice of Peace ... that teacheth to kepe a courte Baron, or a lete* (London, 1539).

Fitzherbert, John, *The Boke of Surueyinge* (London, 1523).

Horace, *Horace, the Odes and Epodes*, C.E. Bennett (trans.), Loeb Classical Library (Cambridge, MA: Harvard University Press, 1927).

———, *Satires, Epistles and Ars Poetica*, H. Rushton Fairclough (trans.), Loeb Classical Library (Cambridge, MA: Harvard University Press, 1939).

Hughes, Paul L. and James F. Larkin (eds), *Tudor Royal Proclamations*, 3 vols. (New Haven: Yale University Press, 1964–1969).

Kitchin, John, *Le Covrt Leete, et Court Baron* (London, 1580).

Leigh, Valentine, *The moste profitable and commendable science of surueying of lands* (London, 1577).

Littleton, Sir Thomas, *Littleton's Tenures in English*, Eugene Wambaugh (ed.) (Washington: John Byrne & Co., 1903).

Manwood, John, *A Treatise and Discovrse of the Lawes of the Forrest* (London, 1598).

———, *A Treatise of the Laws of the Forest* (London, 1615).

Martial, *Epigrams*, Walter C.A. Ker (trans.), Loeb Classical Library (Cambridge, MA: Harvard University Press, 1961).

Moryson, Fynes, *Shakespeare's Europe ... Unpublished Chapters of Fynes Moryson's Itinerary*, Charles Hughes (ed.) (New York: B. Blom, 1967).

Norden, John, *Civitas Londoni* (London, 1600).

———, *England An Intended Guyde, for English Travailers* (London, 1625).

———, *John Norden's Manuscript Maps of Cornwall and its Nine Hundreds*, William Ravenhill (ed.) (Exeter: University of Exeter Press, 1972).

———, *Orford Ness: A Selection of Maps mainly by John Norden*, James Alfred Steers (ed.) (Cambridge: Heffer, 1966).

———, *A pensiue mans practise* (London, 1586).

———, *The pensiue mans practise. The second part. Or the pensiue mans complaint and comfort* (London, 1593).

———, *A progress of pietie, being the third part of the Pensiue mans practice* (London, 1598).

———, *Speculi Britanniae Pars Altera: Or, a Delineation of Northamptonshire* (London, 1720).

———, *Speculi Britaniae Pars. A Description of Hartfordshire* [sic] (1598), W.B. Gerish (ed.) (London, 1903).

———, *Speculi Britanniae Pars: A Topographical and Historical Description of Cornwall* (London: William Pearson, 1728).

———, *Speculum Britanniae. The first parte of an historicall description of Middlesex* (London, 1593).

———, *The Surueyors Dialogue* (London, 1607).

———, *The Surueiors Dialogue* (London, 1610).

———, *The Surueiors Dialogue* (London, 1618).

————, *The Surveyor's Dialogue*, John W. Papworth (ed.), *Architectural Publication Society: Detached Essays and Illustrations issued during the years 1848 ... 1852* (London, 1853).

————, *A table shewing the distances betweene all the Cities and Shire Townes of England* (London, 1625).

————, *The view of London bridge from east to west* (London, 1597).

Ovid, *Heroides and Amores*, Grant Showerman (trans.), Loeb Classical Library (Cambridge, MA: Harvard University Press, 1958).

Perkins, John, *Incipit perutilis tractatus* (London, 1545).

Pliny the Elder, *Historia Naturalis* [Natural History], 10 vols., H. Rackham (trans.), Loeb Classical Library (Cambridge, MA: Harvard University Press, 1938–1963).

Powell, Thomas, *Direction for Search of Records Remaining in the Chancerie, Tower, Exchequer* (London, 1623).

Powell, Thomas, and Arthur Agard, *The Repertorie of Records* (London, 1631).

Rastell, John, *Le Liver des Assises et Plees del Corone* (London, 1561).

Rathborne, Aaron, *The Surueyor in Four bookes* (London, 1616).

Recorde, Robert, *The Pathway to Knowledg* (London, 1551).

Standish, Arthur, *The Commons Complaint* (London, 1611).

————, *New Directions of Experience to the Commons Complaint* (London, 1613).

Statutes at Large [*The Whole Volume of statutes at large ... since Magna Charta*] (London, 1587).

Statutes of the Realm, 11 vols. (1810–1828; London: Dawsons, 1963).

Suetonius, *Suetonius, II*, J.C. Rolfe (trans.), Loeb Classical Library (Cambridge, MA: Harvard University Press, 1914).

Terence, *Terence, II*, John Barnsby (trans.), Loeb Classical Library (Cambridge, MA: Harvard University Press, 2001).

Theophrastus, *Theophrastus, II: Enquiry into Plants, Books VI–IX*, Arthur F. Hort (trans.), Loeb Classical Library (Cambridge, MA: Harvard University Press, 1961).

Vadianus, Joachim, *Epitome trium terrae partium* (Zurich, 1534).

Varro, Marcus Terentius, *Rerum rusticarum libri tres* [*On Agriculture*], in *Marcus Porcius Cato, On Agriculture; Marcus Terrentius Varro, On Agriculture*, William Davis Hooper and Harrison Boyd Ash (trans.), Loeb Classical Library (Cambridge, MA: Harvard University Press, 1960).

Virgil, *Virgil, I: Eclogues, Georgics, Aeneid I–VI*, H. Rushton Fairclough (trans.), Loeb Classical Library (Cambridge, MA: Harvard University Press, 1999).

Wilkinson, John, *A treatise collected ovt of the statvtes of this Kingdom, ... for the keeping of a Court Leet, Court Baron, and Hundred Court* (London, 1618).

Worsop, Edward, *A Discouerie of sundrie errours and faults daily committed by land–meaters, ignorant of Arithmetike and Geometrie* (London, 1582).

Secondary Sources

Allen, Robert C., *Enclosure and the Yeoman* (Oxford: Clarendon Press, 1992).

Ash, Eric, *Power, Knowledge, and Expertise in Elizabethan England* (Baltimore: Johns Hopkins University Press, 2004).

Banerjee, Sukanya, *Becoming Imperial Citizens: Indians in the Late-Victorian Empire* (Durham: Duke University Press, 2010).

Bartolovich, Crystal, 'Boundary Disputes: Surveying, Agrarian Capital and English Renaissance Texts', unpublished Ph.D. dissertation, Emory University, 1993.

Bell, H.E., *An Introduction to the History and Records of the Court of Wards and Liveries* (Cambridge: Cambridge University Press, 1953).

Bennett, J.A., *The Divided Circle: A History of Instruments for Astronomy, Navigation and Surveying* (Oxford: Phaidon, 1987).

———, 'Geometry and Surveying in Early-Seventeenth-Century England', *Annals of Science* 48 (1991): 345–54.

Bennett, J.A., and Olivia Brown, *The Compleat Surveyor. Published to Accompany a Special Exhibition at the Whipple Museum of the History of Science* (Cambridge: Whipple Museum of the History of Science, 1982).

Bourdieu, Pierre, *Outline of a Theory of Practice* (Cambridge: Cambridge University Press, 1977).

Brenner, Robert, 'Agrarian Class Structure and Economic Development in Pre-Industrial Europe', in T.H. Aston and C.H.E. Philpin (eds), *The Brenner Debate: Agrarian Class Structure and Economic Development in Pre-Industrial Europe* (Cambridge: Cambridge University Press, 1985), 10–63.

———, 'The Agrarian Roots of European Capitalism', in Aston and Philpin (eds), *The Brenner Debate*, 213–328.

Bruckner, Martin, and Kristen Poole, 'The Plot Thickens: Surveying Manuals, Drama, and the Materiality of Narrative Form in Early Modern England', *ELH* 69 (2002): 617–48.

Buisseret, David (ed.), *Monarchs, Ministers, and Maps: The Emergence of Cartography as a Tool of Government in Early Modern Europe* (Chicago: University of Chicago Press, 1992).

Coote, C.H., 'John Norden', *Dictionary of National Biography*, vol. 14 (New York: Macmillan, 1909), 550–53.

Cormack, Lesley B., *Charting an Empire: Geography at the English Universities, 1580–1620* (Chicago: University of Chicago Press, 1997).

Cox, Virginia, *The Renaissance Dialogue: Literary Dialogue in its Social and Political Contexts, Castiglione to Galileo* (Cambridge: Cambridge University Press, 1992).

Darby, H.C., 'The Agrarian Contribution to Surveying in England', *The Geographical Journal* 82 (1933): 529–35.

———, *The Draining of the Fens* (Cambridge: Cambridge University Press, 1956).

Dobb, Maurice, *Studies in the Development of Capitalism* (New York: International Publishers, 1947).

Dubrow, Heather, *Shakespeare and Domestic Loss: Forms of Deprivation, Mourning, and Recuperation* (Cambridge: Cambridge University Press, 1999).

Eden, Peter, 'Three Elizabethan Estate Surveyors: Peter Kempe, Thomas Clerke and Thomas Langdon', in Sarah Tyacke (ed.), *English Map-Making, 1500–1650* (London: British Library, 1983), 68–84.

Edwards, Jess, *Writing, Geometry and Space in Seventeenth-Century England and America* (London and New York: Routledge, 2006).

Feingold, Mordechai, *The Mathematicians' Apprenticeship: Science, Universities and Society in England, 1560–1640* (Cambridge: Cambridge University Press, 1984).

Finer, Samuel E., 'State- and Nation-Building in Europe: The Role of the Military', in Charles Tilly (ed.), *The Formation of National States in Europe* (Princeton: Princeton University Press, 1975), 84–163.

Floyd-Wilson, Mary, *English Ethnicity and Race in Early Modern Drama* (Cambridge: Cambridge University Press, 2003).

French, Henry, and Richard Hoyle, *The Character of English Rural Society: Earls Colne, 1550–1750* (Manchester: Manchester University Press, 2007).

Gay, Edwin F., 'The Midland Revolt and the Inquisitions of Depopulation, 1607', *Transactions of the Royal Historical Society* 18 (1904): 195–244.

Gieskes, Edward, *Representing the Professions: Administration, the Law, and Theater in Early Modern England* (Newark: University of Delaware Press, 2006).

Gillies, John, *Shakespeare and the Geography of Difference* (Cambridge: Cambridge University Press, 1994).

Hadfield, Andrew, *Shakespeare, Spenser and the Matter of Britain* (New York and Basingstoke: Palgrave, 2004).

Hall, Kim F., *Things of Darkness: Economies of Race and Gender in Early Modern England* (Ithaca: Cornell University Press, 1995).

Halpern, Richard, *The Poetics of Primitive Accumulation: English Renaissance Culture and the Genealogy of Capital* (Ithaca: Cornell University Press, 1991).

Harley, J.B., 'Silences and Secrecy: The Hidden Agenda of Cartography in Early Modern Europe', *Imago Mundi* 40 (1988): 57–76.

Harrison, Christopher, 'Manor Courts and the Governance of Tudor England,' in C.W. Brooks and Michael Lobban (eds), *Communities and Courts in Britain, 1150–1900* (London: Hambledon Press, 1997), 43–59.

Harvey, P.D.A., 'English Estate Maps: Their Early History and Their Use as Historical Evidence', in David Buisseret (ed.), *Rural Images: Estate Maps in the Old and New Worlds* (Chicago: University of Chicago Press, 1996), 27–61.

———, *Maps in Tudor England* (London: British Library, 1993).

Helgerson, Richard, *Forms of Nationhood: The Elizabethan Writing of England* (Chicago, 1992).

Hill, Christopher, *The Century of Revolution, 1603–1714* (1961; New York: Norton, 1982).

Hindle, Steve, 'Imagining Insurrection in Seventeenth-Century England: Representations of the Midland Rising of 1607', *History Workshop* 66 (2008): 21–61.

————, *On the Parish? The Micro-Politics of Poor Relief in Rural England, c. 1550–1750* (Oxford: Oxford University Press, 2004).

Holmes, Clive, 'Drainers and Fenmen: The Problem of Popular Political Consciousness in the Seventeenth Century', in Anthony Fletcher and John Stevenson (eds), *Order and Disorder in Early Modern England* (Cambridge: Cambridge University Press, 1985), 166–95.

Holstun, James, *Ehud's Dagger: Class Struggle in the English Revolution* (London: Verso, 2002).

Iyengar, Sujata, *Shades of Difference: Mythologies of Skin Color in Early Modern England* (Philadelphia: University of Pennsylvania Press, 2005).

Jardine, Lisa and William Sherman, 'Pragmatic Readers: Knowledge Transactions and Scholarly Services in Late Elizabethan England', in Anthony Fletcher and Peter Roberts (eds), *Religion, Culture and Society in Early Modern Britain* (Cambridge, 1994), 102–24.

Kerridge, Eric, *Agrarian Problems in the Sixteenth Century and After* (London: Allen & Unwin, 1969).

King, H.W., 'The Lawless Court of the Honour of Rayleigh', *Essex Archaeological Society* 4 (1891): 179–95.

Kitchen, Frank, 'Cosmo-Choro-Polygrapher: An Analytic Account of the Life and Work of John Norden, 1547–1625' (unpublished D. Phil. Dissertation, University of Sussex, 1992).

————, 'John Norden (1547–1625), Estate Surveyor, Topographer, County Mapmaker and Devotional Writer', *Imago Mundi* 49 (1997): 43–61.

————, 'John Norden', *The Dictionary of National Biography*, vol. 41 (Oxford and New York: Oxford University Press, 2004), 5–7.

Klein, Bernhard, *Maps and the Writing of Space in Early Modern England and Ireland* (Basingstoke: Palgrave, 2001).

Korda, Natasha, *Shakespeare's Domestic Economies: Gender and Property in Early Modern England* (Philadelphia: University of Pennsylvania Press, 2002).

Lachmann, Richard, *Capitalists in Spite of Themselves: Elite Conflict and Economic Transitions in Early Modern Europe* (Oxford: Oxford University Press, 2000).

————, *From Manor to Market: Structural Change in England, 1536–1640* (Madison: University of Wisconsin Press, 1987).

Latour, Bruno, *Politics of Nature: How to Bring the Sciences into Democracy* (Cambridge, MA: Harvard University Press, 2004).

Lawrence, Heather, 'John Norden and his Colleagues: Surveyors of Crown Lands', *The Cartographic Journal* 22 (1985): 54–6.

Leslie, Michael, and Timothy Raylor (eds), *Culture and Cultivation in Early Modern England: Writing and the Land* (Leicester: Leicester University Press, 1992).

Linebaugh, Peter, *The Magna Carta Manifesto: Liberties and Commons for All* (Berkeley: University of California Press, 2008).

Macherey, Pierre, *A Theory of Literary Production* (1966; London: Routledge & Kegan Paul, 1978).

Magnusson, Lynne, *Shakespeare and Social Dialogue: Dramatic Language and Elizabethan Letters* (Cambridge: Cambridge University Press, 1999).

Manning, Roger B., *Village Revolts: Social Protest and Popular Disturbances in England, 1509–1640* (Oxford: Clarendon Press, 1988).

Martin, John E., *Feudalism to Capitalism: Peasant and Landlord in English Agrarian Development* (London: Macmillan, 1983).

Marx, Karl, *Capital: A Critique of Political Economy, Vol. 1*, trans. Ben Fowkes (Harmondsworth: Penguin, 1976).

McRae, Andrew, *God Speed the Plough: The Representation of Agrarian England* (Cambridge: Cambridge University Press, 1996).

———, 'Husbandry Manuals and the Language of Agrarian Improvement', in Leslie and Raylor (eds), *Culture and Cultivation*, 35–62.

Moore, Stuart A., and Hubert Stuart Moore, *The History and Law of Fisheries* (London: Stevens and Haynes, 1903).

Neeson, J.M., *Commoners: Common Right, Enclosure and Social Change in England, 1700–1820* (Cambridge: Cambridge University Press, 1993).

Netzloff, Mark, *England's Internal Colonies: Class, Capital, and the Literature of Early Modern English Colonialism* (New York: Palgrave, 2003).

Nolan, John S., 'The Militarization of the Elizabethan State', *Journal of Military History* 58 (1994): 391–420.

Ong, Walter J., *Ramus, Method, and the Decay of Dialogue* (Cambridge, MA: Harvard University Press, 1958).

Oxford English Dictionary, eds J.A. Simpson and E.S.C. Weiner (New York and Oxford: Oxford University Press, 1989).

Plucknett, Theodore F.T., 'Revisions in Economic History: III. Bookland and Folkland', *The Economic History Review* 6 (1935): 64–72.

Pocock, J.G.A., *The Ancient Constitution and the Feudal Law* (1957; New York: Norton, 1967).

Pollard, Alfred W., 'The Unity of John Norden: Surveyor and Religious Writer', *The Library* 7, 3 (1926): 233–52.

Poovey, Mary, *The History of the Modern Fact: Problems of Knowledge in the Sciences of Wealth and Society* (Chicago: University of Chicago Press, 1998).

Rackham, Oliver, *History of the Countryside* (London: Dent, 1986).

———, *Trees and Woodland in the British Landscape* (London: J.M. Dent, 1976).

Richeson, A.W., *English Land Measuring to 1800: Instruments and Practices* (Cambridge, MA: M.I.T. Press, 1966).

Serres, Michel, *The Natural Contract* (Ann Arbor: University of Michigan Press, 1995).

Shapin, Steven, *A Social History of Truth: Civility and Science in Seventeenth-Century England* (Chicago: University of Chicago Press, 1994).

Snyder, Jon R., *Writing the Scene of Speaking: Theories of Dialogue in the Late Italian Renaissance* (Stanford: Stanford University Press, 1989).

Sullivan, Garrett A., *The Drama of Landscape: Land, Property, and Social Relations on the Early Modern Stage* (Stanford: Stanford University Press, 1998).

Tawney, R.H., *The Agrarian Problem in the Sixteenth Century* (1912; New York: Harper & Row, 1967).

Taylor, E.G.R., *The Mathematical Practitioners of Tudor and Stuart England* (Cambridge: Cambridge University Press, 1954).

Thirsk, Joan (ed.), *The Agrarian History of England and Wales*, vol. 4: 1500–1640 (Cambridge: Cambridge University Press, 1967).

———, 'Industries in the Countryside', in *The Rural Economy of England: Collected Essays* (London: The Hambledon Press, 1984), 217–33.

———, 'Making a Fresh Start: Sixteenth-Century Agriculture and the Classical Inspiration', in Leslie and Raylor (eds), *Culture and Cultivation*, 15–34.

———, 'Tudor Enclosures', in *The Rural Economy of England*, 65–84.

Thompson, E.P., 'Custom, Law and Common Right', in *Customs in Common: Studies in Traditional Popular Culture* (New York, 1993), 97–184.

Tilley, Morris Palmer, *A Dictionary of Proverbs in England in the Sixteenth and Seventeenth Centuries* (1950; Ann Arbor: University of Michigan Press, 1966).

Turner, Henry S., *The English Renaissance Stage: Geometry, Poetics, and the Practical Spatial Arts 1580–1630* (Oxford: Oxford University Press, 2006).

———, 'Plotting Early Modernity', in Henry S. Turner (ed.), *The Culture of Capital: Property, Cities, and Knowledge in Early Modern England* (New York, 2002), 85–127.

Underdown, David, *Revel, Riot, and Rebellion: Popular Politics and Culture in England 1603–1660* (Oxford: Clarendon Press, 1985).

Vinogradoff, Paul, *Villainage in England* (1923; New York, 1967).

Williams, Raymond, *The Country and the City* (Oxford and New York: Oxford University Press, 1973).

———, *Marxism and Literature* (Oxford: Oxford University Press, 1977).

Wilson, Kenneth J., *Incomplete Fictions: The Formation of English Renaissance Dialogue* (Washington, DC: Catholic University of America Press, 1985).

Wilson, Richard, 'Against the Grain: Representing the Market in *Coriolanus*', *The Seventeenth Century* 6 (1991): 111–48.

Wood, Andy, 'The Place of Custom in Plebeian Political Culture: England, 1550–1800', *Social History* 22 (1997): 46–60.

Wood, Ellen Meiksins, *The Origin of Capitalism* (New York: Monthly Review Press, 1999).

Yates, Julian, 'Towards a Theory of Agentive Drift; Or, A Particular Fondness for Oranges in 1597', *Parallax* 22 (2002): 47–58.

Index